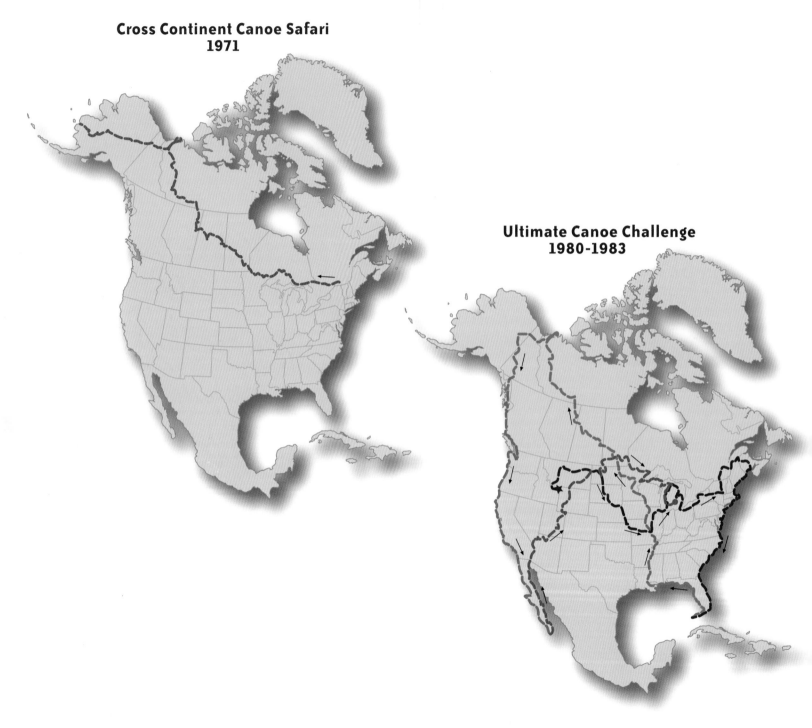

Cross Continent Canoe Safari
1971

Ultimate Canoe Challenge
1980-1983

Two Continent Canoe Expedition
1986-1989

Mississippi Challenges
1984, 2001, 2003

All Things are Possible

The Verlen Kruger Story: 100,000 Miles by Paddle

BY PHIL PETERSON SR.

Adventure Publications, Inc.
Cambridge, Minnesota

Main cover photo by Kip Brundage

Introductory chapter photo credits listed by photographer and page number:
Lloyd Fons: 144; **Valerie Fons:** 156, 168, 178; **Steve Landick:** 124; **Kruger Archives:** 14, 20, 30, 36, 44, 60, 74, 86, 102, 110, 116, 130, 138, 194, 200, 234, 254, 274; **Jenny Kruger:** 264; **Verlen Kruger:** 220; **Norman Miller:** 206; **Dan Pahman:** 244; **Phil Peterson:** 216, 280

Copyright 2006 by Phil Peterson Sr.
Published by:
Adventure Publications, Inc.
820 Cleveland St. S
Cambridge, MN 55008
1-800-678-7006
www.adventurepublications.net
Printed in China

ISBN-10: 1-59193-138-X
ISBN-13: 978-1-59193-138-6

Dedication

For the Kruger family, and all who hold Verlen in reverence.

From Governor Jennifer M. Granholm, State of Michigan

"Verlen Kruger was a legend and a hero far beyond the waters in Michigan that he loved and lived on. His passion grew from his Michigan home and spread to other states, countries, and continents. His greatest legacy is that he sparked that same passion in a whole new generation, and I know this memorial will inspire generations to come."

SPEAKING OF THE LIFE-SIZE BRONZE STATUE AND MEMORIAL TO BE ERECTED ON THE SHORES OF MICHIGAN'S GRAND RIVER IN PORTLAND, MICHIGAN.

Verlen Kruger Remembrance

As a paddlesports writer first, and later a friend, I have followed Verlen Kruger's amazing, and I do mean AMAZING, canoeing career from many perspectives—from his epic Ultimate Canoe Challenge that still remains one of the greatest canoe journeys ever made, to his record-setting Mississippi River race against the clock, to his Two Continent Canoe Expedition that inspired the armchair traveler in all of us.

No matter the challenges, as far-flung and impossible as they seemed to us mere mortals, Verlen never lost sight of his goals, never called it quits. Put him in his canoe, and despite all obstacles, he just kept paddling on... and on... and on... until he arrived at his destination—even if it was 28,000 miles away!

I had the good fortune—the privilege—to canoe with Verlen on several occasions and spend hours with him, notebook and pen in hand, listening to his tales of adventure, be it exploring some distant land, designing the perfect canoe, or navigating life's many currents, some easy and smooth, some rocky and treacherous. Through my association with him, I know this about the man: He was one of the most humble, generous, steadfast, intensely motivated persons I have ever met, a true legend among legends. In this wonderful world of canoeing, he was one of a kind. There will never be another like him.

LARRY RICE, CONTRIBUTING EDITOR, *CANOE & KAYAK* MAGAZINE

Preface

The unique breadth and scope of the quests Verlen Kruger undertook, alone, or with others, provide insight into an ordinary man following his own extraordinary dreams. Few would ever have heard of Verlen Kruger had he stayed on the farm.

Paddling a canoe through the world's arteries enabled Verlen to connect his routes and pass through or along the edge of nearly every state in the nation and North and South America and their oceans. Upstream, or down, didn't matter, which included paddling and portaging up the Colorado River through the entire Grand Canyon!

The price he and others paid to accomplish his long list of Guinness and World Records goes beyond the rational, yet made sense to him at the time. He has portaged farther than most will ever paddle. Canoe trips, with different partners, of 7,000, 28,000 and 21,000 miles, which took him from near the Arctic Circle to Cape Horn of South America are incomprehensible to most. Yet, when combined with his canoe racing career, his Mississippi challenges and his years of tripping added up to over 100,000 miles by paddle!

At different times you might both admire and reject his behavior, but you will take special note of his skills, his vision, his physical and mental strengths, and above all his courage, his faith and his will. In the end, most love him. If there are exceptions, even they must stand in awe of Verlen Kruger because of what they learned from him, saw in him, and wished to replicate in themselves.

From a sharecropper family of nine and a school dropout at the age of 14, Verlen Kruger grew into a man of unbelievable accomplishment. He is internationally respected and an inspiration to ordinary people with their own extraordinary dreams. He became wealthy in faith, philosophy, friendship, and in the stature lauded upon him by his peers. His inspiration can be attached to the dreams of anyone in any field. Knowing Verlen's story will inspire you to never quit, to never tire, and to never be bored.

This is a story that had to be told, and a labor of love for me in the telling. I am grateful to those who sent in their own feelings about Verlen. I couldn't include them all, but they are not forgotten. This then, is the story of Verlen Kruger, the man Larry Rice, of *Canoe & Kayak* magazine, called "Arguably the world's greatest canoeist."

PHIL PETERSON SR.

To All Who Helped Make it Possible

During the writing of this book, I've met a core group of friends of Verlen Kruger, and now count them mine as well. All repeatedly helped me with research, interviews, photos and an occasional paddle. Clint Waddell, Steve Landick and Valerie Fons all contributed from their background as former partners in canoe trips. I called again and again on those who had paddled more recent trips like the Yukon Odyssey; Dan Smith, Stan Hanson, Jon Young, Bob and Janet Bradford, Clark Eid, Dan Pahman and so many others. My thanks to Governor Granholm, of Michigan, for use of her endorsement of the Verlen Kruger Memorial efforts and to Dr. Roger Payne for the photo and reliving his meetings with the TCCE team on the shores of Golfo San Jose.

Planned interviews were cut short by Verlen's loss to the prostate cancer he fought for so many years. I needed a lot of help from Verlen's circle of friends to piece together bits of information and photo identification. At Verlen's suggestion I have used the Kruger Archives as my primary source of information and photos. A special thanks to all who graciously granted use of photos and info and to Tom Foeller for photo enhancement help, and to Pastor Terry Cathcart for biblical reference. We worked very hard to identify. photos and provide proper credit, but some were so old we could not find sources. If you notice a misidentified or miscredited photo, please contact Adventure Publications.

My most helpful supporter in the effort has been Jenny Kruger. Her unending support has caused her to retread through both good and bad times. She never hesitated in the process and incorporated the Kruger family willingly into the effort.

With nearly 300 pages and over 300 photos it becomes impossible to thank each individual involved in the help provided me. I owe a preeminent thanks to the Slabaughs and all at Adventure Publications, who helped to make *All Things are Possible* happen. To all I have not mentioned... thank you!

I am grateful to Larry Rice for his heartfelt foreword and his quotes used. A very special thank you to my wife Joanne, a.k.a. Wild Flower of the North (while on canoe trips), for her ruthless editing, which helps make it appear I can write. Special thanks to Polly Peterson for all the computer aid.

Most of all, thanks to Verlen for selecting me to write his biography! Though we only skimmed the surface of his incredible life, I hope the book gives to others what it gave me in the process. I still see Verlen's reflection in the swirl my paddle leaves on the water's surface. I always will.

PHIL PETERSON SR.

Table of Contents

"You can do it, Verlen, you can!"

VERLEN'S SCHOOL TEACHER

Birth and Early Life of Verlen Kruger

Verlen Emmet Kruger was born at home near Francesville, Indiana, on June 30, 1922. He was the second child and second son to young Daisy and Emmet, who married when Daisy was sixteen. After Leland and Verlen, his parents welcomed seven more children: Doris, Lawrence, Louise, Carolyn, Alvera, Marilyn, and the youngest, Donald. Emmet supported his new family by sharecropping. From an early age, help with farm chores was needed and expected from this active group of four sons and five daughters. Emmet and Daisy worked hard, enjoyed their children and shared a good life. The family worked together and remained close and supportive throughout their lives.

When Verlen was two years old, his aunt visited them on the farm. While she talked to Daisy, the two of them lost track of Verlen. When they realized he was out of sight, a small panic ensued. His mother went around the barn and heard him above her. When she looked up, she found Verlen

Verlen's parents, Emmet and Daisy Kruger *(photo from Kruger Archives)*

on the metal ladder at the top of the windmill. His aunt kept shouting, "Verlen, get down from there!" His mother kept shouting back, "Don't scare him, he might fall!" Nine months pregnant, Daisy climbed to the top of the windmill and retrieved him. Adventure began early in Verlen's life.

Verlen's father, Emmet Kruger, on the farm
(photo from Kruger Archives)

As they grew, the nine Kruger children tended to make many of their own toys. Verlen had found an old wheel from a child's wagon and had attached to it a piece of stiff #9 wire twisted into a long handle. "It was just like a broom handle with a wheel on the end of it. I could push and steer it ahead of me as I ran," he said. One day, he went out to the pasture to bring the cattle home for the night and was pushing his wheel across the field when one of the cows let out a bellow and charged him. This had never hap-

Adventure began early in Verlen's life.

Verlen at six months with older brother, Leland
(photo from Kruger Archives)

Verlen, second from right, with his siblings and his parents, Emmet and Daisy Kruger (photo from Kruger Archives)

pened before and was unusual behavior for a milk cow. As she bore down on him, he swung the wheel at the cow's head; he didn't know what else to do. The wheel hit the cow on the nose, and she skidded to a stop. Verlen quickly backed away and was over the fence and running for his father, leaving the cow bellowing in the field. His father and neighbor went out to the field and determined the cow to be sick with hydrophobia, also called rabies, and so shot and destroyed it. His father praised Verlen's quick thinking and behavior; the nose-hit had saved him from a worse ending. Verlen never forgot the incident or what saved him.

Verlen became quite accomplished handling teams of work horses. He experimented with how he paired different horses and was proud when he was able to team up two stallions. Most farmers strictly avoided teaming stallions, which would both rather kill each other. Verlen repeatedly harnessed a pair of stallions and found that they, in fact, could work pretty well together with proper guidance. Unharnessing them again, however, was always a problem. There was no way, according to Verlen, to make the two stallions like each other, particularly when there were mares in the vicinity.

Verlen learned to identify the moves, looks and stares that the animals used when they were trying to intimidate him. He then developed the skills and confidence to outwit the animals at their own game. He learned how to be in charge of animals five times his size and alter their behavior when needed; essentially, he beat them at their own game. This game happened frequently with the work horses, mules and cattle, and Verlen enjoyed such encounters. He claimed that observing the behavior of farm animals gave him insight and effective reactions to handle other aggressive animals in his life.

Verlen recalled his childhood times on the family farm with genuine fondness and spoke with warmth in his eyes as he described his past. Though it was not an easy life, he remembered it as a good life. In those years, sharecropping was near the scale of subsistence living. No one got rich at it. Sharecroppers tended to earn what was needed, but little extra.

For the Kruger family of eleven, there was seldom any extra money, no family car until later in his parent's lives, and the Krugers were considered by some to be poor folk. He didn't remember, even as a child, feeling they were poor. Verlen said, "We didn't have much, but we didn't know we were supposed to. After the crash of 1929, many people lost their farms because they could no longer handle their mortgages. Banks and wealthier people took over the farms—they knew how to own them, but not run them. Sharecroppers were needed then. There were lots of farmers who had lost their holdings and whose only route, then, was to become sharecroppers. Sharecroppers usually raised a crop or two for resale and then raised a variety of livestock and crops, which were their primary food sources."

Verlen and his siblings grew up with chores being a natural part of daily life. He usually had more chores than the rest, but liked his chores and felt he was better at accomplishing many of them than his brothers and sisters. His sisters were spared some of the outdoor chores but were expected to support their mother with the demanding household jobs of laundry, baking, canning, cleaning and helping with the younger children.

(l to r) Louise, Leland, Verlen, Lawrence and Doris Kruger and the family car *(photo from Kruger Archives)*

Verlen remembered raising chickens, ducks, pigs, milk cows, beef cattle on a small scale, and the farm's dogs and cats. In those almost tractor-less days, they used real horsepower: mules for plowing, fertilizing, cultivating, harvesting and hauling goods needed to raise the farm critters. There were no days off, just the times when they occasionally went to church on Sundays. When problems arose, solutions had to be fit into the daily routine. There was more than enough to keep the chore roster filled.

Verlen attended the one-room country schoolhouse with his siblings and neighbors for the first eight grades. He liked school and did well in all of his classes. His favorite teacher, who taught multiple grade levels in that one-room country school, was able to teach him for several years. He remembered her handling up to five different grade levels at once and bringing the best out of her students. She used to ask the students, "What do you want to be when you grow up?" After each had answered her with their dreams, Verlen said she would reply "You can. You can do that—you should do that!" Verlen was inspired by her encouragement and, because of it, he wanted to become a teacher or a doctor. With those memories of his teacher's encouragement, he almost never doubted that he could do whatever he set his mind to. In his rare moments of doubt, he would hear her voice in the background saying, "You can. You can do that Verlen. You should do that!" Verlen felt it was that teacher who made him into a life-long learner and teacher.

He had been taught by his teacher to be curious, which resulted in his ability to dig a little deeper into whatever interested him. His driving curiosity would constantly push him to

His driving curiosity would constantly push him to know more.

know more. When something broke, Verlen would fix it. If he didn't know how, he would learn. He never seemed to feel there was anything he couldn't do. Some things were difficult and might take more time, but Verlen would work through it.

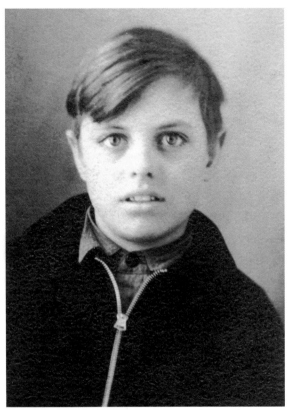

Verlen dropped out of school at 14 to become a full-time farmer after his father's heart attack *(photo from Kruger Archives)*

Throughout his childhood, Verlen tended to grasp responsibility quickly and fulfilled the requirements of each task. His farm chores did not allow anything but completion of the tasks. He knew he must feed or water on schedule. He needed to plant when the seasons called and harvest when the crop was ready, not when he was ready. He was heard by many saying throughout his adult life that he never considered not finishing something he set out to accomplish. From such roots, Verlen developed a strong work ethic and strength of will that sustained him throughout his life. He believed that people, in general, are more capable than they often think and, as a result, do not demand enough of themselves.

Verlen's older brother, Leland, had other jobs outside of the farm. Consequently, much of the responsibility of organizing and performing daily chores fell to Verlen. The demands cultivated his growing work ethic and, to some extent, probably denied him some childhood aspects of fun and freedom. Verlen, however, did not feel that his childhood had been lacking. In fact, his chore-load became significantly heavier when he reached the age of fourteen.

A disabling heart attack struck his father and brought a new crisis to the Kruger family. The senior Kruger could no longer handle the family farm alone. Even with his children doing chores, he still needed more help. Due to the crash of 1929, jobs were still scarce, but his older brother already had work in the city. Just as his father had before him, Verlen dropped out of school at the beginning of his freshman year to take over the farm. This would have been his first year attending the consolidated high school in the nearby town, which offered not only academics, but high school sports as well. There was no choice in his mind; Verlen felt he was the only one capable of handling the farm at that time. He took over the family's sharecropper acreage as a full-time farmer—with the aid of his siblings—at the age of fourteen.

He quickly adapted to his role during his father's long recuperation. He had his father as an advisor and, during the first year of this arrangement, his father regained adequate health to help with some light-work tasks. During his second year, because the farm was flourishing under Verlen's direction, his father felt the need to try to find some additional income from work that he could do. He left Verlen to run the farm and found a job in the nearby town of Hammond, Indiana, fifty miles north of their home in Francesville. The money he earned—added to that from the farm income—improved the Kruger lives.

Verlen knew he was good at what he was doing, and liked being in charge. But his father and mother were separated for the first time by his father's town job. Without a car to commute, his mother remained on the farm with the kids, which was a bad scene to Verlen. He knew his father and mother would be happier together and that his father had liked working the farm far more than he liked his town job. Since his father appeared adequately healthy again, Verlen volunteered to switch jobs with him. They agreed. Verlen had his first factory job and soon understood why his father had not liked it. Instead of being in charge, someone was in charge of him! But his father was back on the farm, his parents were again together, and Verlen could split his monthly check with them to help the family make ends meet. His efforts were worthwhile and Verlen felt things were going just about the way they should be.

The routines of the sharecropper and a factory worker life continued in similar fashion into Verlen's seventeenth year. He worked the weekly town job and returned weekends to the farm to help with planting and harvesting and whatever else needed to be done. For a time, he laid track for the railroad, and took any work that helped supplement the family income. He continued sending part of his paycheck home until he married. He was too busy to return to school; he didn't even consider it. He was learning skills, loved being as productive as he was, and wondered—at seventeen years old—what was next.

Verlen just prior to being drafted into the Army *(photo from Kruger Archives)*

Verlen's brothers and sisters and their spouses *(photo from Kruger Archives)*

"I always knew I belonged in aircraft."

⏤VERLEN KRUGER

The Military and Verlen Kruger

In June of 1941, President Franklin Delano Roosevelt formally declared war on the Axis and the United States entered World War II. Verlen Kruger was eighteen years old and still a full-time factory worker and part-time farmer. Verlen was a patriotic young man who was full willing to give his life to fight for the country he loved. He knew exactly where he thought he should be involved in this war. Like so many young men, he wanted to join the Air Force and fly. His father had other plans.

Because of his health and the demands of sharecropping, Verlen's father felt he could not spare Verlen to the war effort. He applied through the county seat to have Verlen declared exempt from military duty due to farm hardship. The board agreed and granted the exempt status. Verlen didn't like it. He felt he had a duty to be a part of the war and that the Krugers could continue to sharecrop without him for whatever time it took to win the war. He still wanted to fly.

He soon hatched a plan. Unbeknownst to his family, Verlen "borrowed" the family's Model A Ford, drove it to town and attempted to enlist in the Air Force. The recruiter could not process him because Verlen did not have a birth certificate with him. Not having told his parents that he was enlisting made it more difficult for him to get his hands on that certificate. His parents had the only copy. On his way home, he had two bald tires go flat. He managed to talk his mother into loaning him his birth certificate and found his way on only slightly balder tires back to the recruiter. By then, the recruiter had discovered that Verlen was an inch too short to be a pilot, so he could not accept him as a volunteer for the Air Force. Disappointed, Verlen returned home, not telling his parents of his attempted enlistment, and returned to his factory and farm jobs. There was another surprise coming soon.

A month later, Verlen's presence was requested by the County Draft Board. Verlen had not realized that by attempting to enlist in the Air Force, he had voluntarily given up his exempt status. He was now eligible for draft and the Board wanted him in the Army. His dreams of flying were gone. "The Army... the Army," Verlen kept repeating to himself the day he was told. His father was unimpressed with Verlen's secret efforts to volunteer for service in the military. His long-term farmhand and second son was gone in thirty days.

Verlen, the two-striper, at home on leave from Tank Battalion
(photo from Kruger Archives)

Following basic training at Fort Polk, Louisiana, Verlen was assigned to an armored division and wound up in the tank mechanic pool. He performed well, completed the training, but still felt strongly that tanks and motor pool activities were not where he wanted to spend his wartime duty. With his background and talents, he became an accomplished member of this tank operation and his officers all liked his presence, but Verlen repeatedly requested that his commanding officer allow him to take the Air Force Qualification Test. His commanding officer, however, wanted Verlen right where he was and refused each request. To further influence Verlen to settle down as a tank man, his CO gave him two stripes prior to the completion of tank training and sent him off to a three-month tank mechanic school at Fort Knox.

Verlen was twenty, turning twenty-one, when he began courting his Sweet Genevieve.

He completed mechanic school with high ratings, but while there, Verlen continued to plead his case by asking his new commanding officer at tank mechanic school to allow him to take the Air Force Qualification Test. This CO was of a different nature and admired Verlen's determination. The CO granted his request and set up an opportunity for him to test for the Air Force. Verlen passed the tests with flying colors and was on his way to the skies. He was ecstatic.

The Air Force immediately sent Verlen to Jefferson Barracks, Missouri, which was a collection point for new Air Force recruits. The developments of World War II demanded that the Air Force manufacture pilots quickly, and, at that time, one of the requirements to be in the Air Force was a minimum of two years of college education. Verlen had not even finished high school. Because of this, and the fact that he had done so well on his qualification test, Verlen was sent to Michigan State College (MSC; later called Michigan State University) in East Lansing, Michigan. Those recruits who passed the qualification exams had a variety of educational backgrounds. Many had college degrees, but there were others with no college experience. Consequently, the Air Force invented a three-month condensed college prep course for would-be pilots, which sort of leveled the playing field for those who became pilots. Those who had no college background could say that they had gone to MSC. The Air Force felt that the college course made it easier for all of the pilots to transition through flight school and what followed. Verlen claimed that while he did well in all of those condensed courses thrown at him at MSC, he never really understood how they benefited him as a pilot.

MSC study notes found in Verlen's archive files. Note the "Jenny PRINCESS" artwork. *(photo from Kruger Archives)*

A life-changing event did happen while attending the Air Force's MSC crash course. He had a blind date with a seventeen-year-old junior from Lansing Eastern High School named Genevieve Mae Seavolt. Genevieve (called Jenny) had reluctantly agreed to come along with friends and was surprised to find Verlen Kruger an interesting fellow. They toured Lansing in the rumble seat of a Model A Ford Coupe. Verlen was twenty, turning twenty-one, when he began courting his Sweet Genevieve. Jenny came from a small family and found it hard to believe Verlen had eight siblings. They biked through campus, and Lake Lansing was a favorite spot in the summer heat; they loved the ferris wheel and roller coaster there at the amusement park. Both were young, excited about life and strongly attracted to each other. Throughout Verlen's ninety-day presence at MSC, they went out on weekend dates to the town carnival, movies, roller skating and, frequently, just for something to eat.

Following his compressed college education at MSC, the Air Force sent Verlen to Tulsa, Oklahoma, for preflight training. At that time, the Air Force did most training in three-month cycles. As Verlen described these cycles he remembered, "About twenty percent of the original group of pilot-trainees washed out in each of the three-month cycles of training." The Air Force did not encourage making intimate friends during air combat training. They wanted young, highly motivated, unmarried pilot trainees who had little to worry about besides air combat. They did not want cautious pilots. Only about two percent of the recruits actually became fighter pilots. Those who didn't qualify still had the opportunity for other flight duties such as navigation, bombing and gunnery duties.

Verlen continued pursuing Jenny during her senior year through long letters from Tulsa. He scored well in preflight training and remained highly motivated.

Genevieve (Jenny) Mae Seavolt wearing Verlen's silver flight wings *(photo from Kruger Archives)*

2nd Lt. Verlen Kruger, walking with 2nd Lt. Frank Carpenter, in San Antonio, Texas, 1945
(photo from Kruger Archives)

Jenny swimming with Verlen and friend
(photo from Kruger Archives)

Love letters from Jenny helped. Verlen was in the process of becoming what he had dreamed of: a pilot for the U.S. Air Force.

From Tulsa, Verlen was sent to Wichita Falls for primary flight training. During this cycle, he soloed for the first time in a single-engine aircraft. Because his flight instructor was the cautious type, he made Verlen train a full twelve hours (instead of the normal ten) before allowing him to solo. During that solo flight, he took off, flew his pattern and then approached for a landing. As he approached for touchdown, the aircraft wanted to float farther instead of land. Verlen, feeling he'd already used up too much of the runway, poured the coals to the throttle and took the plane around again as if shooting touch-and-go landings. The second approach was good, the landing better, but his flight instructor was still not satisfied. He made Verlen do another flight accompanied with a test pilot to double-check his flight prowess. When they landed, the test pilot gave him an excellent rating, which was exactly what Verlen thought the first test pilot should have done. Verlen was awarded his silver wings.

Silver wings were also worn proudly by Genevieve Seavolt in a high school photo that she mailed to Verlen. Verlen returned to Lansing to spend the Christmas holidays with Jenny. On the way home from a movie, he pulled the car into the Mount Hope Cemetery near her home. "What in the world are we doing here?" Jenny asked. Verlen said, "I thought this would be a great place to propose marriage." Genevieve accepted, and they were engaged. It was then that Verlen gave her the costume jewelry set of silver wings, like those he earned, that she wore in the photo.

Back in Wichita, Verlen could solo at will. Consequently, he spent considerable time testing himself and his aircraft. At one point, he was asked to again fly with an instructor who said that he was going to show Verlen how to fly upside-down. Verlen took great satisfaction demonstrating that he could already fly upside-down better than his guest. He had also privately practiced dives, loops, rollovers, and a variety of other maneuvers he had yet to name. Much of what combat pilots were doing in 1942 was new and innovative and Verlen liked it that way. Early on in his training, he made note of the fact that two pilots fighting in similar aircraft would have equal opportunity to survive the fight, unless one pilot knew how to get more from the aircraft or himself. Verlen pushed to have that edge and flew all the extra time he could handle. When Verlen talked shop with the other trainees about the number of times they practiced each maneuver, he was surprised to find he had practiced those new skills far more times than others.

Waco, Texas, was the next stop for another three-month cycle. This time, it was basic combat flight training in a radial engine trainer aircraft called the BT-13. Verlen and the other trainees had a lot of freedom in their flying time. He flew his own practice combat missions, during which he would attack everything he could find in the sky. He would sneak up behind all aircraft, and if they did not wave their wings—the signal that they knew he was back there—he would count them as a kill. He took pleasure in notifying them, via radio with a chuckle, that they were no longer among the living.

Verlen again did well during this air combat training and was soon bound for Moore Field in McAllen, Texas, for advanced air combat flight training. Most of this training was flying the AT-6 and P-40 aircraft, which brought him ever closer to his goal of becoming a fighter pilot. Again he sought all the extra flight hours he could and became proficient with both aircraft.

Next came six weeks of gunnery training, which consisted of dive bombing, air-to-air combat, machine gun training, and staying alive during the performance of air strategies. Verlen loved every moment of it. He thrived on the excitement, the learning, and the action. This was the most fun he had had since entering the military. One afternoon, he was assigned to go up and machine-gun a target being towed by another aircraft. He zeroed in on the target, fired his rounds, and

Verlen flying an AT-6 in Texas *(photo from Kruger Archives)*

landed, confident of his success. On the ground he was advised that there was not a single hole in the target. Verlen didn't believe it. Up he went again. Again he zeroed in on the target, fired his rounds—making doubly sure to strategically abuse the towed device—and then landed. He was again advised that there was not a single hole in the target. Both he and his instructor were now suspect of these results. Up went his instructor in the same aircraft. He fired, landed, and was told there was not a single hole in the target. They then sent Verlen up in a different aircraft, which provided dramatically different results. He needed a score of thirty hits to pass this gunnery test. He scored sixty-seven. The aircraft mechanics then went to work on the other aircraft Verlen had been flying...something about sighting adjustments.

Verlen liked to test the limits of his piloting skills and the aircraft he flew. The maximum flight ceiling for the AT-6 aircraft was said to be 20,000 feet. He couldn't understand that because the plane had behaved perfectly well for him at 23,000 feet, though a little "mushy." It also dove at full throttle all the way down to near ground altitude with no ill effects. His instructor had told him that if the plane exceeded its maximum prescribed speed (which Verlen had done repeatedly by more than 100 miles per hour) it was apt to disintegrate. "Loved those tailspins on the way down!" he grinned.

At the end of his Moore Field training in McAllen, Texas, President Franklin Delano Roosevelt commissioned Verlen Kruger a Second Lieutenant in the Air Force. Verlen

Verlen and Jenny shortly after their wedding
(photo from Kruger Archives)

was a certified air-combat fighter pilot. He was ready and anxious to go into action wherever the war demanded. After graduation and commissioning, Verlen was asked what he wanted to do next. His response was, "Combat fighter pilot. The sooner the better!"

Verlen patiently awaited assignment, but it was some weeks later when his CO informed him that, instead of a combat flight assignment in the war, he had been assigned to air-combat flight instructor status and was to be stationed at McAllen, Texas. Verlen was bitterly disappointed to find he was not assigned to active duty combat for his country and made it known to his CO. He was immediately given an attitude adjustment speech by his CO, which resulted in Verlen seeing the merits of his assignment as a greater service than as a single combat pilot. He was also advised of many worse assignments he could have been given. Only the top ten-percent of any class were eligible to become instructors, so this was another major accomplishment for an ex-sharecropper with little formal education.

Verlen and Jenny were married in McAllen on June 30, 1945, Verlen's twenty-third birthday.

At the ripe old age of twenty-two, Verlen was on his way to Randolph Field in San Antonio, Texas, for advanced fighter pilot instructor training. At Randolph Field, he was once again flying AT-6 trainers. Following this ninety-day training cycle, Verlen was sent back to Moore Field in McAllen where he was assigned as a permanent air-combat flight instructor.

Victory in Europe (VE) Day signified the war was approaching an end. This event allowed Verlen and Jenny to believe it was safe for them to head down the matrimony trail. With the war ending, Verlen felt being married would no longer be frowned upon by the Air Force as it had in the past, and he wanted to marry Jenny. Verlen didn't want Jenny to have to move from one base to another, but they had both made up their minds they wanted to be together, starting now. Jenny was a gutsy young woman and she was determined to be with Verlen whenever and wherever she could. She was soon on a train bound for Texas.

We're getting married in the chapel! *(photo from Kruger Archives)*

One week after graduation in June of 1945, Jenny packed two heavy suitcases. Her parents wished her a good life and a happy marriage, gave their blessing, and waved goodbye as Jenny embarked on her first train ride ever. Jenny later said, "I was surprised to hear later in my life that my calm and composed father had tears running down his face as I pulled out of the train station." A younger sister and a cousin accompanied her as far as

Chicago, the first of several transfers, then returned to Lansing, leaving Jenny on her own. Jenny found her train and hauled her luggage aboard. She anticipated the next transfer in St. Louis, a large train station, with trepidation. During the St. Louis transfer, she realized she had lugged her suitcases far across the train yard to the wrong train. Peering across all the tracks, she hefted one suitcase and, with the other lengthening her arm, charged straight across the rail yard, leaping track after track. She wasn't going to miss that train. Jenny said, "My heart nearly stopped when I boarded. It was a troop-train loaded with veterans returning from the European front." She spotted the only other female aboard, a Mexican woman, and quickly stowed her luggage and sat beside her. The soldiers were courteous, but she admitted they made her nervous. It was a long two-and-a-half-day trip to McAllen, Texas. Jenny arrived on June 28, 1945.

Verlen and Jenny were married in McAllen on June 30, 1945, Verlen's twenty-third birthday. Genevieve Seavolt was eighteen years old. Their military married life took them to various little apartments—even to an aluminum mobile home—in Texas, Arizona, Illinois, and back to Texas. It wasn't until six months later that they were able to spend a holiday with Jenny's parents by commuting back to Lansing for a short period in between Verlen's moves. Jenny never got to meet Verlen's parents until Christmas of 1945.

He loved to fly! *(photo from Kruger Archives)*

Each flight instructor at Moore Field had five students permanently assigned to them. Verlen spoke of the traumatic times when a student-pilot crashed during training. Many near-accidents occurred to most instructors during flight training, and Verlen was no exception. He had taken up one student in a two-seater trainer, an AT-6, for some precision maneuver practice to fine-tune his formation flying tactics. As they came in on their final approach turn to the runway, the student lost speed and went into a dive. At only 500 feet, Verlen quickly pushed stick and throttle forward to achieve adequate speed to regain control, went around again, and made the student perform a proper landing. He said those things became almost routine to the instructors, but he was always amazed at how much he would sweat while flying with students during practice.

One of his students was the son of an Air Force commanding general. Verlen knew his instruction methods were under scrutiny, but only received positive feedback from his superiors. He loved flying and teaching and felt confident of his skills. He believed he could both out-fly and out-teach most of the other instructors, then added with that blue-eyed grin, "But that's how most of us instructors felt." Verlen's students rated high with their check pilots, a tribute to his methods of teaching. He didn't push his students to be rated higher or to win awards. He pushed them to demand more of themselves and their aircraft so that they had a better chance to out-fly their opponents and, therefore, a better chance to survive.

Jenny and firstborn Nancy
(photo from Kruger Archives)

Verlen's last year as a flight trainer provided him a lot of flight time in the P-51 aircraft. He

BASIC TRAINING SQDN 2 FLIGHTS A&B CLASS 44-10 RANDOLPH FIELD, TEXAS

Verlen with flight class, front row, second from right *(photo from Kruger Archives)*

loved that airplane! At that time, the Air Force was short on pilots, so student pilots from different countries that were our allies came to the U.S. to be trained and incorporated into the Air Force. In addition to his U.S. students, Verlen trained pilots from the Philippines, China and Brazil. These carefully selected pilots had already completed basic flight training and spoke fluent English. "These were interesting people to rub elbows with," said Verlen. Since the end of the war was now in sight, the action was slowing down. While there was a shortage of pilots a few years previously, they would soon have a surplus; thus, training assignments slowed. Verlen saw the end of his current instructor status might arrive in the next few months and, after talking it over with Jenny, he made another move in the military. Because of his officer status, by re-upping for another two years he would receive considerably more money and retain the opportunity to fly and teach. He liked what he was doing, so he did not want to be converted into a ranking officer, which is what would happen to him when he was no longer needed as a flight instructor. Jenny agreed, and Verlen signed up.

After that, he was TDY (assigned temporary duty) while awaiting new orders. Verlen's temporary duty assignment allowed him to fly when he chose to and, otherwise, have a good deal of time off with Jenny to enjoy the great states of Texas and Arizona, where Verlen was temporarily assigned in November of 1945. Jenny became pregnant with the first of their nine children in December of 1945. In that same year, after years of brutal fighting, the atomic bomb ended the war with Japan. A month later, Verlen was surprised when new orders shipped him to Tokyo, Japan, in July of 1946. Jenny moved back to Lansing to be with her parents during her first pregnancy and Verlen's absence. Nancy, their first child, was born in September while Verlen was in Japan and Korea.

When Verlen arrived in Japan, no one seemed to know what to do with him. He flew his time-required in P-51s, his aircraft of choice, to keep his flight certification active. Verlen was told to spend time in the air over Japan, but he never understood why. No one seemed to care when or where he flew. As he put it, "I got to know Japan well from the air." He felt he accomplished little in Japan, except the further honing of his flight skills in the P-51 and helping less-experienced pilots to do the same.

With the considerable free time between flying sessions, since he was no longer involved in active training classes, Verlen began to develop an intense interest in world religions. The free time activities of many pilots didn't much interest him. During his time in Asia, he read the Qur'an and two versions of the Bible. He said, "I never really knew why my interest in the Bible developed. The more I read, the more wisdom I found, so I kept reading." By the time he left Japan, he had read it through cover to cover. He was not involved with any church at that time and no one else was motivating him. He just liked what he read.

Verlen with his P-51, *Sweet Genevieve*, in Japan
(*photo from Kruger Archives*)

Six months later, he was reassigned from Japan to Korea, where he joined a flight group serving as a recon squadron assigned to keep the Air Force highly visible in the region around Seoul with their P-51 aircraft. This was a good assignment in Verlen's mind; he could, once again, fly as much as he wanted. His orders provided him a responsible assignment, there was still a military presence to maintain, and since he had to complete his tour of duty, he would rather do it flying. The scaling down of the U.S. war machine changed most military personnel's lives and he, too, adjusted to a less challenging assignment. Despite the absence of his Sweet Jenny, Verlen liked the fact that he was still serving his country, though not actually in combat. The Air Force needed to justify his presence and wanted to use his piloting skills. To make his stay in Korea official, the military had to have a duty assignment status for him. Since they didn't have enough pilot openings, the Air Force assigned him mess-officer. He knew absolutely nothing about that field, but it didn't matter; they only wanted him to fly.

After six months in Korea, Verlen was reassigned to Japan where he flew out of two more airbases. The Air Force had one more bonus for him in Japan. He was assigned his own P-51 for the balance of his service, proudly named *Sweet Genevieve*. Jenny was impressed. Verlen Kruger had given his best to his country and came home in May of 1947. After four and one-half years in the Air Force it was time to go home to Jenny and their baby, eight-and-one-half-month-old Nancy.

"Nine was fine with Jenny and me."

VERLEN KRUGER

Beginnings of the Verlen Kruger Family

Verlen spent the last three months in Japan planning the next moves for his young family that would follow his discharge. Fellow pilots speculated about the bright futures available to Air Force pilots in the developing U.S. commercial airlines. Major travel would be an integral part of a career with the airlines and he felt strongly that he wanted to be home and, like his father, be an important part of rearing their children. While thinking his way through the commercial airline scenario in letters to Jenny, they both felt he had been away from home enough and the lifestyle no longer suited them. He had accrued leave time from the Air Force, and with the additional savings from officer's pay, was able to fund the move and start-up expenses for a new life. Home from Japan in 1947, Verlen moved back to Lansing, Michigan, to rejoin Jenny and his baby daughter. He carried good memories of Lansing: his three-month collegiate experience, court-ing Jenny, plus her family lived there. It seemed like the thing to do. Verlen never piloted an aircraft again.

Verlen, Jenny and his parents on farm *(photo from Kruger Archives)*

They settled into a Lansing apartment across the street from a plumbing contractor busi-ness. Noticing that contractor's sign, and since he wanted to work with his hands, Verlen thought plumbing would be a natural extension from his farm background and mechanical training. He optimistically visited the Plumber's Union office to check it out. This first meet-ing with Union officials turned out to be pivotal for both Verlen and the Union. The officials made it clear that he needed to join the Union and become a dues-paying member before they would talk with him about plumbing. By then, Verlen had had enough of bureaucracy in the military and was a bit tired of being pushed around by rank. He was more than ready to be in charge of his affairs again. Verlen refused to join that Plumber's Union section, walked out and looked elsewhere.

Back at their apartment, he again spotted the plumbing contractor's sign and walked across the street. After a brief discussion with the woman managing the business for the owner, who was absent that particular day, Verlen was instructed to come back the follow-ing Monday morning. He started work for the company that same Monday and, within two years, had his journeyman's plumbing license. In another three years, he had earned his master plumber's license and was training other plumbers for the firm. Verlen's boyhood

Jenny with first baby, Nancy, at two months
(photo from Kruger Archives)

goal of being a teacher had surfaced as a combat pilot instructor and resurfaced in the commercial plumbing trade. He loved to teach.

Their involvement with the church increased. At that time, the American Sunday School Union was trying to promote growth in rural areas by using churches left empty. They encouraged their members to do some missionary work in that effort. Verlen agreed to give it a try. He and Jenny both felt a calling to help country families know and serve the Lord. With another couple, Verlen and Jenny held Bible Studies and Sunday School for the children in a rural, empty church. About thirty-six people showed up with their children for the first service, indicating the receptivity for small rural church services. Verlen and Jenny were at that time ready to go anywhere in the world to help the church. Verlen decided to accept the missionary role and return to his original home territory in Indiana. There, he was to attempt to bring some of his new church's gospel into his old church, its members and his other acquaintances in the region.

Barn on sixty-five-acre farm burns in 1975 (photo from Kruger Archives)

Both Verlen and Jenny were happy with the way their lives were unfolding. Their family grew by four more. Verlen and Jenny were invited to the Walker Bible Church in Lansing and attended there for one year before getting involved with helping to organize the East DeWitt Bible Church in DeWitt, Michigan, just north of Lansing. At that time it was a small, newly formed church, which Verlen helped to fund, build, and organize. At first, not having adequate room, they met in an abandoned church for Sunday School classes. They didn't have enough money to hire a minister, but Verlen, then a member of the church board, invented a way to do it. On Verlen's plumbing paydays, he would pick up the minister, proceed to the bank, cash his check and then split it with the minister. To Verlen, there was always a way.

Verlen and Jenny had saved some money during those plumbing years and had bought an 80-acre farm North of DeWitt in Clinton County, which they also worked while he was in the plumbing trade. Verlen had nearly six years of satisfying work with the plumbing company. The Union, however, was not happy with the company because, so far, they were not Union members. All during that six-year period, the Union kept pressure on the company to have their employees join. As the pressure increased, things became more difficult for Verlen, who still harbored his Union grudge. It became obvious to the owner that it was important for the firm to have Union cooperation if they were to have more Union contracts. Verlen had already made up his mind about Union pressure and he would not join. When all employees but Verlen agreed to join, it put the spotlight specifically on him. The company offered to make him the head man if he would agree to join. Verlen made their decision easy; he resigned.

They sold the eighty-acre farm and, in March of 1954, purchased another sixty-five-acre parcel closer to DeWitt where they lived for the next twenty-two years (from 1954–1975). Eventually, and after considerable effort, Verlen saw that he would not be able to earn an adequate living for the family by farming. Ultimately, they sold this acreage too.

Seven of nine *(photo from Kruger Archives)*

Verlen and Jenny felt they had enough money to coast for a little while, and perhaps they had had enough of the plumbing trade and unions. The church life of the Krugers was growing stronger. Verlen continued to read the Bible, which aroused considerable interest in both him and Jenny. At Walker Bible Church, they met other Born-Again Christians and attended Bible study classes and Sunday school sessions with their kids. It was there that Verlen dedicated his life to Christianity. Later, at the East DeWitt Bible Church, first Verlen and then Jenny became Born-Again Christians. They were both beginning to think Verlen might pursue an even stronger involvement with the church.

Verlen and Jenny moved onto the sixty-five-acre farm and turned their attention to raising the family and church activities. With the church's encouragement, they headed south each weekend to be ambassadors for Christ in Verlen's old home town. He still needed to create income, so he tried to find plumbing work in the region. He would earn a living during the week and work for the church nights and weekends. Verlen's urge to teach had surfaced again, unexpectedly, as a calling.

He found no work. Either there was no need for plumbing business in the region or those needing it were not willing to hire Verlen. Whatever he tried to do, he found doors closed to him. The local banks wouldn't grant him a mortgage. Homes or farms for sale became unavailable to him. With hindsight he realized that his evangelical approach to bringing the gospel home was resented by the community. Who was Verlen Kruger to begin preaching a new gospel to them? He and Jenny put forth a valiant effort for a couple of months before realizing they had made a mistake. Though they had accomplished some of their gospel-

He and Jenny both felt a calling to help country families know and serve the Lord.

spreading mission, they realized further efforts would be futile without work and with doors closed to them.

They both knew there were other ways they could help the church and they were both determined to properly raise their family without this added hardship. They returned to that sixty-five-acre farm they had bought in DeWitt. Verlen used the barn to store plumbing supplies and the enclosed porch for an office, and aggressively created his own commercial plumbing contracting business.

By then he already had his master plumber's license. He looked around the Lansing region and found a small motel under construction. Through a conversation with the builder he found that they did not yet have a plumbing contractor secured. Verlen successfully bid the job and was on the way into his new business. He continued to focus on smaller motels and other small commercial contracts, thereby avoiding direct conflict with his old nemesis, the Union, which hadn't yet noticed his reemergence in the region.

His plumbing business flourished as he used the barns on the 65-acre farm to store his plumbing supplies. The family had more money to spend than ever before. Verlen brought his mother and father up from Indiana and built a home for them in the region. His father's heart ailments and age prevented him from being very active in the plumbing trade, but he took over the tasks of inventory control and job preparation, freeing the plumbers to do their work and enabling them to be more productive. Verlen hired a brother, and his brother-in-law as well. They all worked for the business. When Verlen encouraged his brothers and additional members of the Indiana Kruger family to come to join the business, they often lived with Verlen, Jenny and their large family for about a year while getting settled in Lansing.

Verlen was approximately thirty-six, and Jenny, at thirty-two, had given birth to Sarah, their ninth and last child.

Kruger family, 1959; (front row l to r) Christine, Jon, Philip, Verlen, Deborah, Mary and Sarah on Jenny's lap; (back row) Nancy, David, Daniel next to Verlen. *(photo from Kruger Archives)*

Within ten years, Verlen had over twenty other employees and, for a time, claimed to be the second largest commercial plumbing contractor in the city of Lansing. As Verlen began to want more time off to vacation with Jenny and the kids, he trained his brother Lawrence into managing the business with him so he could handle it when Verlen was gone. It was a good arrangement and Verlen began to have more fun with Jenny and the kids.

By then, Verlen was approximately thirty-six, and Jenny, at thirty-two, had given birth to Sarah, their ninth and last child. It was about this time that Verlen decided he needed a recreational vehicle that would enable the eleven

Krugers to vacation inexpensively. He built his own camper trailer that he and Jenny used for vacations into Canada, to the Grand Canyon, and around the Great Lakes. When they weren't vacationing for longer periods of time, it was weekends here and there. The Kruger family liked to be on the move!

It took constant effort by both Verlen and Jenny to keep up with their nine children. The morning ritual included awakening by Verlen, serving eleven breakfasts, dressing for school, and standing inspection for the parents before heading out the door. Living on a farm, as Verlen and Jenny had wanted them to, enabled the kids to have freedom to play. They used the barn more for playing than for animals. Verlen would climb after the boys through the rafters of the barn. The bear, as the kids called him, could always be stimulated into the chase; how they all loved it! The kids grew up with chores, as Verlen had, and they all developed a strong work ethic as they matured. Farm life was a good life for the Krugers. He was far from wealthy, but they were more comfortable than ever before. Verlen said, "I never wanted to be wealthy, just to have enough." He never was wealthy and was at times borderline, but he always managed to keep the family secure, comfortable and active in an atmosphere of fun and love.

Krugers on the church steps; (back row l to r) Philip, Jon, Daniel; (middle row) Christine, David, Mary; (front row) Jenny, Deborah, Sarah, Nancy and Verlen. *(photo by Caroll Ramsey, courtesy of Kruger Archives)*

Creating his own business provided ten years of prosperity for him and Jenny and the family. It had been a good move. Verlen was approaching his forties and was about to discover canoes. Nothing would ever be the same again.

"Recreational paddling and canoe tripping was my first real recreation. It started when I was forty-one."

VERLEN KRUGER

Discovery of Canoes and Racing

Since Verlen's plumbing business concentrated much of the Indiana Kruger family around Lansing, the extended family naturally shared lots of time together on recreational outings, picnics, and multi-generational gatherings over the years. In 1963, Verlen, at forty-one, Jenny, and his brothers all took their families on a vacation into Canada. They rented canoes and tried out a short excursion into the Canadian bush. The first trips were brief, mostly weekends due to the business demands, but in the next years became longer and more frequent. Verlen soon owned a seventeen-foot, sixty-five-pound Grumman aluminum canoe.

It was on one of their week-long visits to the bush country of Ontario that Verlen began to dream of the possibilities canoeing presented. He envisioned simply cruising by canoe. He saw longer canoe trips that he didn't have to abort after a weekend or a week-long paddle—a canoe trip that would enable him to just keep going. He said, "I would look down some of those long, serpentine coastlines and I could see myself just continuing on to wherever I chose to go. What a dream that was!" In a book written by Verlen and Clayton Klein in 1984, Verlen wrote of canoeing, "It was the first hobby or sport I had ever engaged in. It seemed to fit my long-suppressed dreams and disposition perfectly!"

> *It was on one of their week-long visits to the bush country of Ontario that Verlen began to dream of the possibilities canoeing presented.*

Verlen Kruger at forty-two
(photo from Kruger Archives)

In the 1960s, Verlen had little knowledge of canoe paddling other than what he had taught himself. He knew nothing of canoe racing, or even of canoe tripping, except what he could find to read. It was then that he became interested in canoe racing, began to paddle and to read everything he could find on the subject. It was from those experiences that Verlen began to think of ways to make canoe paddling more efficient. His piloting experiences enabled him to have a cultivated grasp of things like friction, drag, and the behavior of air currents and machines that flew in them. Why should water be that much different? Verlen was falling in love with canoeing. Canoeing, as recreation and a sport, was about to have its limits tested, Kruger fashion.

From 1965 on, though operating his plumbing business full-time, Verlen read everything he could find on canoeing. In his typical fashion, he devoted one hundred and twenty percent of his efforts into his newfound interest in canoes. He read all of the history of canoeing he could find, including the fur trade throughout Canada and America. He read diaries, history books and personal sagas. Verlen also learned that Michigan had a rich history of canoeing of its own. The state was loaded with great canoeing rivers like the Au Sable, the Raisin, Manistee, the Manistique, the Chippewa, the Shiawassee, the Titabawassee, the Red Cedar,

Verlen teaching children to paddle a flooded canoe (photo by Jenny Kruger)

the Grand, and more. In his home, he began to build a specialized reference library about canoeing and tripping. Because of the demands of his business and their family, Verlen became used to burning the midnight oil for these extracurricular studies. During those years of research, the Krugers continued to do more and longer canoe trips into the Canadian bush. During the summers, Verlen and Jenny would take the kids on most paddling adventures, but each fall reserved one trip for just the two of them.

Jenny told a good story of early paddling: "Verlen and I were canoeing in Canada in the Rocky Island area, during our annual trip we took alone with no kids. We noticed a dam on the map that looked interesting. So we portaged into another lake to check it out. We paddled far down and around the shore of that lake for a long time, looking for the dam, but couldn't find it. We noticed there were no cabins or homes anywhere on the lake. Meanwhile it got dark and cold, because it was October. The lake seemed to be in flood, the water was high, now it was dark, and we couldn't find the portage back to the lake where our campsite was. We weren't dressed warm enough to be out there at night, and were getting colder fast. We thought we saw one light way down the lake so headed for it. When we finally reached it, we stumbled out of our canoe, exhausted, wet and *really* cold. It looked like some kind of a lodge so we knocked on the main door several times with no response. Finally a woman called out, 'Whoever is there, go to the guide cabin.' We explained our situation and she said, 'There is no dam, it's gone.' The owner had just flown out with hunters this day, and the guide took us over to a cabin the woman had told him to put us in for the night. He helped make a fire in the stove and left. We were grateful and quickly fell asleep laughing about our 'lost-in-the-dark dam adventure.' An hour later, we both awoke choking from smoke throughout

Swim time at the campsite (photo by Jenny Kruger)

OPPOSITE: You can do it! Racing with Clint Baird.
(photo from Kruger Archives)

the cabin. The stove pipe had become too hot where it passed through the wall and was glowing and about to burst into flames where the wood was smoking. We poured buckets of water on it to cool the wall, let the fire go out, and leaped beneath the warm covers on the bed!"

Verlen soon discovered the Michigan Canoe Association, the variety of annual races it sponsored, and how he could join and learn new skills from its members. Soon Verlen and Jenny were paddling with members of the canoe association, practicing after work and on weekends for upcoming races. Verlen loved it. He found, as with most things, that he was a fast learner and was quickly becoming a skilled paddler. He began to envision Verlen Kruger winning races. As he developed his technique and endurance, he began translating his combat pilot competitive strategies into canoe race strategies.

The first race Verlen ever won was a friendly race on the Red Cedar River in Lansing, sponsored by the Michigan Canoe Association in the spring of 1965. He and Jenny paddled their old Grumman, hardly a racing canoe by today's standards, but it got them to the finish line before the rest. Verlen said, "I didn't really have a strategy, I was just trying to keep up with Jenny in the bow!" The nine Kruger kids soon became bank runners, chasing the Kruger team down the streams of the canoe associations rivers. Verlen continued to meet with the Association, devouring their information, meeting new members and found some who practiced more often and were always seeking paddle-partners. Verlen loved racing. It was his favorite canoe activity at the time. He knew racing would hone his canoeing skills, but what he enjoyed more were the miles of long-distance marathon paddles. He liked cruising by canoe, discovering and exploring new country along the way. If a race was what drew him to a specific area, that was fine; but when the race ended he always wanted to keep on paddling. He continued to dream about what it would be like to just keep going. He said, "I was born 200 years late. I should have been an explorer with Lewis and Clark, Mackenzie, and Peter Pond."

Kruger's three-month tour of the United States and the nation's capital (photo by Verlen Kruger)

He credited a portion of his success at racing to his pilot navigation skills. The longer the race, the more important navigation became. His skills at reading topographical maps made him able to expedite routes through the bush. Through more than 100,000 miles of paddling, he was seldom lost, though he admitted to times when he was "misplaced for a few days." In the slow-moving currents of the braided, flat mouths of large rivers, he would sometimes have to watch the direction underwater grasses pointed to select the branch of the outlet on which he could reach the sea. Backtracking seemed to take so much longer after the discovery that he'd made the wrong choice and had to paddle back and try again.

It was Verlen's experience as a flight instructor that helped him choose partners for races and marathons. He was careful with whom he teamed up. Often, it was a mutual respect for each other's talents and attitudes that brought teams together. Verlen competed in nearly every big race on the North American continent at least once. On many competitions, his partner was Clint Waddell. Clint could remember twenty-five such events and said he and Verlen would always try to paddle a minimum of 500 miles before each race, just to be in shape for the event.

Clint Waddell as a racer in Michigan
(photo from Kruger Archives)

Teaming up with Clint Waddell was an easy decision. Clint had spent four years in the Air Force as a weapons technician, had been a short-order cook while in school, had a degree in Biology and was working for the Forest Service in Michigan when he and Verlen met. His friendship with Verlen blossomed quickly because they were from similar molds. "We would sort of dare each other into trying something. Verlen would suggest that after a winter blizzard they should paddle the Looking Glass River in the snow. I would agree, but then suggest, 'Why don't we paddle all night?' We would usually try to one-up each other." When they first teamed up and started daring each other they often heard, "You're crazy, you'll never even finish!" That was the talk that inspired both of them to do a quick 500-mile practice before the event. The more they heard it the more determined they became.

The wins and near-wins he and Clint enjoyed inspired Verlen to think of bigger challenges. Clint had taught Verlen most of what he had learned about competitive paddling and Verlen was ready to test it out. When Verlen and Clint first met and started paddling a couple of nights a week, Clint told Verlen about the Boundary Waters Canoe Area Wilderness (BWCA) on the border between Minnesota and Canada. Verlen had read of it, but had never seen it. When Clint told Verlen about one of the toughest races in America, Verlen's eyes lit up. The race was nonstop from Atikokan, Canada, through the Quetico Canoe Country of Canada, across the border and through the BWCA to Ely, Minnesota, then back to Atikokan. If you were one of the fortunate few who managed to finish, the race usually took about five days. Most did it with little more than fast food stops and catnaps. Verlen and Clint thought this would be the perfect race. They were now a good team, in top condition, and the BWCA seemed a suitable destination for the next challenge.

When Clint told Verlen about one of the toughest races in America, Verlen's eyes lit up.

This was Verlen's first highly competitive long-distance canoe race. Most other races he had paddled as a competitor were completed in one day. Verlen recalled that he talked Clint into going. Clint remembered that he talked Verlen into it. Verlen wrote in *One Incredible Journey*, "I still don't know why Clint let a forty-three-year-old greenhorn talk him into something like that, as at that time I had not yet seen a hard-core long-distance canoe race!" Once they agreed to go, they trained aggressively around the Lansing area whenever they could. Verlen and Clint found an eighty-pound cedar strip canoe they thought would be suitable. Prior to the race date, the two of them with Jenny and the kids drove to Atikokan. They found fifteen canoes had entered, but only ten actually showed up for the event. Jenny was fired up over this race. She and Verlen had won a couple's race not long before and she was sure he and Clint were headed for the winner's circle. The Kruger kids were, by now, also expecting their dad to show up in the winner's column.

During the planning stages for the Atikokan-Ely race, Verlen and Clint strategized on how to maximize their combined strengths to win. Verlen's "rule of maximum efficiency" led him to study how to get the most from the least. He learned it to get more out an aircraft or a pilot, but it easily translated into canoe racing as well. He and Clint both knew that time spent ashore for any reason other than portaging would cost them paddling time. The more time they paddled, the shorter the race would be. They concluded they should avoid doing any meal preparation or cooking ashore and make eating as effortless and efficient as possible while afloat. Verlen decided that they needed a portable and drinkable concoction, similar to the power drinks invented later. It would take no refrigeration and no preparation (other than shaking), and enough could be prepared in advance to complete the entire race. It would, in Verlen's opinion, certainly contain maximum nutrition and nourishment, and involve minimum hassle during consumption. It sounded like a great idea to both of them; thus, the infamous invention of Verlen Kruger's Moose Juice!

By the afternoon of the second day, Moose Juice had made Clint so sick to his stomach that he was crippled by cramps and nausea. They dropped out of the race that night. Clint said, "That was horrible stuff—the worst I have ever run across—and I let Verlen talk me into drinking it. By late afternoon, I was so sick and so weak I could not continue." He added, "Verlen was always known to take everything with him but the kitchen sink. We were so heavily loaded and I was so sick. And worse, it didn't bother Verlen a bit! That man could put anything into his stomach." That was the only race Verlen or Clint ever aborted. It was also the thundering end of Moose Juice. Verlen never applied for a patent.

The following year, better prepared, sans Moose Juice, and with another year of paddling under their belts, they were back in the Atikokan race. They won, besting Ralph Sawyer and Buzzy Peterson. Verlen said in *One Incredible Journey*, "It was an upset victory against most of the winners from previous years, including a team, both previ-

A curious bear checking out Verlen and Clint's canoe in the BWCA *(photo by Clint Waddell)*

ous winners and considered the U.S. National Professional Champs. That was high wine for a new paddler."

Clint remembered an interesting race strategy used by some contestants in those wild days. In another race, a couple of the contestants spent some time the day before the race modifying and disguising one of the real portages, then cutting a new and attractive "short-cut" that competitors would see, and perhaps use, during the race. The inviting turnoff looked well used, and Verlen and Clint ran hard and fast, over a portage with their canoe and gear straight into a dead end. By the time they backtracked, found the real portage and continued across to water, they had lost nearly a half hour on the leaders. Clint and Verlen always wondered how those leaders managed to miss that dead end portage.

Verlen invented a new dare for Clint, a sort of test for the both of them. He had read in history books of Sir George Simpson setting a six-and-one-half-day record paddling 269 miles from International Falls, Minnesota, to Grand Portage on Lake Superior during the fur trade era. Verlen wanted them to break that record. Clint agreed to try. To do it they would have to paddle the entire Minnesota–Canadian border route nearly nonstop, round the clock, for over three days. In 1969, Clint and Verlen paddled the exact Sir George Simpson route in eighty hours and forty minutes, a record that still stands today.

"Considering their canoe for the Ely-Atikokan race." *(photo by Jenny Kruger)*

Clint said about that trip, "We got lost more on the Rainy Lake to Grand Portage route than we did on the whole 7,000-mile Cross Continent Canoe Safari! BWCA portages are sometimes tough to find, especially at night. Lakes like Lac La Croix are easy to get lost on, even on a sunny day. During the second night above Gunflint Lake, while on the Granite River, we wound up dragging and lining our canoe right down the river because we couldn't find the portages. On Gunflint Lake, I told Verlen I could see fishermen in a boat ahead of us, and asked 'Why not ask them where the portages are?' He said, 'Go right ahead, but those are logs.' It seems I was hallucinating a little. This was the only canoe trip Verlen Kruger ever packed sparingly. We were so determined to beat that 1800s record we didn't even bring a tent. When we needed to eat or rest, we'd stop, build a small fire, cook and eat, then catnap by the fire until it went out and we were awakened by the cold. Then we'd get up, grab our gear and move on. To beat the record there was no time to make camp. No one has ever attempted to beat that record. There's probably no one foolish enough to try," Clint laughed. "We were young, strong and dumb then."

When told he couldn't live on junk food, Verlen responded, "This is fuel. Think of your stomach as a furnace. When the fire is raging, you can throw anything in it and it will be consumed. Only a sputtering fire has to be primed and babied."

VERLEN KRUGER

Cross Continent Canoe Safari

Winning the Atikokan to Ely and return race, and with the mad dash across the BWCA from International Falls record firmly clinched, Verlen and Clint knew they could handle bigger challenges as a marathon team. They agreed to partner up again, and named the canoe trip the Cross Continent Canoe Safari (CCCS). The route they would follow was sometimes called the Fur Trade Route.

Clint and Verlen planned to paddle a tandem canoe from Montreal to the Bering Sea, the route that the French voyageurs and English explorers traveled during the fur trade era. The trip had never been done in less than one year because of the annual freeze-ups on the rivers. The Voyageurs would usually make the journey in about a year: complete half of the route, winter over at some location, and then finish the trip come spring and summer. During that era the trips were in large freight canoes with six to ten paddlers.

Verlen and Clint right after the eighty-hour BWCA record *(photo by Jenny Kruger)*

Verlen could find only two other men who had tried this route in a tandem canoe: Sheldon Taylor, age twenty-four, and Geoffrey Pope, age twenty-three. Both were from New York City and they had paddled it in 1936. They made the trip in eighteen months, finishing in 1937. Verlen and Clint planned to complete the trip in six months. Experienced paddlers told them it could not be done. It is plausible that Verlen had a special, extra-competitive gene that was triggered into action by phrases like "It can't be done." Clint had one, too.

Verlen knew the bigger challenge of the Cross Continent Canoe Safari would be psychological, not physical. Once launched, he and Clint would not be farther than ten feet away from each other while paddling, and would remain in that proximity for ten to twenty hours a day for six months. There was only so much room in a tandem canoe. Ashore, they would make or break camp, build fires or cook and eat together, then try to get much needed sleep within a two-man tent, snoring and nightmares included. They would have two ways to communicate: talk to each other, or not.

A photo of Francis Hopkins's famous Voyageur painting, which has inspired so many canoeists, hangs in Verlen's office. *(photo from Kruger Archives)*

The planning was intense, Kruger style. Verlen did the bulk of the research and communications for mail-stops and food replenishing sites along the planned route. It took him more than a year. He wrote letters to post offices, stores, trading posts, and small communities telling them of their plans for the CCCS and was amazed at the response he received. People were interested in what they were attempting and wanted to help. Some also tried to discourage their attempt to make it in just six months. "Don't try it," they heard. "It's never been done in just a year. You're crazy if you think you can do it." The more they heard things like that, the more determined they became.

Cross Continent Canoe Safari good-bye from Jenny, May 1971
(photo from Kruger Archives)

Friends heard Verlen or Clint talk about the upcoming trip and some asked to join them. Verlen and Clint made it their policy to turn them down. Two paddlers were less prone to accident, sickness, or other complications than a larger group. Two paddlers in one canoe could likely adhere to the dictates of that carved-in-stone time and distance schedule to get them to the Bering Sea before freeze-up. A greater number of paddlers would likely slow them down. They learned this from their marathon and competitive events and stuck to their policy.

During the last year before the CCCS, Verlen built what he thought at that time to be the ultimate canoe for the challenge. In the early 1970s, the availability of commercially available canoes was limited. There were a few standards like Grumman and Alumacraft in aluminum, and a small variety of other wood and canvas or fiberglass models, but the choices were few. Most of the racing canoes were custom built by their owners and used designs usually found through the canoe associations. Verlen and Clint could find nothing commercially available that suited them, so Verlen decided to build. He and Clint were pretty much up to speed on the variety of racing canoe designs, and Verlen was always dreaming up ways to make canoes faster, more efficient, capable of carrying the desired load, and seaworthy. He designed and built a twenty-two-foot, cedar strip, fiberglass-sheathed canoe, and they were both quite happy with it. But Verlen felt that it could still be improved with a wider beam, so he built a second canoe, one foot shorter and with a thirty-four-inch beam. That one they loved! They could find no paddles tough enough, so Verlen built them as well, and spares too, from fiberglass components. This canoe was one of over 200 that Verlen eventually built. It was also one of the last he built without a rudder. After the CCCS, Verlen's canoes morphed into a sort of half-canoe, half-kayak designs.

This second canoe proved worthy. Its twenty-one-foot waterline and thirty-four-inch beam width made it fast. Its combined length and beam enabled it to carry whatever load of bulk and weight needed. It would carry the two of them through bigger seas and weather than either of them had ever paddled. The full-length canvas cover would keep it dry when needed, and should help keep the paddlers warm when they neared the Arctic end of their route. The fiberglass sheathing of the cedar hull was designed to hold up well with almost no repairs throughout the Safari. Portage-ready (empty), the canoe weighed in at 144 pounds.

Verlen planned to portage the canoe plus a backpack, bringing his load to 170 pounds. Sometimes during training, to her delight, Verlen would portage his ten-year-old daughter, Sarah, along in his backpack. They tried to keep the loads as even as possible, but Clint remembered that there were many times he carried 200 pounds. "Like I said, we were strong, young and dumb then." Both admitted that they had overestimated their ability to carry that kind of weight for long distances, and paid a high price in sore muscles, wear and tear on knees (which haunted Verlen's later years), aching backs and feet for their self-declared and rigorous standards.

In *One Incredible Journey*, Verlen said, "It was a strong matter of principle to us, that we would go all the way under our own power and at no time would we use a motor, sail, guides, or follow-up crew. Neither would we accept help of any kind in paddling, portaging, towing, or trucking on land or water. Being true to the elemental spirit of canoeing seemed to give us a more satisfying sense of earned enjoyment."

On the morning of April 17, 1971, Jenny and the kids dropped Verlen and Clint and their gear off by the St. Lawrence River in Lachine, Quebec, a suburb of Montreal. Jenny said, "This was no easy task for the kids and me. Verlen had been the love of my life since I was 18. I was engaged in the excitement of what they were undertaking, but both the kids and I knew how much we were going to miss him." Verlen and Clint had to search for enough ice-free, open water to launch. Real breakup would not come for another few days and in the meantime they had Verlen's carved-in-stone time and distance schedule to reckon with. "The ice was haunting our start," said Verlen. "After several false starts for cameras and media, I turned back a couple of times to hug and kiss Jenny and to tell her goodbye, before I finally stepped into the canoe where Clint had been patiently waiting."

It turned into another false start; three-foot thick ice soon stopped them again. Because of anticipated freeze-up at the Bering Sea, they had no days to spare waiting for the ice to break up. Thus began the legendary, three-day, forty-four-mile

Jenny's RV in background, Verlen and Clint load canoe in Montreal (photo by Jenny Kruger)

Too much ice, no place to paddle! *(photo by Verlen Kruger)*

Starting a three-day portage! *(photo by Phil Pemberton)*

portage up the St. Lawrence River to find ice-free and open water. The Cross Continent Canoe Safari was underway. During those three days of portaging, Jenny and the kids drove ahead of them, reporting ice conditions in the evening. She wondered why Verlen and Clint didn't just start where open water began. "Too stubborn, I guess," he responded.

Their route from Montreal took Clint and Verlen several hundred miles onto Lake Superior, whose reputation still prevents many from plying those waters. Gitchee Gumi, as the Ojibwe called her, is renowned for the storm-sinking of ore ships, freighters, sailboats and fishing vessels designed for her waters. In the canoe, it was primarily the paddlers who enabled the boat to weather the waves and squalls of Lake Superior. It was also up to them to determine when they were better off windbound ashore. Verlen and Clint had good judgment and a tripping canoe up to the challenge.

In *One Incredible Journey*, Verlen wrote of racing the wave's surf on the Lake Superior paddle: "It was crazy, for we had paddled thirty-eight-hours and had moved 115 miles since our last camp. We had been cold, wet, miserable and very tired only a few minutes before. Then, we raced the wind and the waves, and enjoyed it. We no longer felt tired. It was just the thing we needed to make our hearts pump harder and faster, to force the circulation of blood through tired muscles, and to stimulate our bodies. We both remarked how good it made us feel. To sprint like that, to make the heart beat faster is part of a long-distance, marathon canoe racer's strategy. It pumps some life back into a dead-tired body."

The danger of freeze-up on the Bering Sea at end of the trip demanded that they adhere to the planned schedule. Freeze-up coming early could cause the end of the trip before they accomplished their six-month goal and could also make it difficult to return to civilization from the Bering Sea. Being caught in freeze-up near the Bering Sea could be life-threatening. There are no roads, almost no people and, therefore, no help. Their marathon racing experiences had already made them aware of their abilities to go well beyond what others might call normal limits of perseverance. If needed, they could paddle on for twenty-four-hours and more. As they sought their limits, they discovered new capabilities they never dreamed they had.

Verlen and Clint paddled from sunup to sundown, and often into the night when conditions were right. As they paddled west, their daily routine began to average sixteen-hour days. Because of the tight time and distance schedule, they would frequently try to gain extra distance when they could. Several days of going farther than planned gave them a cushion, which allowed them to lie over in extreme weather, or if they became wind-bound or ill. They could always count on the weather to do something to steal valuable paddling time. When it did, they would make up the time with a longer, harder day's paddle to come back on schedule.

Already built into the schedule were the visits from Jenny and the kids, who met them along the route with goodies, news from the home front and the fun and enjoyment of reuniting. These rendezvous stops were a boost and everyone parted feeling better for the contact.

Verlen and Clint loved to physically pull on the paddles. They would sometimes paddle for hours without saying a word. Clint, the stern paddler, steered as he paddled and Verlen, the bow paddler, provided plenty of propulsion and set the pace, sometimes in fast water calling out obstacles or deflecting them. Their rhythm was an inspiring sight. They didn't need to focus on staying in rhythm, or at pace. As part of their muscle memory, it just happened.

Ice behind them, upstream into the Ottawa's current! (photo by Phil Pemberton)

Being experienced canoe racers, Verlen and Clint used the racer's power stroke exclusively throughout the trip. They cruised at fifty to fifty-five strokes a minute using the short power stroke, which enabled them to continue that pace, hour after hour. As simple as the power stroke looks, professional racers sometimes spend years bringing it to a level they call satisfactory. It seems they are never quite finished perfecting the stroke, and someone is always coming up with a new tweak to make it better. Subtle improvements that can't be seen in a single stroke can be seen in the result of several thousand. Technical paddling in marathon canoe racing is an art and there are many artists out there. Verlen and Clint were among some of the first and best of them.

Verlen and Clint avoided conflicts by taking turns being captain for a day. Clint would captain on even dates and Verlen on odd dates. The captain would make decisions: best routes through the day's waters, when and where to stop for breaks, camp site selection and other major decisions du jour. The day's captain often shared or discussed decisions as well. This captain-for-a-day routine brought out the best in both men and was an effective system; the effort required to keep it working was less than what might be required to deal with the controversies that could easily develop in close confines.

Based on general moods, needs, weather and circumstances, sometimes conversation flourished; at others, each quietly pondered his own thoughts. Verlen was a fountain of history and Clint, a forestry biologist, was at home in the wilderness and could hold his own. If they wished, there was always something of interest to share. Boredom was never a part of their trip. When they needed space, Verlen or Clint would go off for a walk alone in the evening. Clint would sometimes go fishing, which usually provided a change of diet. When the strains were greatest, they separated the longest in the evenings, but generally it was easy for them to be together. Clint and Verlen tried hard to accommodate the other's moods and they were both good at it. Verlen was married, had the loving support and blessing of Jenny and their kids. Clint had been divorced for a couple of years and was missing his four children. The trip was good for Clint, who at the time was getting serious over another lady in Minneapolis (whom he later married). Family life was a frequent subject of their conversations. Clint, too, enjoyed the visits of Jenny and kids.

When they came ashore at night, they really had no assigned tasks. They both knew what needed to be done and would automatically go about their chores. If they needed wood for a fire, which they did almost every night of the trip, one would gather it while the other chopped or broke it up and kindled a fire. Both Verlen and Clint preferred an open fire for cooking and, after eating, could enjoy its warmth while drying gear. Verlen would more often cook, but Clint enjoyed making supper, too. While one cooked, the other would set up the tent and prepare their camp for the night. A good meal in a well secured camp site with a peaceful, friendly campfire left them comfortably ready to rest through the night.

Clint said, "I can only remember two times during the entire trip that Verlen and I had harsh words. Verlen was so easygoing and easy to paddle with. He was, of course, older than I by some fourteen years. He was more mature, had married and raised a family of nine children. I was newly divorced, missed my kids, and was wrestling with new directions in my life at this time. He was a stabilizing influence, a great navigator with his flight training experience, and was a good planner." Clint went

Clint complained that Verlen wore out his shoes, then would borrow Clint's spares and wear them out, too!
(photo by Clint Waddell)

A portage on the Canadian side (photo by Phil Pemberton)

OPPOSITE: It doesn't get much better than this, Clint!
(photo by Clint Waddell)

Portaging another rapids *(photo by Clint Waddell)*

Verlen writes his journal during lunch on the BWCA's Canadian Shield rock *(photo by Clint Waddell)*

on, "Once, when we were both frustrated by the conditions we were in, Verlen sensed my frustration and said, 'Do you want to quit?' He received no answer, and that was the end of that topic of discussion. It never came up again."

"The biggest frustration for me on the CCCS, and I think for Verlen too, was all the times we had to just sit and wait for Phil Pemberton to show up." Phil Pemberton was a film specialist Verlen had hooked up with before the CCCS began. Verlen felt it would be a great opportunity for a movie to be made on the trip. Pemberton was to do the filming at different times and locations from the beginning in Montreal to the end at the Bering Sea. Verlen and Pemberton set up filming locations and dates on the time and distance schedule for the trip. That way he and Clint could continue to race against time by paddle, and Pemberton would be waiting for them at strategically selected filming locations when Verlen and Clint arrived. "The plan was great," Verlen said, "but often we'd paddle in, and there would be no Pemberton. When you are racing freeze-up at the Bering Sea and haven't a day to lose, it is impossible to sit around waiting for the camera man when you should be paddling."

Clint echoed this frustration. "The second time Verlen and I exchanged harsh words during the CCCS was over Pemberton. Over the length of the trip, we had waited several days for him to show up at the designated locations. He always seemed to me to have some lame excuse for being late, and didn't seem to care that he was late. Then, when he finally did get there, we'd spend more time filming things again and again, using up more valuable time. Perhaps I just didn't see the potential value of the film, as Verlen did. Anyway, in usual fashion, once we had our harsh words, it was over. I can't remember another time we were upset with each other. We both wanted to be doing just what we were doing, as long as it wasn't waiting for Pemberton."

But there are always two sides to every story. Imagine chasing Verlen Kruger and Clint Waddell through the rough country they passed through on this trip, and then asking them to slow down for pictures. The movie was eventually made and distributed, but never reached critical mass, as Verlen put it, and ended up nearly bankrupting him. Phil Pemberton's photography skills were exceptional, though, and have provided an array of wonderful images chronicling the CCCS.

During their miles of paddling, Verlen and Clint ate well in their own fashion. To get underway in a hurry, they usually had a cold breakfast: canned fruit, leftover pancakes, peanut butter and jelly sandwiches, and whatever else was handy. During the day, they often ate something cold while paddling. They carried several thermos jugs for coffee, soup or hot water. Leftover soup and sandwiches were big during the day. At night, they made hot food, as gourmet as they could make it: usually beans, soups, canned meats and vegetables, with bread and a variety of topping. Macaroni and cheese was a staple throughout the trip and, indeed, on every one of Verlen Kruger's trips. Verlen also claimed that one pancake equaled four miles. So pancakes were one of the most-used recipes on the entire trip and pancake flour was an easy base food to carry. Verlen became famous for measuring or projecting a day's paddle by the number of pancakes eaten at the start of the day.

The before (and after) pictures of Clint's Northern pike
(photos by Phil Pemberton)

Clint told an interesting story about Verlen's eating habits. Early into the trip, they agreed that Verlen was bowman and Clint took the stern. Clint said, "The canoe was usually covered with its full-length cover to help keep us dry and warm. Verlen never seemed to eat a single meal, but usually the volume of two meals at one sitting. Then I would hear him occasionally speak of an upset stomach, which I knew would soon result in the stern-paddler being overcome by a blue cloud of methane, the source was sitting in the bow. Because of the forward motion of the canoe, that cloud would exit the canoe cover through the opening in the stern where I sat. Verlen and I had many discussions about this phenomenon as we progressed toward the Bering Sea, but he was never able to fix it. Even worse, he didn't even seem to notice when it occurred!" Verlen never mentioned this phenomenon.

Verlen had an interesting theory about eating while canoe tripping. He said, "One should look at their stomach as a furnace. In a poorly built fire, much wood will not ignite, burn hot, or provide warmth. But in a raging fire, one can put almost any burnable material, including green wood, into the fire and it will burn famously." It was important to Verlen to eat a lot, and to eat a lot often to keep his stomach functioning well. Most who paddled with Verlen were amazed at the amount of food, the variety of food, and the frequency with which he devoured that food no matter where they were. Shortly after breakfast, Verlen would invariably ask "How about a Coke or a cookie?"

There was really nothing special about the clothing and gear that Verlen and Clint used on

We'll get there even if we have to walk.
(photo by Clint Waddell)

They loved their twenty-one-foot canoe in fast water (photo by Phil Pemberton)

the CCCS. In 1971, exotic, high-tech tripping gear was commercially available, but not to the degree it is today. As is evident from the photos, most everything they had—except their canoe and paddles—appears rather run-of-the-mill. Their tent, especially, was nothing to crow about. They had not tried for clothing sponsors for the CCCS, so they wore basics: blue jeans, wool shirts when cold, t-shirts when hot, simple wind breakers, and rain jackets when it was dripping, but you see no brand names or labeled gear. Verlen and Clint spent very little on gear and clothing. They expected to be wet, cold, hot, to sweat and shiver as the price to be paid for such an adventure. They were excited about paddling to the Bering Sea with what they had. They dried what got wet, ignored it, dressed for the temperature in wool and, more than once, spent the night in wet sleeping bags. Years later, both could think of many items available in today's market that they would have liked to have had with them then.

One hundred and seventy-six days from the Montreal start, on the exact day the time and distance schedule called for, Verlen and Clint, covered with a thin film of ice, dipped their paddles into the waters of the Bering Sea. They reached their destination approximately 10,368,398 paddle strokes from Montreal. They had made 133 portages covering 153 miles, had towed or lined their canoe for forty-miles upstream in the Richardson Mountains, and had portaged around seventeen dams en route. According to the book, *One Incredible Journey*, "Unbeknownst to them at the time they had set records, such as the only two people in history to paddle the full route by manpower only, in less than six months. They had also established a record for the most miles ever traveled in a two-man canoe in less than six months." Even more amazing than the fact that they arrived on the Bering Sea on the exact date their time and distance schedule called for, was the fact that they were still friends and continued to be lifelong friends.

The wilderness staple of macaroni and cheese in gourmet hands (photo by Phil Pemberton)

The first truly long-distance canoe trip of Verlen Kruger was accomplished. He had not found his limits, nor had Clint, and neither one of them thought they had really gotten close to them. On October 10, 1971, when Verlen Kruger and Clint Waddell arrived at the Bering Sea, they were lodged in the history of canoe tripping through their success on the Cross Continent Canoe Safari. They had accomplished exactly what they had set out to do, to the very day. They established new records along the way, which still stand today. Better still, Verlen had learned that he was right about most of his feelings about his limits. They

Graffiti by an unknown on a lonesome portage in Yukon Territory *(photo from Kruger Archives)*

Lining upstream on the Rat River *(photo by Clint Waddell)*

That way, or this way? "Not Lost," said Verlen, "just temporarily misplaced." *(photo by Phil Pemberton)*

Campsite on the Yukon beside some lumber piles *(photo by Phil Pemberton)*

"North, Clint!" "No, south, Verlen!" Always time for a little fun. *(photo by Phil Pemberton)*

(l to r) Clint, Verlen, Tony Mercredi (Phil's guide) and Phil Pemberton, the movie producer
(photo by Phil Pemberton)

Indian fish camp. Drying salmon on the Yukon. *(photo by Phil Pemberton)*

Pemberton got some great photos! Breaking camp on the Rat River headed for snow! *(photo by Phil Pemberton)*

Heavily iced the day before reaching the Bering Sea *(photo by Verlen Kruger)*

Lunch and a quick nap as Clint dreams on a bed of rocks *(photo by Verlen Kruger)*

had left as tough men, came home tougher, and still had not found those limits. What's more, they had a blast doing it! Clint's face glowed as he remembered the Cross Continent Canoe Safari that was his and Verlen's.

Author's Note

The daily details of the journey are well presented in the book, *One Incredible Journey*, by Verlen and Clayton Klein. Read it if you can find it. As you read those details, it becomes clear that Verlen and Clint were indeed a well-matched team. Throughout the entire trip record, there is only a single reference to possible dissent between them (and that one unexplained by Verlen). He apparently forgot about Clint's grumbles about waiting for photographers. Both had expertly managed the stress of the trip. Each trained himself to concentrate on their goal, instead of being sidetracked by positives or negatives, daily weather or experiences. Neither of them glamorized or dramatized their situations or accomplishments.

10,368,398 paddle strokes from Montreal! *(photo by Phil Pemberton)*

"We were like brothers."

VERLEN KRUGER

A Brotherly Loss

Verlen Kruger and Jerry Cesar, and occasionally some of Jerry's family, canoed together for several years, mostly after Verlen's 1971 Cross Continent Canoe Safari with Clint Waddell. Verlen and Jerry met in Michigan canoeing circles through the Michigan Canoe Association, practiced and raced in some of the amateur events, and then began canoe tripping together. They and their families visited Coffee Lake, above the Sault Saint Marie region of Michigan and became fond of that area.

Jerry was inspired by the long distance paddling Verlen had done with Clint in 1971, when they did the 7,000-mile Cross Continent Canoe Safari, and was itching to do something similar with Verlen. Verlen was self-employed in the plumbing contracting business in Lansing, so had a more flexible schedule and could take time off in longer

Jerry in his new canoe, tripping with Verlen *(photo by Verlen Kruger)*

stretches. Jerry was limited to a ten-day work leave. Consequently, ten-day trips became the norm for Verlen and Jerry. They started taking up to ten-day trips together into the Boundary Waters Canoe Area Wilderness of Minnesota, and the Canadian regions of Lake Superior along with the rivers that feed it. They soon began to dream of longer trips they both wanted to make. In an article for *Canoe & Kayak* magazine, written by Larry Rice in July of 1999, Verlen is quoted as saying, "We first got to really know each other when canoe racing. Paddling as a team, you learn a lot about a person when you run a hard canoe race. Jerry and I were kindred spirits, like born brothers. We used to joke that our butts were identically conformed to a canoe seat."

Jerry and Verlen shared more than just their love of canoes and paddling. They both had firm religious convictions. They were both Born-Again Christians, they read the Bible together on occasion, prayed before meals, and often discussed their individual philosophies during their paddling ventures. Their relationship was so close that at a northern Michigan Bible Camp during a Christian Retreat in 1974, Verlen was the one to baptize Jerry, at Jerry's request.

Jerry was an accomplished canoeist. In 1973, he and Verlen had made a 400-mile canoe trip up the Kaministikwia River near the Thunder Bay region of Ontario and then looped

Their relationship was so close that at a northern Michigan Bible Camp during a Christian Retreat in 1974, Verlen was the one to baptize Jerry, at Jerry's request.

back down the Pigeon River Canadian Border to Lake Superior. What made that trip unique was that they bypassed the Grand Portage from Fort Charlotte down to historic Grand Portage, Minnesota, and instead paddled and portaged the rapids, falls, and fast waters of the Pigeon River all the way to Lake Superior. Jerry and Verlen were both into physical training and loved to pick long, tough, routes. Jerry Cesar wrote an article about that trip with Verlen. He said, "This story is about the experiences of two Christian men as they retrace one of the almost forgotten fur trade routes from Thunder bay, Ontario, to Fort Frances on the International Boundary. Verlen Kruger and myself, Gerald Cesar, were the second canoeists over the first portion of this route in the past hundred years or more. Both of us have a deep love for the wilderness and being physical fitness advocates we enjoy traveling in the footsteps of the bygone age of the voyager and try to match or surpass their records for time and distance. Even with our modern equipment and nutrition; one is often hard pressed to match their pace."

Jerry's family: Jerry, Jill, Todd and Nancy Cesar
(photo from Kruger Archives)

In that same article, Jerry painted more of a picture of him and Verlen as canoeing partners when he wrote "I consider Verlen an expert on all phases of canoeing. He has been quite successful in professional canoe racing by winning or placing quite high in a number of the larger Canadian races. Verlen is from De Witt, Michigan. He is 51 years old but I often think of him as being younger than myself. He stays in condition by doing a lot of race paddle training and some jogging. In the past 5 years he has set some very impressive time and distance records by canoe. Fort Frances, Ontario to Grand Portage, Minnesota of Lake Superior in 80 hours, 250 cross country miles! Ottawa, Ontario to Moosonee on James Bay, 540 miles in 10 days! In 1971, the historic Cross Continent Canoe Voyage never before accomplished, establishing new long distance endurance records, 7000 miles in 176 days, from April 17th to October 10th. I'm 32 years old and from Ashley, Michigan. By using a combination of weight-training, jogging and paddling, I stay in fair shape the year round. I have about 15 years canoeing experience, including 5 years of racing. Most all of my leisure time has been spent afield hunting, trapping, fishing, hiking, backpacking, canoeing, cross country skiing and snowshoeing. So the wilderness and I are old acquaintances."

Verlen loved the northeast coast region of Lake Superior from the moment he first paddled it with Clint Waddell during the CCCS, the first of Verlen's big canoe adventures. During that trip, he and Clint paddled the entire northeast coast of Lake Superior from Sault Saint Marie to Grand Portage, Minnesota, and Verlen had mentally recorded several regions to which he wanted to return. One region in his bull's-eye was the summit of Tip Top Mountain, which at that time Verlen thought was the highest elevation in Ontario, Canada. Verlen had made two previous attempts to reach the top of Tip Top Mountain; one with Jerry and one with other friends. Both had failed. The terrain of smaller mountains, which surround Tip Top, combined with swamps, rugged tree and underbrush growth, had prevented them from ever reaching the top within their ten-day time limits. But Verlen was determined that on the next attempt they would have success.

Verlen and Jerry planned to reach the summit of Tip Top Mountain and began to plan carefully and strategically. They had studied the region and decided to drive Canada's highway 17 to the White River, launch there, and paddle and portage the fifty-odd miles down to the shores of Lake Superior. Arriving at the mouth of the White River, they would paddle east along the shoreline until they reached the point estimated to be about twelve miles due south of Tip Top's summit. Those twelve miles would be the shortest overland route they had found to attempt to reach their goal.

Jerry and Verlen always said grace before meals *(photo from Kruger Archives)*

By the time he and Jerry settled on the Tip Top Mountain goal, Verlen had gained much experience at canoe design and construction through years of race training, races, ten-day canoe trips, and lots of canoe building. He and Jerry spent a good deal of time looking for what they thought would be an adequate boat for this trip.

Verlen and Jerry needed canoes that would handle both the river waters and the big waters of Lake Superior. Verlen said, "Jerry and I were doing a lot of tripping together then. Mostly into the Ontario bush country on those ten-day trips. We both wanted to be able to do longer trips and it looked like the best way to do it was to have a good solo boat for each of us. We had done considerable paddling in tandem racing canoes, but for this kind of tripping we felt solo boats would be better. Neither of us could find such a thing." Verlen had tested existing boats through canoe clubs and commercial manufacturers, but in those days solo boats were not readily available as they are today. These were the years when kayaks were just being discovered again, and canoes were not being used that much on big waters. Verlen even ordered a Rob Roy out of Denmark, but it wasn't big enough for their needs. Though well designed and built, neither he nor Jerry felt it was big enough to carry what they needed. Finally, they decided to design and build their own. Verlen felt they must have canoes that could hold a couple of hundred pounds of gear, plus themselves. They also had to be tough enough to take the anticipated beating.

By 1974, Verlen had built about twenty-four racing and modified racing canoes, using existing designs with his own innovations added.

By 1974, Verlen had built about twenty-four racing and modified racing canoes, using existing designs with his own innovations added. He had done extensive research on canoe design and construction and studied other manufacturer's boats as well. His flight training knowledge of air flow, drag, friction and resistance made it easy for him to envision different designs for building faster, more efficient, and larger capacity boats. Each of the boats he built for canoe racing had either been faster than the last, or was discarded for being shy of the performance desired. These boats were all of cedar strip construction, some with fiberglass skins added after they proved to be fast. With each new boat he improved his designs, construction skills, and understood more about working with the new high-tech miracle boat materials of fiberglass and Kevlar. By the time he and Jerry decided to build, Verlen was ready to accelerate his design skills and wanted to do more experimenting with Kevlar—a new, stronger, lighter type of fiberglass for the White River Tip Top Mountain trip.

Verlen's psychedelic-floral canoe for the White River *(photo from Kruger Archives)*

In 1974, Verlen drew plans, scaled models, made full-size patterns, and began the first of his solo, single-passenger canoes. From the finished cedar strip boats he made a fiberglass mold, which was needed to make a pure fiberglass or Kevlar canoe, which had no cedar or wood content between its multiple layers of fiber-mesh. These two solo boats were Verlen's entry into pure glass design and construction of canoes. In a later interview, he said, "I believe I may have made the first Kevlar canoes in the state of Michigan at that time." He and Jerry were not only going to have two state-of-the-art canoe designs, but the lightest and strongest as well. The boats were experimental and bold in colors. Verlen's was yellow and covered with psychedelic flowers. You could see them coming for miles.

During that winter, Jerry would stop in to help Verlen with construction and to continue strategic planning to reach the summit of Tip Top Mountain via the White River. The first solo canoe Verlen made was an undecked canoe for Jerry, who preferred a more open version. Jerry liked a fixed seat with two boat cushions, which, in those days, were Coast Guard-approved life cushions. He liked that height off the canoe's floor while paddling and he enjoyed the comfort of the cushions. While Verlen believed that a lower center of gravity was important in rough water, they had both agreed at the outset that each boat would be built exactly the way each wanted and each would have their chosen idiosyncrasies.

Verlen finished Jerry's canoe first, and then began his own. Verlen wanted his to be more enclosed, with a decked bow and stern surrounding an elongated cockpit area for the paddler. (Unknown to Verlen at the time, this decked-over design was the forerunner of his now-famous Loon, Monarch, Sea Wind, Dream Catcher, and Kruger Cruiser canoe designs, several of which are still built today.) The covered bow and stern section would readily shed turbulent water and wave crests. His boat now had the elongated and roomier interior, which Verlen felt was necessary for both comfort of the paddler and access to whatever gear might be needed while underway. He also felt that the more open cockpit would greatly speed the loading and unloading process when portaging.

Verlen's was the first canoe he knew of, or had seen built, with the feature of a multiple-height seat adjustment. He could elevate or lower the tractor-style seat at will, to either lower the boat's center of gravity in rough water, or increase the paddler's comfort by raising the seat in calm water. Being able to lower the center of gravity in rough water was a breakthrough over existing canoe designs, which then had fixed, stationary seat heights built in. Verlen felt his tractor-style seat was better for both comfort and control, because of the way it surrounded and comforted the paddler during long sessions of paddling. (Most canoes to this day still have fixed seat-heights, but the adjustable tractor seat was so popular and practical that it remains in all Kruger designs today.)

Another Kruger innovation was that each of these boats would have a rudder and foot-pedal steerage system. This was pioneering for canoe design at this time, because kayaks were just beginning to be rediscovered and manufactured. During his search for the ultimate boat, Verlen tested some of the few sea kayak designs then available. It was while doing this that he discovered the merits of rudders. Verlen, with his rule of maximum efficiency, immediately homed in on the fact that with a rudder for steering, one hundred percent of the paddling effort could be used on propulsion. In marathon racing, this saving of whatever amount of energy was directed to steering could win races. Steering by means of foot pedal also eliminated the tiring procedure of paddling harder on one side of the canoe when wrestling with winds and currents. (After this experiment, all of Verlen's future designs had foot-pedal rudders. There stands today a long list of wins and records that will likely stand for years to come. Some portion of each of those wins must be credited to this design innovation of rudders on Verlen's designs.)

In the spring, after they had finished the boats, they continued to play with the small design improvements each wanted in outfitting their hulls. In May of 1975, Verlen and Jerry loaded their boats and gear and headed for Canada. After driving all night, they arrived at the park where they would leave their cars and launch onto the White River. They loaded the canoes and had breakfast before daylight. They didn't need or want sleep.

They launched and paddled down the river 60 miles toward Lake Superior for the entire

Another Kruger innovation was that each of these boats would have a rudder and foot-pedal steerage system.

The part of Angle Falls hidden from the portage *(photo from Kruger Archives)*

day, reaching White Lake by late afternoon. They were pleased with the canoes and pushed themselves hard. The waters were high and they had made good time.

They approached their last planned portage of that day, just above a small lift-over called Angle Falls. They could see the portage sign above the high water level on the shoreline, which indicated where to come ashore for the short portage. Because of the flood stage of the White River, there was fast water flowing by the portage sign, not a rapids, but a strong downstream current against the rocky shoreline. Verlen watched from a few canoe lengths behind while Jerry nosed up to the rocks beneath the portage sign attempting to land. He grabbed the rocks on the shoreline, but the water's downstream tug and the slippery rocks prevented him from hanging on. As the water forced his canoe past the portage sign, he reached up and grabbed an overhead cedar branch to slow his drift. The current immediately pulled his canoe out from under him and swept it downstream, leaving Jerry immersed to his neck in the cold water. Verlen backstroked above him, to slow his canoe, as the swift waters pulled him toward the portage sign. Jerry made a decision to save his boat. He released the branch and looked at Verlen as he swam for his canoe. Their eyes locked, but neither was alarmed. Jerry was a strong swimmer, and their maps indicated there was no real danger immediately downstream. Verlen thought Jerry was thinking of what the loss of a canoe would do to the rest of their trip, which was why he swam for it. Jerry was right behind his canoe when he went over the slight drop in the river rounding the corner downstream of the portage.

Verlen paddled hard and rammed his bow far enough onto the slippery rocks to grab hold of the shoreline and got out of his canoe. He yanked his boat ashore and ran over the short portage and downriver to help Jerry pull his canoe ashore. Cresting the portage trail, he broke through the underbrush. He could now see downriver and immediately realized Jerry was in trouble. The river worsened quickly into a severe rapids, which, near the bottom, disappeared over what looked like a falls. Verlen continued running down the shoreline through the trees hollering for Jerry. He heard no response, just the roaring of the water cascading through rapids and boulders. He continued to run down the rapids to the big basin at the base of Angle Falls Portage. There was no sign of Jerry or his boat.

Verlen kept hollering, hoping to hear or see Jerry. The roar of the wild water became louder and more intimidating as the weight of a new possibility began to settle on Verlen. He saw Jerry's backpack floating farther along the shoreline of the basin's quiet water. The sight of anything of Jerry's produced hope. Verlen ran back up the portage, dumped everything from his canoe, then portaged his canoe at a run back down to the basin. He quickly launched and paddled all the way around the basin, and then did so again, and again, and again. During the next two or three hours, he found more of Jerry's gear, including the two boat cushions Jerry used as a seat. Both had been ripped, as though torn on the rocks. There was no sight or sound of Jerry.

Lagoon at the base of Angle Falls on the White River *(photo by Dan Smith)*

Dark approached and Verlen knew there was nothing more he could do but pray and hope. He built a big fire on the beach of the basin, hoping against hope that Jerry would see it and walk up for warmth. He found a stored fishing boat on the shore, which he tipped up and braced on its side with logs. He then set his sleeping bag beneath it and maintained his fire and vigil. He kept the fire blazing throughout the night as if adding more wood would encourage things to change and bring Jerry back. Sleep evaded him. Verlen said, "That was the longest night of my life."

At daylight, Verlen searched for two more hours, both around the basin and up and down the rapids that weren't there, according to their maps. No Jerry, no canoe, no more gear. Verlen continued to holler, "Jerry!" throughout his morning search, but finally realized there was nothing more he could accomplish alone. He felt fairly sure that Jerry was somewhere lodged within the rapids. He left Angle Falls Portage and paddled and portaged his boat, gear, and Jerry's recovered gear back upstream to their car in the park on highway 17. It was nearly dark, but there was a phone there in the park. He called the Canadian Mounted Police number posted on the payphone, reported their tragic accident, and arranged for the police to meet him there the next morning. He slept fitfully in his car, a second long night, awaiting the arrival of the Royal Canadian Mounted Police early the next morning. Verlen knew he had to call Jerry's wife, son, and daughter to tell them her husband and their father was not coming home. He had to call Jenny too. The weight was crushing, but he knew it fell to him to communicate the loss.

When he finished the call,
he cried and prayed for
Jerry and his family.

Though he knew better, Verlen had clung to the faint hope that the police might accomplish something in their search that he had not. They drove Verlen from the park to a seaplane on a nearby lake, then flew into the stretch of the White River just above Angle Falls Portage where they landed and tethered the plane to shore. Climbing over the rocks and through underbrush, they combed the edge of the rapids and shoreline of the basin below, just as Verlen had done, but found nothing more. They searched the day, farther downstream, verified Verlen's story in their report, then delivered Verlen back to his car via the plane where they left him alone. He put off making the phone call until the police left. He called Jenny first, near midnight, to break the news. After hearing the story, she told Verlen she would leave immediately for Nancy Cesar's home to be with her all that night after Verlen's call.

Now he knew he must call Jerry Cesar's family. "It was the hardest thing I have ever done,"

A piece of Jerry's canoe found two portages below Angle Falls the following September
(photo from Kruger Archives)

said Verlen. Though brief, it was the longest call he had ever made. When he finished the call, he cried and prayed for Jerry and his family.

Then he drove home alone.

The Kruger and Cesar families had been friends for several years prior to Jerry's death. Verlen followed through with post incident inquiries, and family support for the Cesars as much as he could. Larry Rice's article in the July 1999 issue of *Canoe & Kayak* magazine summarized it best: "Since that fateful day when Jerry Cesar was lost to the river, Verlen and the Cesar family had lost touch. Verlen resumed his paddling exploits with a passion beyond reckoning; the Cesar family struggled to make do without a husband and father."

Verlen said of the incident: "It should never have happened. We didn't have any idea we were even in trouble when Jerry turned

Erecting the first cross for Jerry at Angle Falls *(photo by Steve Landick)*

his boat over. There were no rapids shown on the map. I was confident that I would find Jerry around the corner below the portage, and just help him come ashore with his boat. Jerry was a strong man and a good swimmer. He was confident that he could retrieve his boat and make the shore. I'm sure his thoughts were, if he lost his canoe while we were still miles from Lake Superior, we would then have a real problem on our hands. Two people, with gear for two people for ten days, will not fit into a one-man solo boat. That's why he went after it." The loss of Jerry didn't stop Verlen from more canoeing. He knew Jerry would not have wanted this. Verlen never felt anyone was to blame for the accident. It just happened. Verlen canoed the White River several more times after the loss of Jerry.

In September of 1975, just a few months after the accident, Verlen and Steve Landick went back to Angle Falls to try to find Jerry. They found parts of his canoe two rapids and two portages below Angle Falls Portage where Jerry was lost, but no further signs of Jerry's gear or body were ever found. During that September trip of 1975, Verlen and Steve erected a small wooden cross on the rocks where Jerry had been swept into the rapids below Angle Falls Portage. It was observed there for years by infrequent canoeists who paddled the White River. While Verlen and Steve went by canoe, they flew Jenny and Jerry Cesar's wife in for a memorial ceremony. Verlen and Steve paddled down to Angle Falls Portage. When the seaplane carrying Jenny and Jerry's wife arrived, the weather was too threatening for the pilot to land. They returned unable to participate in the memorial service Verlen and Steve held before moving on down the White River to Lake Superior. After reaching Lake Superior, Verlen and Steve climbed to the top of Tip Top Mountain, just as Verlen and Jerry had intended to do the prior spring. They accomplished it for the three of them: Verlen, Steve and Jerry.

Bronze plaque on first cross *(photo from Kruger Archives)*

Steve Landick and Verlen Kruger on their way home from the White River, after finding parts of Jerry's canoe in 1975. (Steve's favorite photo of himself and Verlen) *(photo by Verlen Kruger)*

In 1998, someone informed Verlen that the cross was gone, either removed by spring ice breakup, flood, or people. It had been nearly twenty-three years since he had spoken directly to the Cesar family. Following the incident, both Verlen and Jenny had tried to support the Cesars through their grief, but it had been difficult to maintain a relationship. Now Verlen again called the Cesar family. Remembering the trauma of his last call to Jerry's wife filled him with those same emotions as he reached for the phone.

Bridging those years of absent communication, Verlen called Jerry's son, Todd, now twenty-eight years old, explaining he had heard of the disappearance of the cross he and Steve had erected at Angle Falls in 1975. He told the family he wanted to replace it and he invited them to be involved with that activity. According to Verlen, "I kind of blindsided them with this call out of the blue and I am sure I also stirred a considerable amount of dormant anxiety. I just thought Jerry would have wanted me to do it, especially involving his family in the process. I didn't push for an immediate answer, but asked them to consider it and get back to me. I suggested that both Todd and his sister, Jill, could be a part of this trip, and I hoped they could make it."

Steve Landick on Tip Top Mountain, which he and Verlen summited in remembrance of Jerry. To make the difficult climb, they "siwashed," meaning carried no gear, tents or sleeping bags.
(photo by Verlen Kruger)

According to Verlen, the Cesar family wrestled with their decision for twelve days before he heard back from them. Todd was filled with dormant fears from his childhood, which he had not yet faced. He also knew he did not have the skills his father had when the river claimed him. He was scared and no one in his family wanted him to go. He also knew that if he did go, he would finally have to admit that his father was gone. He had so far been able to avoid that last stroke of closure. Todd had made a decision. In the Larry Rice article, Todd Cesar said, "I said, 'Mom, look. I'm going to finish my father's trip, and I'm going to climb that damn mountain.' She broke down and bawled, and said, 'I knew you were going to go up there someday, but why the whole trip?' 'Because it's something I've got to do,' I said. 'I've got to face my fears.' That's when I called Verlen. Two days later we started training."

"He was a chip off the old block and I loved again being with a Cesar on the water."

Verlen was happy that he would finally be able to help the Cesar family come to grips with Jerry's death. He invested heartily in the education of Todd Cesar, teaching him canoeing skills. Verlen was going to bring closure to Jerry's untimely death, replace the memorial cross, and Jerry's son was going to be with him when he did it. It seemed to Verlen that it was just the right thing to do, and he could feel Jerry's approval.

For the next thirty days, Todd and Verlen paddled most evenings on the Grand River in front of the Kruger home in Lansing, Michigan. Todd called it "Voyageur Boot Camp." Verlen put Todd into one of his Loons, a solo boat he developed long after those he had built for Jerry and himself, and began to teach Todd how to paddle the stream, avoid the rocks, negotiate the currents, and paddle efficiently. Todd was in the hands of a master, *the* master in many canoeists' minds, and he was determined to recreate his father's skills. Verlen worked his magic of teaching, passing his skills to Todd. Todd soon knew how to portage, launch, pack, prepare, navigate, and to take care of himself and his gear, as well as his fellow canoeists. Todd was highly motivated, learned fast, and loved the training. He would be able to carry his own weight as a fellow paddler on this memorial trip for his father. Verlen said, "I could see Todd's confidence building as he learned the skills that had made his father such a good canoe tripper. He was a chip off the old block and I loved again being with a Cesar on the water."

Verlen enlisted two of his paddling friends, Dan Smith and his brother Scot, with whom he'd canoed often and whose skills he could count on for great support on this trip. They and Verlen, with Todd and his sister Jill's help, built a new cedar-post cross in Verlen's boat shop. Todd and Jill attached a beautiful brass plaque to the cross in memoriam to their father. Jill would be unable to join the trip, but Verlen and Todd felt sure that helping to build the cross also helped her with closure. By late August of 1998, the four canoeists and their cross were back on the waters of the White River headed for Angle Falls Portage.

Verlen reflected, "Todd wrestled with emotions as he paddled that whole day. He had to deal with a lot. Twenty-three years of wondering about the loss of his father to this river began to surface as we closed with the imminent and haunting site of the portage above Angle Falls Portage. We had negotiated several portages before Angle, but as we approached this one we let Todd paddle ahead when he wanted to, staying close enough that, should he need help of any nature, one of us could provide it. Since it was August, the water was much lower than it had been during the May of Jerry's loss. Todd was pretty good in a canoe now, but he needed to be alone with his emotions in this geography. I was comforted by the fact that I was instrumental in this process of bringing Jerry and his son into closer proximity than they had been since his death. Since accepting to be part of this trip, Todd had dedicated himself to training and learning what he needed to make the trip. No matter what the emotions or outcome of this event were going to be for Todd, I was sure this was a good thing for him to be doing. That whole first day of paddling and portaging was fueled by Todd's emotional adrenaline. The rest of us just let him set the pace so he had sufficient time to process whatever it was he had to deal with. I was grateful Dan and Scot Smith were with us.

"We stayed behind Todd as we approached Angle. I could only imagine what was going through Todd's mind, but I knew what was in mine. We had verbally rehearsed landing at Angle Falls Portage, and with current water levels, I had no doubt that Todd would not

"Right away Todd unloaded the cross and carried it to the top of the rocky point at the edge of the water's first drop into Angle Falls, the place where I had last looked into Jerry's eyes."

Jerry Cesar's daughter, Jill, and son, Todd, with the cross for Angle Falls (photo by Dan Smith)

Todd Cesar carrying cross to its final site *(photo by Dan Smith)*

repeat Jerry's fate at that same landing. I had been back to the site several times, and in different seasons, since that fateful incident, and was not about to risk Todd. I was sure nothing could be more prominently focused in Todd's mind than a successful landing at that site. We beached in single file on the rocky shore of the portage. All were respectfully quiet. This was Todd's time. Right away Todd unloaded the cross and carried it to the top of the rocky point at the edge of the water's first drop into Angle Falls, the place where I had last looked into Jerry's eyes. I have never forgotten them, no fear showing, just determination, and perhaps a little aggravation at his situation. He was going to get his boat."

Verlen and Steve had piled a cairn of rocks at the site of the original cross. They were still there to be used with the new cross Todd carried. He rested the cross at the site and then proceeded to walk down the edge of the rapids that had claimed his father. Larry Rice wrote: "For a long time he just stared into the dark, turbulent depths. Chills ran down his spine. The falls were in tiers, and the water churned into the rocks. 'I knew now that my father didn't have a chance,' Todd said, his voice cracking. 'He was strong, but no one could have survived being forced through those boulders. My God, I could see how they didn't find his body.'" The four canoeists then erected the new cross. Verlen led them in prayer and read the 23rd Psalm. Then, with Todd in the lead, they portaged their gear and canoes to the base of the rapids and paddled downstream. Todd wanted to get on with the rest of his life. He finally had closure to the loss of his father. Tip Top Mountain lay ahead.

Scot, Todd and Verlen. 23rd Psalm, then downstream again. *(photo by Dan Smith)*

Verlen said he was pleased to see Todd successfully negotiate the remaining rapids between Angle Falls Portage and Lake Superior. Their month-long training efforts had prepared him well. Todd had told his mother that he was going to finish his father's trip. He, too, had wondered for a long time of Tip Top Mountain, never dreaming that he would one day attempt its summit. As they approached Lake Superior, that was exactly the plan. Instead of mountain climbing, however, they were forced ashore by high winds, which used up their remaining time for this trip. Tip Top had won again. When they were finally able to launch onto Superior's waters again, they had just enough time to make it to the take-out spot before the families hit the alarm buttons. To be even an hour late on this particular trip would have panicked those aware of the history of the White River/Cesar tragedy. "As Todd paddled by," Verlen said, "he hurled a glove at her summit. He pledged he would one day sit on top of that mountain." Todd went on in further years to become an accomplished canoe tripper, owner of several Kruger-designed canoes, and fulfilled what must have been many of the canoe tripping goals of his father, Jerry.

Author's Note

Another attempt on the summit of Tip Top Mountain was made by several of the same people. On July 22, 2005, Todd Cesar, his 16-year-old son, Jacob, Mark Przedwojewski, Dan and Scot Smith, who had accompanied Verlen and Todd on the memorial expedition, and Larry Rice of *Canoe & Kayak* magazine left again for the White River and Tip Top Mountain. Todd Cesar reached the summit of Tip Top Mountain, which his father had sought with Verlen. The story, by Larry Rice, appears in the May 2006 issue of *Canoe & Kayak*.

"God bless you Jerry."

Closure for Todd, Jill and the Cesar family *(photo by Verlen Kruger)*

Dan Smith paddles by Angle Falls Portage sign on left of photo. Cross shown in upper right hand corner. *(photo by Verlen Kruger)*

"One pancake equals four miles."

VERLEN KRUGER

Planning the Ultimate Canoe Challenge

Once Verlen returned from the Cross Continent Canoe Safari, his first big canoe trip, he poured himself back into his plumbing contracting business in Lansing and reengaged in helping Jenny raise their family into young adults. Verlen was always a man possessed of extraordinary energy and, even while engaging in multiple activities, still had time to devote to his family. He was committed to his church and congregation, designed, built and paddled more canoes, and spent all the free time he could muster in researching the next big canoe trip that lurked in his soul.

When he returned from the CCCS, he found his plumbing business had slowed some from what it had been when he had left, primarily because no one had been chasing contracts as he had previously done. This was bad news for Verlen because he was facing debts left over from the CCCS. Verlen had invested in the movie, *Never Before, Never Again*, and became a partner in producing the film with Phil Pemberton. The movie took several years to fail, and never produced the needed return on investment. This cost Verlen a lot of money he had not planned on spending. He had to pay off the debt of the film-production costs, and finally gave up on the movie ever succeeding. With a faltering plumbing business, there wasn't enough commercial work happening at the time to turn a profit. Verlen had to forfeit one of his properties, including his home, and he and Jenny temporarily moved in with one of their kids for a year. To resurface from this debt, he had to focus attention on getting more plumbing and heating contracts. He decided to specialize in apartments and motels since there seemed to be a boom in that part of construction around Lansing. Verlen was able to slowly pay off his film costs and other bills, and built up the business to the point where it again had reserves. He became the business finder, and provided those contracts to his brother, who was now running the Kruger plumbing business, for a finder's fee.

Once he'd regained his financial footing, Verlen began thinking about a trip from the Arctic down to the Gulf of Mexico. The more he studied the possibilities, the bigger the trip became. His first approach was to scrutinize the rivers of North America and try to tie them together with a minimum of portages. Looking further, he realized that by using the Atlantic on the East coast and the Pacific on the West coast, and then combining them with the rivers of the country, he could quadruple the number of states to paddle through in North America. The plan soon grew into the challenge of paddling as many states as possible in a single canoe trip.

It was during the time that Verlen first started contemplating his Ultimate Canoe Challenge that he had first met Steve Landick. Steve Landick befriended Verlen shortly after paddling solo from an Outward Bound camp in Maine all the way back to Mackinac Island in his home state of Michigan. He was only eighteen years old at the time. He had heard of Verlen and he even bumped into some boaters who had seen Verlen and Clint Waddell on their Safari as Steve was paddling back from Maine. He wanted to be like Verlen. Verlen inspired him to make his own dreams come true.

Their friendship just clicked when they first met. Steve saw Verlen as a mentor and they immediately liked to paddle together. Verlen saw potential in Steve and recognized it when he saw him in Michigan races. They were kindred spirits, similar to what Verlen and Jerry Cesar had been, but with a thirty-year age spread. Steve began to partner up with Verlen on several smaller canoe trips (small by Kruger standards), such as the September trip on the White River following the loss of Jerry Cesar. Being a well matched pair, it was easy for Verlen and Steve to dream of and plan major trips to come. Steve felt fortunate to be able to partner with the living legend Verlen was becoming. Verlen felt fortunate to partner with a man of Steve's skills and experience.

Soon Steve was a regular visitor at Verlen's boat shop and they began to talk enthusiastically about the potential of the UCC. They agreed to partner up for what would eventually become the UCC, but there was much planning left to do. Verlen always said "The way to select a potential partner is to find the one that most wants to be there." He used that criterion before measuring capabilities such as experience, physical condition, paddling and camping expertise. While Steve was indeed an accomplished paddler, Verlen could see that Steve wanted to undertake the UCC as much as he did.

They were friends for more than a year before Verlen recognized there were two reasons for Steve's visits. Verlen's youngest daughter, Sarah, was usually there too! She went from an Outward Bound camp in Colorado to San Diego and married Steve while he was training to become a Navy SEAL. He served three years. During the time Steve had to be away in the Navy, Verlen continued to study and plan the trip. When Steve was discharged from the Navy, he and Verlen continued to plan the Ultimate Canoe Challenge.

Before they made the first stroke of the UCC, Verlen and Steve confirmed their agreements. One of the first was that the Ultimate Canoe Challenge was theirs alone, and the team was to be just the two of them. No one else could join them as part of the team; in fact, they had already turned down others. They also agreed that they would paddle single canoes. Single boats enabled them to be as close, or as far away, as each chose to be on a daily basis. They could separate from each other at any time, by personal decision, without having to explain their reasoning to the other. To accommodate that option they packed their canoes independently. Each had whatever he needed in terms of food, shelter, water and comfort to be able to go on for days without the other. Neither carried anything the other could not do without.

When Verlen and Steve chose to paddle separately, the man in the lead would leave a trail of pink surveyor tape with dates and times written on them for the other to find. This form of trail marking became one of their foremost methods of communications when separated. In those years, there were no cell phones, towers, or payphones in the bush.

Because of Verlen's involvement in professional canoe racing and his growing reputation among canoeists, he always received support from the canoe associations and clubs. They helped with money-raising, logistics, communications, and would always muster the troops at various points along the routes of his races or marathon trips to cheer him on. This support enabled Verlen to have a communicative grapevine along most of his routes over the years. During the 1971 Cross Continent Canoe Safari, he had established a chain of mail drops from Montreal to the Bering Sea. He could retrieve mail and gear, or mail out newsletter installments, film, and unnecessary gear. This grapevine also provided willing participants along the way who were looking forward to helping in any way they could. That array of support would often make immediate help available for whatever Verlen needed as he passed through. Meals, company, repairs and advice were graciously provided and, often, many would paddle with Verlen as an escort for some distance. They also frequently provided a night's respite with warm lodging and food and camaraderie that could ease built-up tensions. Verlen's history and relationship with the Christian Church community created similar support wherever he went.

Verlen's office library *(photo by Phil Peterson)*

As the departure time for the UCC neared, Verlen applied himself to the pursuit of more commercial plumbing contracts, which would help sustain the flourishing business while he was gone for the three and one-half years the Challenge would take. Years before, when he and Clint left on the Cross Continent Canoe Safari, three of Verlen and Jenny's children had already married. One married while he was gone, and six were still living at home and in school. But now, Verlen and Jenny's children were all out of high school and into the labor force or post high school education, which would allow Jenny to fly in for an occasional rendezvous somewhere along the UCC route. Those rendezvous had worked well for both of them during the Cross Continent Canoe Safari. Verlen being gone for that length of time was never an issue with them on that trip. This time, her husband would be gone

REALITY OR DREAM?

REACHING OUT -

EXPLOREING A CONTINENT
NEW WORLD -

MATH 6.35

p.19

HE ULTIMATE CANOE CHALLENGE

28,000 Mile Odyssey by Paddle and Portage

ULTIMATE CANOE CHALLENGE .... highlights

" WE PROCEED ON "

THIS WAS PUT
TOGETHER ALMOST A YEAR
BEFORE STARTING -

A beginning with no end.. (in sight)
Up in the Mountains... headwaters of the Missr.
Full length of the MIssouri Rv...
★ Lewis and Clark Trail...   RACE
Huge back-waters...   historic St. Louis..   the gigantic arch
Up the Illiois Rv., thru Chicago ★...   Stove
What kind of Canoe country is this ?
Around Michigan.... sand dunes ... Mackinack bridge...
A Challenge within a Challenge......   RESCUED BY COASTGUARD — ?
Nationaly famous Au Sable Rv. MARATHON CANOE RACE....WITH STEVE
Thru 4 of the Great Lakes..
JAIL ? Niagara Falls,.... to portage or not to portage !
Historic Erie Canal... 53 locks...
Hudson Rv. .... Lake Champlain and Northward
Fur trade route.... Montreal.. St Lawrence Rv.
Up the Chaudiere Rv. ... over the Heigth of land
Over the border from Quebec to Maine.... long portages.. ·
Maine waterways.... full length of the famous Allagash Rv.
~~Another Challenge.... to the top of Mt. KATAHDIN.... a rare panorama.~~
St. Johns Rv. (New Brunswick) to the Bay of Fundy....
World record tides, up to 53' .... Reverseable Falls. (unusual)
Rugged , stormy Maine coast. ...
Boston, Plymouth Rock,.... & on to New York City
★ Statue of Liberty.... Land of the FREE and home of the brave..
Start of the Inter-coastal waterways...
Huge Delaware & Chesapeake Bays.... to Taverse or NOT to Traverse !
Land of sail-boats, cabin cruisers & Yachts.
Rubbing elbows with th best. !
Full length of the eAST COAST & the Inter-coastal waterway.
Dolphins, sharks, & asst. Marine life.... + COLLISION — MANTA RAY
Dismal Swamp... Okee fenokee Swamp..
Paddling out of winter.. going south with the tourist...
Daytona Beach, Cape Canaveral, Miami...
Fla. Keys... The bridge highway... KEY WEST, southern most poi
Canoeing in the Tropics ... Mangroves, Orchids, Pink Flamingoes,
Pelicans, asst'd exotic birds... all kinds of fish..
Everglade National Park..
sponge capital of the world..
Worlds largest fresh water spring, scuba diving, manatees....
Deep sea fishing... big ones... free tow ! fish power!
Heading west on the Gulf Coast.
Gap in the Inter-coastal waterway.
Mississippi Rv. at New Orleans.
Down to mile zero at Mouth of the passes.
The nature of our journey cahanges.
WE PROCEED ON.... DETERMINATION.....

The skids were greased, the boats and paddlers were ready, the gear and vehicles were packed...

Some of the planning pages with Verlen's penned notes

NEAR RUN OVER BY TUG BOAT IN FOG

" GULF OF MEXICO TO THE FROZEN SEA "

LOTS OF HISTORY + GEOGRAPHY

The Challenge before us... the long uphill grind....
Miss. Rv. from mile zero to Lake Itasca... 2340 miles. 2348 MILE
RECORD... first to ever paddle UPSTREAM the full length of the Rv.
Miss. Rv.   statistics.... history....   impact....
Great tributaries... Red Rv., Arkabsas Rv., Ohio Rv., Missouri Rv.
Huge delta system....   mouth of the passes... mile zero.
Paddling against spring flood waters all the way....
29 locks all between St Louis & Minn.
14 dams above Minn.
North to adventure...   race with spring....
Perpetual spring... the 6,000 mile spring...
Traveling north with the speed of spring....
pushing ice break-up clear up to the Arctic...
On the edge of ice most of the way...
We plan to be there when the headwaters of the Miss. breaks up in Apr.
Likewise we will be pushing to be there when the ice breaks up
on Great Bear Lake in july....
Our strategy...from Itasca to the Artic to Skagway, a distance of
5,978 miles, we plan to push to the limits of our endurance.
To beat freeze up in the Mt's. of Chillkoot Pass.
A time schedule forced on us by ice....
Miss. Rv. wing dams, Levees, flood control...
Floods.... big fast water.... hard spots..
LOwer Miss. Mile zero to St, Louis.
MIddle Miss. St. Louis to Minn.
Upper Miss, MInn. to Lake Itasca.
Historic St. Louis.... the big arch...
Locks .... dams.... backwater...   Huge barges...
Huckleberry Finn..
Meeting the frist floating ice....
Minneappolis,   end of river transportation... home of Clint Waddell..
Change in the river.... faster , harder work.
Headwater Lakes... frozen lakes ? ice break-up....
Headwaters of the great River.... Lake Itasca...
Portage,... Hudson Bay water shed... Red Rv. of th North...
Up the Assiniboine River...   LAKE WINIPEG
Portage La Prairie.... how long ? ....   BACK ON ICE FUR TRADE RW
Prairie lakes.. Lake Manitoba, Lake Winipegosis....   more ice?
up fast waters... to Flin Flon, end of civilization....
Indian country.. good fishing ....   living off the land....
Riendeer Lake, Wollaston Lake, Athabasca Lake   large & remote
Near the edge of the Barrens ...
Off the main canoe routes... the more remote trails...
Great Slave Lake....   more ice?
Intricate waterways... no traffic...
Great Bear Lake...   wild & free..!!
Steep climb out of Great Bear.... lineing & portageing 65 mile!
Barren lands of the far North......   Anderson River & northward
Into the Arctic.... land of long & lonely days....
Permafrost.... Tundra... Land of little sticks....
 Arctic Ocean... Permanent shelf ice...
White whales.... seals... polar bears... etc.
Eskimo country..... life style... culture...

While planning the Ultimate Canoe Challenge, Verlen continued to hone his racing skills. Early photo of him and Clint. *(photo from Kruger Archives)*

for possibly three years, but Jenny was fully supportive of the trip. She alone knew how important these trips were to Verlen and said she truly didn't mind what he was doing with Steve Landick and the UCC. She and Verlen agreed that it was a once in a lifetime opportunity. Jenny would continue to work at the hospital and save vacation time for the rendezvous along the UCC route.

Before embarking on the UCC, Verlen made certain that his plumbing business was built up with reserve funds and an adequate number of contracts to sustain it until he returned. He was able to leave Jenny with a fat bank account and a business that was once again in good shape—in fact, bigger and better than it had ever been before. Verlen and Jenny both felt positive about this new canoe trip.

By this time, Steve was home again, as a civilian. He and Verlen each had built their own new Loon during 1979 and 1980, designed to be the canoes of the Ultimate Canoe Challenge. By then, Steve had built quite a few canoes, most of them designed for racing or tripping.

The UCC was the first trip that they would be able to test out Verlen's new catamaran method of joining the two boats Polynesian-style when necessary. Each of the Loons had a fiberglass pole stored within it. When they wanted to catamaran the boats they would each slide their pole through the shaft-holes on the cockpit, then across the five-foot space between the boats and into the adjacent boat's shaft-holes. A spring-loaded, vertical holding button would pop up on the outside of each hull to hold the shafts firmly in place. Once joined, the two boats were stable as a catamaran, and could be paddled by one or two paddlers. This enabled one of them to sleep while the other paddled, and made it easy to accomplish other tasks that would normally have to be done ashore. The catamaran concept also enabled them to handle much rougher water than they could in single canoes, which really proved its worth on the Pacific Ocean. They later improved their method of attaching the boats with an enclosed connector for the poles that didn't leak, and so had much dryer boats for the ocean.

But as he continued to plan, an unanticipated problem confronted Verlen. The Board of Deacons of the church that he had helped to build and finance and had worked hard over the years to help grow, began to take issue with Verlen's UCC plans. Verlen had been a member of the Board for some time. Other Deacons felt Verlen's canoeing quests were causing him to behave irresponsibly toward his wife. But Verlen was certain that he had been a devoted husband and a good father; besides, he already had Jenny's blessing and support. Further, Verlen believed that the Lord was on his side, had answered his prayers, and was steering him toward the UCC. He also felt it was none of the Deacons' business to meddle in his private family affairs. When the Church realized Verlen was ignoring their criticism they turned up the heat by threatening to kick him off the Board of Deacons if he continued with the Challenge. Verlen did not take this lightly. He believed in his religion, the Church, and did not want to have this all happen. Verlen's brother and some friends told him that he was being irresponsible by leaving his wife at home alone for that length

of time. Even Verlen's mother tried to talk him out of going on the UCC. He was under considerable pressure. Nevertheless, he was Verlen. The more people told him he couldn't do something, the more likely he was to do it. The Church lost the argument and voted him off the Board; they also lost Verlen for some years. Throughout this unpleasant experience, Jenny continued to believe in him and support this once in a lifetime dream trip.

And yet more resource books (photo by Phil Peterson)

The last big obstacle for Verlen and Steve on the Ultimate Canoe Challenge was money. Steve did not have much. He was young, newly married, and just one year out of the military; there had been little time for earning and saving. Verlen's business was in good shape so he agreed to finance much of the trip. Verlen and Steve had accrued some sponsorship, which provided money, equipment and clothing, and some of the funds needed to support their cash requirements for food, phone calls, and postal fees for gear and mail coming and going from their planned stops. Verlen had again worked up an agreement with Phil Pemberton, who had filmed him and Clint on the CCCS. Pemberton and a friend would act as agents for the UCC and attempt to line up sponsors who would contribute to the operational fund for Verlen and Steve to draw against as needed. In addition, they arranged to have an installment newsletter produced and circulated for subscription fees, which would bring in some money. That newsletter ultimately turned out to be one of their best supporting tools for the trip. They wound up with more than one thousand subscribers, which helped them to have 33 organized mail drops spread along the route. There were also impromptu hosts for warm meals, an occasional overnight and local transportation for provisioning, as needed. That newsletter, called the "Ultimate Canoe Challenge," also carried the name of the United States Canoe Association, who helped to support the trip. Verlen took what he could from savings, from the plumbing business, and combined that with what he anticipated would be produced by the newsletters and Phil Pemberton. Hoping more would be invented along the way, he and Steve were ready to embark on the three-and-one-half-year Ultimate Canoe Challenge.

The skids were greased, the boats and paddlers were ready, the gear and vehicles were packed, and Jenny and Sarah were ready to launch their husbands and canoes at Red Rock, Montana, for the start of the Ultimate Canoe Challenge. Though it was not without some trepidation, they wanted this launching to be a celebration. Their drive to Montana was bittersweet.

When they launched the UCC on April 29, 1980, Verlen was fifty-eight-years old. Verlen had been happily married for thirty-five years, and he and Jenny had already raised their family of nine children. He was a former flight-trainer of combat air pilots, an officer, a successful plumbing contractor and president of his own firm. He was thoroughly used to being in charge, and he had already established himself as one of the country's foremost canoe racers.

Verlen paddles a new Loon up the Grand River to a Lansing wedding *(photo from Kruger Archives)*

Steve Landick was twenty-seven years old, an elite Navy SEAL and an accomplished canoeist in his own right. Though he and Verlen had agreed to partner up on the UCC before Steve married Sarah, and though Sarah gave Steve her full support, neither of them relished being separated for the three and one-half years of the UCC. They had only been married for four years, nearly three of which the Navy had kept Steve away. But Steve was inspired to do the Ultimate Canoe Challenge; he wanted to be there. Steve said that Verlen was not only his partner on the UCC and his father-in-law, but also his best friend on earth.

Despite their nearly thirty-year-plus age gap, and their differences in drives and needs, Verlen and Steve liked and respected each other. They had already tripped together for a couple of weeks at a time, and both had accomplished major canoe trips on their own. Both had boundless energy, loved physical competition, and could paddle together for days on end and enjoy every moment of it. They were confident in their abilities and had high respect for each other. Their training and experience also prepared them to step outside of their family relationships as needed, so as to logically and strategically address the demands, risks, and challenges of the trip. They also knew they had to plan and prepare for the physical and psychological demands their quest would require of them. They felt there would be few problems they couldn't handle together.

The ability of these two to have fun was a bonus. They loved to paddle hard. On days that would exhaust many, Verlen and Steve grew stronger. They were having fun! They reveled in the miles behind them and looked forward to the challenge of tomorrow. Most times, they didn't need a break from what they were doing; they needed more of exactly the same thing. They were happy in that environment.

Both men were extremely competitive, which accounted for much of the success they had enjoyed to date. Each was an accomplished canoe racer, though Verlen's track record was longer, and both were comfortable under stress. Steve and Verlen seemed to energize under stress and emerge stronger at the ends of their challenges. They enjoyed competing with each other and also with themselves, always seeking—but seldom finding—their limits. Being as competitive as they were also caused them to occasionally choose to out-paddle each other as if in a race; fun for them, but woe to anyone else who might be temporarily paddling with them.

Steve and Verlen heading up the Mississippi *(photo from Kruger Archives)*

As well-matched as these two men were, the UCC was not without its troubles. Verlen was established with the press because of his former canoeing exploits, and knew how to both work them and work with them. His canoe racing experiences, the 7,000-mile CCCS, and all the follow-up interviews trained him. There are accounts of him being disappointed when the press didn't show as scheduled. That disappointment was twofold: first, without adequate press attention it was difficult to obtain sponsorship and funds to continue tripping. Second, he just plain enjoyed the attention.

Steve had never established a reputation or worked with the press in the ways that Verlen had, and didn't enjoy it much when he had to do it. He did not have Verlen's built-in welcome attitude for reporters, and, initially, almost resisted their attention. Steve relished accomplishing the UCC; he was there to paddle and break records and to participate to the fullest extent—not sell it to the press. Still, when the presence of the press would put Verlen into auto-mode behavior, Steve would sometimes wonder why the press wasn't talking to him, too. He quickly sensed he was in Verlen's shadow when the press was around. He was happily married to Verlen's daughter, Sarah, which made him Verlen Kruger's son-in-law.

Standing next to Verlen Kruger, it was easy to be ignored by the press, and, with any degree of resistance to their presence, a sure thing. The press was not as attractive to Steve, and he actually did not enjoy interviews, despite being an accomplished writer and a speaker of talent.

In Steve's thirty-year-old-mind, he fully respected and admired Verlen for his accomplishments, his friendship, and his partnership. At the same time, he saw himself as an accomplished paddler in his own right, who was not only a Navy SEAL, but had paddled solo all the way home from an Outward Bound camp in Maine to the Mackinac Bridge in Michigan at the age of 18. He did not resent the attention lavished on Verlen by the press, but he did resent the lack of attention to his participation in the trip. Soon into the UCC Steve knew this treatment by the press would be the same throughout the trip.

Steve slipping over an old beaver dam *(photo from Kruger Archives)*

Verlen also said, "Each of us had to deal with our own personal factors. Steve usually wanted to paddle faster, farther, or longer than I did. Part of it was his being half my age and having a greater need or desire to save time to visit Sarah whenever possible. They had just started building a young marriage when we left."

Steve expressed, "I was concerned about my marriage at that time, and I wanted to spend all the time I could with Sarah. I had to finish the UCC, but did not want my marriage to fail. Consequently, I was driven to move faster than Verlen wanted to travel during that time period."

Competitiveness was another double-edged sword for Verlen and Steve. When they faced a challenge together, they could combine into one unstoppable duet of power. They were a formidable team. But if they found themselves at odds, their competitive spirits could motivate them to compete with each other, and separation was usually the salve that could ease the sting of friction between them.

Sometimes it was just their need to test their limits that fueled aggressive paddling between them. It was common for either Steve or Verlen to decide to paddle straight on through the night, ignoring tiredness, pain, hunger, their partner and myriad other details on the yardstick they used to measure their performance. They fueled each other to strive for more. Still, Steve Landick insists that they had far more fun than friction.

Verlen always said that the biggest problems he faced on all of his 100,000-plus miles of paddling were created by

They became accustomed to chasing each other up and down the rivers *(photo from Kruger Archives)*

man. People created the biggest and most dangerous challenges and consequences. He frequently said "The biggest challenge on a journey is making the chemistry work between the partners." In later years, Verlen admitted that he had made many errors during the UCC, but never felt the decision to do the trip was wrong. "The problem with me on the UCC," Verlen said, "was that I really never came back."

"You have to understand your goal.
That's what makes a difference."

VERLEN KRUGER

The Ultimate Canoe Challenge and Mississippi Upstream

On April 29, 1980, two Loons launched from Red Rock, Montana, into the Red Rock River for the ultimate cross country canoe trip, expected to take three and one-half years and 28,000 miles of paddling and portaging to complete. They'd been planning for five years.

With boats loaded on the river's edge, Verlen, Jenny, Steve and Sarah bowed heads and prayed. All four knew they would be mostly without their spouse for the next three and one-half years, but Verlen and Steve could look forward to the adventure ahead. They launched their canoes and paddled into the current and on down the Red Rock River. Jenny and Sarah drove the three days back to Lansing. Sarah lived with Jenny for a time in their cozy Grand River home with the canoe shop, and worked while she took classes.

Verlen Kruger and Steve Landick three minutes from launch in Red Rock, Montana! *(photo by Jenny Kruger)*

The route Verlen and Steve had planned for the Ultimate Canoe Challenge was from Red Rock, Montana, down the Missouri River to the Mississippi, then up the Mississippi to the Illinois River and on up to Lake Michigan. Then up the west side of the State of Michigan and down the east side on Lake Huron to Detroit and into Lake Erie, then to Cleveland, on to Buffalo, N.Y. From there, they'd go through the Welland Canal around Niagara Falls and on into Lake Ontario. Next it would be the Erie Canal, Lake Champlain, and the St. Lawrence River, then through Maine's canoe country and on into the St. John's River to the Bay of Fundy, well known for its monster tides. Next, it would be down the Atlantic coast of Maine on saltwater to Boston Harbor, and then back into the Atlantic all the way down the east coast to Florida, using the Intracoastal Waterway as much as possible.

Ultimate Canoe Challenge

1982

1980

1981

1983

★ START
● FINISH

Once there, they would be 8,000 miles into their trip. From Florida, they would head to the mouth of the Mississippi, another 1,350-mile paddle.

The mouth of the Mississippi was a significant spot. There, they would begin what they wanted to be a record-setting pace up the Mississippi: 2,350 miles against the current to its source at Lake Itasca, Minnesota. They could find no existing record to race against, so aimed to set their own record and submit it to the Guinness Book of World Records.

From Lake Itasca, they would paddle and portage to the famous Red River of the North, which flowed north into Canada, the Northwest Territories, to the Arctic, and Alaska. In Alaska, they would again have to go upstream, this time on the Yukon to its source near the little town of Carcross. From there it was up over the legendary Chilkoot Pass and down to Skagway, then again on saltwater down the entire west coast of Alaska, Canada and the States to the southern tip of the Baja peninsula. They would then reverse their direction and paddle north, up the inside of the Baja, to the mouth of the Colorado River.

Once past Yuma, Arizona, they planned another World Record: they would paddle, portage, line, and climb up (yes, up) the Grand Canyon. Once again, there was no established record because it had never been done. Verlen and Steve planned to be the first to ascend the Colorado River up through North America's Grand Canyon at a pace that would establish a long-standing record. Once through Glen Canyon, they would go on up to the Wind River across the Dakotas and back into Minnesota through the famous Boundary Waters and down Lake Superior and Lake Michigan to Lansing, Michigan, where this dream began.

Verlen and Steve were high on adrenaline and enthusiasm and their paddles ate up the miles. Verlen was physically a little softer than Steve, but Steve said within the first month they were on a par as paddlers.

After five years of strategic planning, Verlen and Steve had records on their minds. In addition to their two World Record goals, they intended to set a speed record for paddling the entire Missouri River to St. Louis faster than it had ever been done before. When they reached the mouth of the Missouri River that emptied into the Mississippi, they had paddled 2,415 miles from Three Forks, where the Missouri began, to the Mississippi at St. Louis, in 33 days, 18 hours, and 45 minutes. That record still stands today. After three days of rest and some fundraising with a local whitewater paddling club that raffled a Kruger canoe, they were off again on the Illinois River headed for Chicago and the Great Lakes.

The lakes are big, the canoe is small *(photo by Steve Landick)*

One of the first times they separated was approaching Chicago. Steve knew that every day he could shave off their time and distance schedule was another day he could spend with Sarah while on Lake Michigan. He arrived in Chicago four days ahead of Verlen, and continued right on through the night to the other side of Lake Michigan, up to the Grand River and home. It was a week before Verlen saw him again. They rejoined at Verlen and Jenny's home in Lansing and, because they were a month ahead of their schedule, entered the established Au Sable Marathon Canoe Race. They hadn't practiced in a tandem for some time, and placed only ninth out of 32 contestants, but thoroughly enjoyed the camaraderie of the event with a lot of old friends. Verlen commented, "We were the only contestants in the Au Sable Marathon who had paddled 3,500 miles to get there!"

The view has changed since they paddled the New York harbor in 1980 *(photo from Kruger Archives)*

Snacks on the water so they can keep paddling *(photo from Kruger Archives)*

They happily spent nearly three weeks with their wives in catamaraned Loons, paddling up the shores of Lake Michigan toward the Mackinac Bridge. For Verlen and Steve, it was a welcome respite to again be with their mates. Jenny paddled with Verlen up the coast toward Grand Haven before having to return to her work, and Sarah and Steve planned to paddle together north to the Mackinac Bridge and down the east side of Michigan to Oscoda where the mighty Au Sable joins the waters of Lake Huron.

Not wanting to separate again, Steve and Sarah actually paddled farther into Lake Huron and then went off to Quebec for ten days of canoe-racing and fun, while Verlen paddled the next 1,500 miles toward the east coast alone. He and Steve enjoyed their independence for a while. It took the remainder of June through October to get from Lake Michigan to the East Coast.

It was not until September 20 that Steve finally caught up to Verlen in time to make a ten-mile portage down a gravel road to Portage Lake, 1,500 miles farther east along the Canadian border. This was the first time just the two of them had paddled since leaving the Great Lakes and they were both glad to be together again.

They raced the fall season with another 1,700 miles of aggressive paddling through the smaller, inland rivers toward the Atlantic Ocean before freeze-up. They knew they were in a race with the elements as they ate breakfast in 16-degree temperatures. They made St. John's, New Brunswick, in Nova Scotia, by

The Statue of Liberty stands over the waters as the team paddles into New York City Harbor *(photo from Kruger Archives)*

October 7, 1980, and paddled on into Portland, Maine, by October 22. Fall was a beautiful time to go through the forests of Maine and on down the coast to New York. They were blown off the water by sixty-mile-an-hour winds in Rhode Island, and wound up staying at Steve's grandmother's home for a week in the town of Lincoln, Rhode Island, where they rested, worked on their Loons and replenished supplies. They still had much of the upper reaches of the east coast to paddle before they were into the warmer latitudes where freeze-up would no longer be a threat. They paddled on down the coast of Connecticut. By November, they were chasing the hazy skyline of New York City. Their business agent, Phil Pemberton, who had

Jenny and Verlen paddled the Carolina coast for a week before he went on alone *(photo from Kruger Archives)*

been chasing sponsors and money, met them in the City and did some filming of Verlen and Steve in New York City Harbor. They next paddled on down the New Jersey coast, aiming for the Intracoastal Waterway after 850 miles of open Atlantic Ocean. For the next 1,500 miles south, they would be protected by the Barrier Islands. They now knew they would win the race against freeze-up.

As they progressed south, the pace they maintained enabled them to stay well ahead of their time and distance schedule. Jenny drove over from Michigan and joined Verlen on the coast of the Carolinas. She brought an extra Loon from home, so she and Verlen catamaraned them for a week of paddling together along the coast. Verlen said, "It was a vacation on the water for us both and we thoroughly enjoyed it." When he reached St. Augustine he met up with Steve and was surprised to find Sarah with him. She had flown down from Lansing to give Steve a plane ticket home for Christmas. These occasional visits with Jenny and Sarah left Verlen and Steve with renewed enthusiasm and encouragement to get on with the UCC. At Christmas, Steve flew home for a week with the family in Lansing. Due to increasing shortages of funds, Verlen elected to spend Christmas paddling solo down the Florida peninsula. He reached Fort Lauderdale on Christmas Eve and

It's been a great week! *(photo from Kruger Archives)*

called home. He said, "The hardest thing about the trip was being separated from Jenny, and while it was wonderful to talk to her by phone on Christmas Eve, it also left me feeling very lonely after I hung up."

Verlen paddled on alone during Steve's Christmas absence, down the Keys from Florida's southernmost tip, then back up the Keys along the Gulf Coast to New Orleans. It took Verlen 44 days to paddle from Florida to Empire, Louisiana, where he was to meet up with Steve again. After his return from Christmas with Sarah, Steve was running about a week behind. By February 2nd, Verlen reached New Orleans and knew that Steve was not far behind. This had been their longest separation, and

"Goodbye, my Jenny! See you in Florida." *(photo from Kruger Archives)*

"The hardest thing about the trip was being separated from Jenny, and while it was wonderful to talk to her by phone on Christmas Eve, it also left me feeling very lonely after I hung up."

Verlen's longest solo paddle, since Red Rock, Montana. Verlen was ready for some company. He met his friends, Pat and Byron Almquist, who owned the Canoe and Trail Shop in New Orleans and flew with them to the National Sporting Goods Show (NSGA) in Chicago. Jenny met him there for another welcome reunion. This gave Verlen and Jenny some time together, after missing Christmas, and the opportunity to visit sponsors at the Show and enjoy Chicago. While working the NSGA Show Verlen discovered a possible fundraising opportunity in New Orleans. He decided to take advantage of it, which meant that they would be in the New Orleans region a week longer. Sarah flew down and surprised Steve when he paddled into New Orleans. Life was good for the UCC Team. By February 16, 1981, Verlen and Steve were ready for their record ascent of the mighty Mississippi River.

The route up the Mississippi for this record attempt began at the Mile Zero Marker, about a mile south of the town of Pilottown. At that time, Pilottown was a simple one-room store where boat pilots could await the freighters they would board for the upstream portion of their trips to unload their cargos. While there, Verlen and Steve conversed with one of the pilots. When he heard their plans of canoeing to Lake Itasca he said, "You can't do it. You'll never make it, too much traffic!" That was just the inspiring message Steve and Verlen needed to get them going. Verlen and Steve left the Mile Zero Marker at exactly 10:00 am on February 17, 1981, and headed north.

Verlen and Steve always got along famously going upstream. One of the things that made upstream paddling fun for them was that it took special skills to accomplish. They made it a practice to paddle close to shore almost all of the time. This enabled them to take advantage of eddys and protective shorelines, which sometimes offered less current. When strong downstream current denied them upstream progress, they would cross the river to find a better upstream opportunity over there. They also had tugs and barges to deal with, as well as powerboats and pleasure craft, all of which were not usually near shore. Sometimes barge traffic would force them out into the river where it would be much tougher to paddle against the downstream force.

This record attempt was a serious venture for these two. They usually paddled from 8:00 am until near midnight. They did not want to waste time making camps or cooking, so frequently ate cold meals such as a can of cold beans and some bread. They would then pitch the tent, drop into their bags and sleep till daylight. Then it was a quick breakfast and back onto the river. They were so driven to keep moving that they only built three fires between the Mile Zero marker and Lake Itasca. It is not difficult to imagine tension building between these two as they tried to outdo each other's strengths and stamina. Though they would both say that it was never a contest between them, they did compete to a degree all the time.

Verlen said just prior to their arrival in St. Louis, they began to argue. Steve wanted to keep going faster and Verlen wanted to slow down a little. Verlen had an old ulcer condition that had begun to act up, and he felt that if he slowed down a little he would feel better. In addition, Verlen felt the pressure of having to deal almost solely with the press and make the various arrangements to meet and talk with them. Steve never denied that. He did not like working with the press. He was involved in setting a speed record up the Mississippi and felt that was where his focus should be. Verlen felt the media was a necessary component that could not be ignored, but did not like having to do most of it himself. Their conflicts were increasing. But then St. Louis arrived, along with Jenny and Sarah. Steve, who had said he would not meet with the press while there, even changed his mind and helped with the event beneath the Arch of St. Louis.

The St. Louis Arch casts a shadow on the Mississippi. Watch those barges! *(photo by Steve Landick)*

Sarah and Jenny left for Lansing on Tuesday and Verlen came down with the flu. This delayed their return to the river another day. When they did start, Verlen was weak. Steve kept spurting ahead and pretty soon was out of sight. Verlen said it made him angry at Steve. It seemed like Steve wanted to race ahead and have the upstream Mississippi record to himself. Steve, at some point, had told Verlen that he would like to have some portion of the records from the UCC to himself. He seemed tired of being in Verlen's shadow when the press was around. They parted for several days again. The next time Verlen was able to contact Steve was when he was in Dubuque, Iowa. Steve was several days ahead in Winona, Minnesota! When Verlen reached La Crosse, Wisconsin, he called Clint Waddell in Minneapolis to find that Steve had been staying there with them for two days. They had agreed to be a part of the Minnesota Canoe Association's Rendezvous on May 2nd and 3rd, so planned to meet there in Minneapolis. Since they were ahead of schedule, Steve decided to paddle on ahead as far as the spring Mississippi ice would allow, stash his canoe and then return to the Twin Cities to meet Verlen at the Rendezvous. He was far enough ahead to have time to hop a bus in Duluth to return to Lansing and visit Sarah while Verlen caught up. Once again, Steve wasn't racing to get ahead of Verlen, but to make more time to visit Sarah. Cliff Jacobson, the well known outdoor writer and canoe guide, met Verlen and took him to his home in Prescott, Wisconsin. Verlen said he was a gracious host and returned him to the river the next morning to continue toward Minneapolis. He knew, by then, that Steve stopped on the river up near

Verlen and Steve always got along famously going upstream.

Brainerd, Minnesota. Verlen reached the same area Steve had left near Lake Bemidji. He then met Steve in Duluth to head for Minneapolis for the Rendezvous, which they both enjoyed. Then they again set out at daylight near Brainerd, Minnesota, to finish the Mississippi record together.

They arrived at Lake Itasca, Minnesota, the source of the Mississippi, at 3:18 pm on May 11, 1981. Steve took an icy dip in Lake Itasca to clean up. One week earlier, the water he bathed in had been covered by remaining winter ice. After the swim, Steve's comment to Verlen was, "I'm glad we arrived here together." Verlen was glad to hear that as they basked in the success of their record setting run; he, too, was glad. Verlen said, "That warmed my heart so

"I'm glad we reached Itasca together! Congratulations, Verlen!" Steve Landick. *(photo from Kruger Archives)*

much after the disagreements we had on the way up. We were a team again and had accomplished our goal of the entire Mississippi, from Mile Zero to Lake Itasca." He and Steve had paddled the 2,350 miles upstream in just over 83 days, and that time included the days they took off along the way. They had averaged about 28 miles per day against the current. Their record still stands today. (There is a very good, detailed, account of that upstream journey in the book, *The Ultimate Canoe Challenge*.) They celebrated their arrival at Lake Itasca by getting back into their canoes at 5:00 pm on the same day to paddle on toward Alaska.

"We were a team again and had accomplished our goal of the entire Mississippi, from Mile Zero to Lake Itasca."

The next forty-nine days would take them 2,100 miles north to Fort McMurray in Alberta, Canada. Verlen and Steve had planned on meeting up with a friend, Mark McCorkle, who at the time was on a long trip across Canada in one of Verlen's Loon designs. Right on schedule, they met Mark on June 8, 1981, on the waters of the Saskatchewan River. They camped there for the night, decided to paddle together for the next days, and enjoyed hearing of Mark's accomplishments in Verlen's boat. Mark had planned some solo long distance canoe tripping for years. Finally, he contacted Verlen because he wanted one of his boats. Verlen built him a Loon, which Mark paid for by working as a plumber's helper in Verlen's business for a few months. By the time Verlen and Steve caught up with him at this Saskatchewan campsite, Mark held the longest nonstop paddling distance record—approximately 8,331 miles—in his Loon. (That record had been set during a 11,979-mile trip by Mark. Now, joining together at this campsite, Verlen and Steve's progress, to date, on the UCC would surpass Mark's existing record. As of that Saskatchewan campsite, Verlen and Steve had paddled some 13,000 miles.)

On June 9, 1981, Verlen, Steve, and Mark paddled their Loons across Lake Amisk. The three of them paddled, portaged, camped and ate together until the night of June 24, 1981. Verlen sensed that Steve was again becoming impatient, and that the warm relations between him and Steve since arriving at Lake Itasca were beginning to cool. Later, Steve remembered it only as his usual impatience with the pace, which caused him to have less time for Sarah visits. Verlen and Mark enjoyed a pace somewhat slower than Steve's. Sarah was now living in Alaska while Steve finished the UCC. They had agreed to meet at Fort McMurray and Steve did not want to be late. On the morning of June 25th, Steve paddled off at the crack of dawn, saying to Verlen and Mark, "I'll see you in Fort McMurray." Verlen and Mark didn't mind. They were a good team and enjoyed each other's company.

They did not meet up with Steve again until Verlen's 59th birthday, on June 30, 1981, in Fort McMurray, and then only briefly. Sarah was flying to Dawson, and Steve was going to paddle on to meet Sarah in Circle, Alaska on the Yukon River. Verlen invited Steve to paddle with him and Mark, but Steve was determined to get to Dawson faster and wanted to paddle alone for speed. He did break some speed records. In one ten-day stretch on the Mackenzie River, he averaged over 100 miles a day. Verlen said in his UCC book, "Steve paddled into Circle, some 90 miles up the Yukon from the Porcupine River and met Sarah on August 8, having covered the 2,500 miles from Fort McMurray in 39 days, a daily average of 64 miles, including three grueling days crossing the Richardson Mountains. Steve called this stretch the 'highlight of my trip so far!'" This was fun for Steve! He arrived almost a full month ahead of Verlen and Mark.

Mark McCorkle and Verlen race the rain through deep water *(photo by Verlen Kruger)*

When Verlen and Mark reached the Arctic Ocean, at the mouth of the Mackenzie River, Verlen had paddled from the mouth of the Mississippi on the Gulf of Mexico to the Arctic Ocean, 40 degrees farther north. They continued up the Rat River to the Yukon and then up the Yukon River to Dawson. Verlen had done the Rat River before with Clint Waddell on the Cross Continent Canoe Safari. Steve was then about three weeks ahead of them on the identical route. After more than two months without him, they again met as planned, on the third of September, in the little town of Circle on the Yukon River. Steve and Sarah arrived by car from Fairbanks, Alaska. Steve had stored his Loon and gear in Circle while he spent time with Sarah. Verlen said this was the point where Mark left them. Mark's original plan had been to paddle all the way down the Yukon to the Bering Sea, but he changed that when Steve paddled on ahead, and stayed with Verlen to keep him company. Verlen always said Mark McCorkle was a fine companion and a world-class paddler. Before they joined up, Mark had told Verlen and Steve he probably wouldn't be able to keep up with them, but in fact he did. Verlen thought Mark improved by being challenged; Mark also said that Verlen's normal pace, when Steve was not paddling with them, was still faster than what Mark normally paddled on his own. That was Verlen Kruger the teacher, leading by example. From Circle, on the Yukon, Mark returned home to Wisconsin.

As usual, Steve and Verlen were glad to be back together again. While Mark was a great paddling companion, Verlen and Steve were so well suited for each other as a team that there was never anyone else they preferred to paddle with when challenged. Their friendship was now about eight years old. Though there was sometimes friction between them, it actually motivated and drove them on. They were best when they were together and faced with a challenge that most said could not be done. Verlen said, "Steve was driven to try the impossible." As if Verlen wasn't! That's a bit of the pot calling the kettle black.

Verlen often said Steve was the better paddler of the two, and that Steve sometimes had the advantage of using a kayak paddle in conditions that warranted it, which Verlen did

Verlen and Steve upstream again! *(photo from Kruger Archives)*

not. Steve was always urging Verlen to learn the use of a kayak paddle, to add knee and hip pads inside his Loon (as Steve had) to lend better control of the boat when needed, and to even consider learning to roll his Loon, in the event that learning to do so could save his life. Verlen always resisted—he hated to get wet! He couldn't swim, and once said, "At best, I can dog paddle a few feet. Then I'm in trouble." He felt rolling to be an unnecessary technique, which was done mostly for show, rather than practical use. He just plain did not like paddling with a kayak paddle and had accomplished all that he had without one, including winning long distance races with a canoe paddle over kayaks. When Steve skillfully paddled some upstream portion that Verlen could not, he would blame it on the fact that he was carrying more gear then Steve. About one such instance, Verlen said, "In this case, with his lighter canoe he made it through. I tried and did not, and aggravated my back too. Why was Steve's canoe lighter? Because I was carrying more gear—cameras, lenses, film, shotgun and shells, a bigger tent, a heavier pad, and when I hit the fast water it made a difference. I had to back out and portage."

Steve, on the other hand, believed any paddling advantage that Verlen perceived in him had far more to do with technique than weight. Steve felt that Verlen too often counted on faith rather that preparedness. This issue has not been settled to this day, but they sure had fun trying! In a recent interview, Steve said, "It was my opinion that Verlen could have done as well as I in nearly all of those circumstances if he had simply prepared the fit of his boat better (as kayakers do, with knee and hip pads, they sort of wear their boats) and been more willing to learn new techniques."

Verlen had established a renowned track record for always carrying more than most. In later interviews about this topic, Steve would always laugh—Verlen, too. They had fun almost constantly harassing each other about their loads. On more than one occasion, they unloaded each other's canoes, sorted the contents to compare them, and then weighed them to settle the ongoing dispute. Steve laughed "The loads we carried was frequently an issue. I was a trained Navy SEAL. The SEALs taught us how to do a lot of things with less, and to never have too much. That's how I packed. Verlen, on the other hand, never seemed to have enough. You should have heard us argue over what we were each carrying. We even went so far as to weigh each other's gear!"

Verlen Kruger could be as stubborn as he was tough when he wanted to be, but then, admitted Steve, "So could I." Sometimes they had stubborn contests, but never while they were up against anything serious. When serious happened, they were a team, and that never changed, even when they were stubbornly refusing to get along.

Steve laughed at how serious Verlen and co-author Brand Frentz made some of these disagreements sound in *The Ultimate Canoe Challenge*. He said, "Sure we had issues. How could we not on a trip like this? But most would have far more issues than Verlen and I

Verlen and Steve were so well suited for each other as a team that there was never anyone else they preferred to paddle with when challenged.

Verlen Kruger descends Chilkoot Pass, of Gold Rush fame, in October of 1981 *(photo from Kruger Archives)*

did. We had so many tremendously good times, and we even had fun with our issues. Verlen and I had far more fun together than we ever had disagreements."

Steve and Verlen were together again, charging hard for the Pacific Ocean, with a different kind of problem looming on the horizon. Phil Pemberton and his partner met Verlen and Steve in the community of Carmacks, in Yukon Territory. They explained they had been unable to raise enough money for them to continue the UCC nonstop. They urged Verlen and Steve to take the winter off and return to Lansing to help them raise more money to continue in the spring. Verlen did not want to do it, but he did not have enough money to finance both himself and Steve further. Steve was in favor of taking the winter off because that would enable him to spend more time with Sarah, who was now pregnant. The debate continued on into Whitehorse, where Steve and Sarah were able to spend more time together. Verlen was still strongly reluctant, but the conclusion they finally reached was that they would go over the Chilkoot Pass, of Gold Rush fame, and on into Skagway. There, they would store their gear for the winter, take the ferry home to Lansing, and spend the winter fundraising for the balance of the trip. Phil Pemberton planned to go over the Chilkoot with them to do more filming. Steve was pleased with the opportunity to earn more money over the winter to help finance his part of the UCC—he never liked it when Verlen had to carry more of the financing.

On October 13, 1981, Verlen headed over the Chilkoot without Steve. He was accompanied by Phil Pemberton, Phil's son, and Christine Hedgecock, the head ranger on the Chilkoot Trail at that time. Steve had planned on joining them that day, but had not made it to the meeting place, so they left without him, hoping that he would catch up. In fact, Steve and Sarah had spent some days together in Whitehorse and then the last three in Carcross. Sarah had paddled with Steve and was going to the Chilkoot Trail to see him off. Wind drove them off the lake and they were wind-bound for two days. Steve finally walked her back along the shoreline of Lake Bennet and then returned alone to catch up with Verlen somewhere between the Chilkoot and Skagway.

Verlen, meanwhile, reached Skagway. He boarded the ferry for Lansing on October 19, 1981, with Steve nowhere in sight, nor did he know his location or circumstances.

By this time, Steve had made it to the top of the Chilkoot in a blizzard. The falling snow made it nearly impossible to see and he dared not attempt the dangerous descent through the maze of broken rock on the west side of the pass. Knowing he was boarding a ferry in Skagway to bring him home for the winter, Steve buried his gear and Loon on top of the Chilkoot Pass and carefully memorized and marked its location so he would be able to dig it out in the spring. With the blizzard still blowing, he walked back to Carcross, caught the train to Skagway, and boarded the ferry for Lansing the day after Verlen had left.

Whether Verlen liked it or not, wintering in Lansing proved to be a good decision. Their fundraising efforts helped replenish their travel funds. They were able to land Dow Chemical and the DuPont Company as sponsors. They also landed more gear sponsors and a freeze-dried food company, which helped to fill the larder for the rest of the trip. Verlen and Steve spent a portion of the winter modifying their canoes to include hard fiberglass spray covers to handle the formidable seas of the open Pacific Ocean, an upcoming leg of the UCC trip. Their new canoes, shrouded with removable spray covers, were only open in a skirted center cockpit, more similar to kayak designs. These modifications made them more seaworthy and watertight, even when catamaraned. They also added the catamaran sleeves from thwart to thwart, as solid hollow tubes, to eliminate water leakage. Verlen even made the boats two inches deeper to increase their buoyancy and capacity. He called the new boats the Kruger Monarch (after the butterfly he loved) and was able to

The falling snow made it nearly impossible to see and he dared not attempt the dangerous descent through the maze of broken rock on the west side of the pass.

Steve Landick, accompanied by a friend who took this photo, climbs Chilkoot into blizzard conditions
(photo by Doug Sanvik, courtesy of Steve Landick)

sell this new design to the Mad River Canoe Company in Vermont. His boat royalties from the sale of that design helped him finance the balance of the UCC trip. Mad River also gave Verlen and Steve four of the first boats they made. Two were given to Steve, provided that he switch to the Monarch for the balance of the trip. They now each had two Monarchs, in addition to their Loons, to finish the Ultimate Canoe Challenge.

They both were attached to their Loons. Verlen, at the request of DuPont, chose to continue in his. Steve switched to a Monarch in Skagway, to have more capacity and to just try it out. Verlen modified his Loon's spray cover to be quite similar to the new Monarch. By doing that, he could comply with the wishes of the DuPont Company that he continue in the Loon. DuPont made the Kevlar that was the fiberglass building fabric of Loons, and they wanted to see the effects of the full 28,000-mile UCC on the original Loon to help measure the toughness of their product.

There was no one they would rather paddle with than each other (photo from Kruger Archives)

Verlen arrived in Skagway a day ahead of Steve, who had gone back onto the Chilkoot several days before to retrieve his Loon and complete his trip down the west side of the famous Gold Rush Pass. He met Verlen in Skagway on April 13, 1982. Because of the design changes in the boats, they needed two days of sorting and packing. Though watertight storage capacity increased, access had become more difficult due to the modifications.

They were both fired up with a winter's rest, had new sea-covers for the open Pacific, and they were again an enthused team headed south. They were at 17,000 miles, halfway through the UCC, and nothing was going to stop them. Verlen was, in fact, happy he had been granted the time at home during the winter with Jenny and family. He also had had the time to modify the canoes and raise more money. They headed south in much better shape, mentally and financially, than they had been the prior fall. Progress was slower on the open ocean stretches that interrupted the inside passage and there was considerably more weather to deal with than they were used to, even than when on the Atlantic Ocean.

Because they were both in newly modified boats, their loads had changed. Steve suggested, while in Ketchikan, they weigh in their loads and try to balance the content-loads of their canoes. It turned out that Steve was actually carrying eleven pounds more than Verlen when they added in the weight of the new boats. Their teamwork balanced their loads, as well as they could, and they were off again. They had a new element to deal with on the open Pacific, where the inland passage had long openings to the ocean, stretching all the way to Japan. Verlen was subject to occasional seasickness and sometimes lost his meals over the side of his boat. Fortunately, it never lasted too long, so his condition didn't weaken from it. Their primary complaint of the west coast, so far, was being wet and cold most of the time. During a free afternoon around the 16th of May, after having been blown off the water by high winds, Steve made the comment that he thought their team was more together than at any time during their first 17,000 miles. Verlen agreed.

Steve Landick in a new Monarch catamaraned to Verlen's Loon, headed for Seattle *(photo by Verlen Kruger)*

It took them from April 13 to June 4 to paddle to Seattle, Washington. They planned to spend at least two weeks there, and become involved with festivities sponsored by the local canoeing associations. Steve's mother and Sarah were to meet him in Seattle. They also used the time to meet some new local sponsors. They were romanced and outfitted with a lot of new gear from the Helly Hansen Company, of foul-weather-wear fame, and given new Thermarest mattresses that soon became their sleep gear of choice. In addition, Dow Chemical, one of their sponsors, gave them an Emergency Position-Indicating Radio Beacon (EPIRB) the same day they left Coos Bay for Cape Blanco. The device was fairly new at that time. It had been invented for use by boats and sailing yachts that got into trouble. This one was so basic it had a simple on/off switch, but no light or indicator showing it was on or sending a signal. When switched on, it transmitted an emergency signal to the nearest Coast Guard station, providing the latitude and longitude of the vessel in trouble and asking for rescue. Steve and Verlen decided to mount it beneath the deck of Steve's Monarch, because they felt his was the safest place to keep it. Both agreed that Steve was the best rough water paddler with his skills from SEAL training, and the fact that he always carried both a single canoe paddle and a double kayak paddle in his Monarch. In rough weather, with a kayak paddle, Steve could better brace and control his boat than Verlen.

They were now 19,191 miles into the Ultimate Canoe Challenge and going strong!

The all-time high of their paddling time together on the UCC delivered them down the coast to Seattle. They were 19,191 miles into the Ultimate Canoe Challenge and going strong!

*"The biggest challenge on a journey is making
the chemistry work between companions."*

VERLEN KRUGER

Cape Blanco

It was during those days in Seattle that Verlen and Steve met Valerie Fons. Valerie had recently discovered canoe racing with the Seattle Canoe Club. While paddling during some canoe race training, she happened to see Verlen and Steve being interviewed by the press on one of the docks being used by her Canoe Club. She listened to Verlen talk to reporters about his and Steve's UCC experiences and immediately became intrigued. At thirty-one years old and after experiencing failed marriage, Valerie claimed her life was not working out as she had hoped. She was quickly impassioned by the adventure these men were having and in a book she would later write, said, "I knew I belonged there too."

At each of their subsequent meetings, all of which were paddle events around Seattle, she broached the subject of paddling with them. Steve was against the idea. As far as he was concerned, his agreement with Verlen that the UCC was theirs and only theirs, was in force and they should not have even been discussing the possibility of someone joining them. Steve remembered that she seemed to him to be too persistent about joining them. He knew she was inexperienced as a canoeist and he was genuinely concerned about the safety of neophyte paddlers on the open Pacific Ocean, with surf launches and retrievals, as well as the extreme weather often found out there. Steve had asked Valerie about her skills and experience with canoes during a paddle on Grays Harbor in Seattle, had warned her about the problems that could arise on the big waters, and explained why he felt she was not ready for it. Though safety was his chief concern, he was also sure that she would be unable to keep pace with him and Verlen and would therefore slow them down. Both Verlen and Steve said on different occasions, "She just kept showing

In one of his legendary nightmares, Verlen called out "I fear the seals!" *(photo by Steve Landick)*

up, saying that she wanted to paddle on with us." "Persistent" was her word of choice to describe her behavior around the UCC team between Seattle and Long Beach, California.

Steve said Verlen had formed a friendship with Valerie during the twelve days they were in Seattle, and that Verlen was always unable to give Valerie a definitive no about paddling with them down the coast. Steve felt that put him in the distasteful position of repeatedly having to explain his refusal to accept her repeated proposal. He felt, because of Valerie's presence, a faint crack had developed in his and Verlen's UCC partnership and friendship, which had seemed so strong since leaving Skagway. One of Steve's original goals, which he had promised himself, was to return to Lansing with the friendship between him and Verlen in as good or better shape than it had been at their Red Rock launching. Despite Steve's unease, Verlen and Steve left Seattle the morning of June 17, 1982, and headed down the west coast of the Pacific without Valerie Fons.

"Steve and I had agreed before we started that we would not allow anyone to join the trip."

Verlen wrote in his book, *The Ultimate Canoe Challenge*, "None of the Seattle paddlers was more enthusiastic about the Ultimate Canoe Challenge than Valerie Fons, a woman of 31. She was a novice paddler, but eager to learn canoe racing. Like many people who met us along the way, she was fascinated with the idea of the Challenge and our stories about it. And like a few others, she wanted to join us."

"Steve and I had agreed before we started that we would not allow anyone to join the trip. Even when Mark McCorkle paddled with us for several weeks, it was clearly understood that he was not joining the Ultimate Canoe Challenge; he was just paddling along for a while. And so, when Valerie raised the question of joining, the answer was no, without even considering the practicalities of taking on a novice woman paddler." The primary reason was her novice status. McCorkle was a seasoned veteran of long-distance paddling when he joined them; there was no double standard at work when Valerie was turned down.

"But the trip still excited her. And when, after nearly two weeks in the city, we gathered our boats and gear at Edmonds Beach to continue the trip, Valerie was among the well-wishers who saw us off. She did more that that—she bought me dinner beforehand, gave us a loaf of homemade banana bread, and paddled the first hour with us as we headed out. On top of that, she gave me a box marked '40 letters for 40 days,' to be read one a day for morale as we made our way down the West Coast.

"Well, of course, in our travels we met lots of people that we wanted to stay friends with, but never saw again. When I left Seattle I never expected to see Valerie Fons again, but I was wrong about that."

A mid-July day found Verlen and Steve paddling out of Coos Bay above their target of Port Orford. To get there they had to paddle around Cape Blanco, the westernmost point of the continental U.S. Verlen and Steve knew that any point of land protruding out into a large body of water tended to produce strong, abrupt, local winds, and Cape Blanco wasn't just a protruding point of land. It towered above the Pacific and was famous for producing winds of magnitude. Since the day started calm, Verlen and Steve had decided not to catamaran the boats, and so paddled solo as they rounded the Cape.

Verlen didn't like the looks of the sea or the winds as they approached Blanco and wished that they had catamaraned before launching. But because they had to be ashore to successfully catamaran the boats, and because there was nowhere safe to land, they were now committed to pass Cape Blanco solo. He said to Steve, "Well, okay. Stick close. I don't like the looks of this."

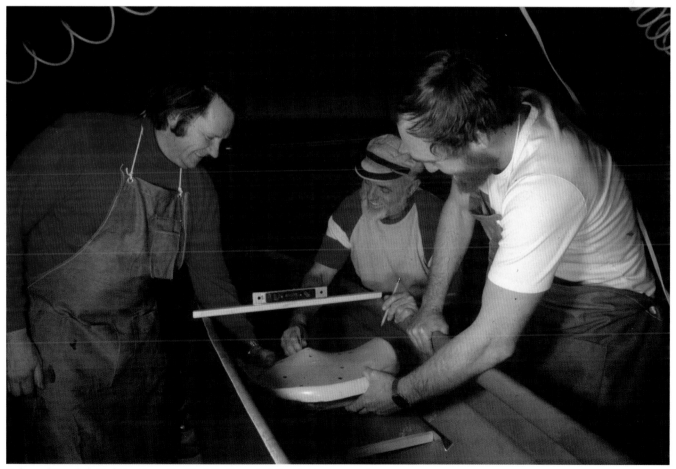

Verlen and Steve help Mad River Canoe President, Jim Henry, install seats (photo by Jim Henry)

As they passed the Blanco reef, the winds increased. They felt they would soon be in worse trouble if they tried to continue, so they both headed toward shore to try to find shelter. They tried to stay close together. Verlen said he would never be sure exactly how it happened, but he suddenly found his Loon teetering on the crest of a big wave. As he tried to stroke to stabilize the boat, he found that his paddle could not reach the water. His boat flipped, dumping him into the cold Pacific. As he surfaced, he felt the bottom of his Loon, but there was nothing to grasp. He tried again, as both he and the boat rose to the crest of another wave, but Verlen was not tethered to his canoe and the wind quickly blew it downwind and out of reach. Neither Verlen nor Steve were wearing their life jackets; they didn't like to paddle while wearing them and usually kept them on deck behind them under bungee cords. And Verlen couldn't swim. He was flopping in sixty-degree water, and he was in trouble.

Steve was about twenty-yards ahead of Verlen when he saw the empty Loon. He saw Verlen surface under the boat, and then watched the wind blow it away from him. He knew Verlen would never reach it. Steve immediately began maneuvering toward him, while still struggling to stabilize his own boat. Steve later related that it seemed to him to take forever to get to Verlen after the capsize. When Steve reached him, Verlen pulled himself onto the back of Steve's canoe, hanging onto the cockpit combing at the rear. There was nowhere else to go. The majority of his body was still in the water. Steve's Monarch, fully loaded as it was, had greater buoyancy than Verlen's Loon, and that extra buoyancy helped support Verlen's added weight. Steve needed his kayak paddle, which was lashed to the deck. Wrestling with the waves and wind, with Verlen on the back end of his canoe, he needed more

Verlen considering Seattle departure route *(photo from Kruger Archives)*

power. Because it was so rough, it took him time to find a wave trough long enough to allow him time to stop paddling and release the kayak paddle from the deck. Once he had it in hand, the double-bladed paddle provided better control and gave him more confidence. But they were still in big trouble.

As Verlen clung to the back of Steve's canoe, Steve removed his life jacket and handed it to Verlen. Verlen wrestled with it for some time, trying to get it on, but it proved too difficult while hanging onto the boat. It was then Steve remembered that his Monarch was equipped with the EPIRB, which they had received from their Dow Chemical sponsors that same day. Had it been in Verlen's canoe, the EPIRB would have been gone as his boat blew downwind. Steve switched it on, but had no idea if it was working, so he never counted on rescue. He had his hands full.

He paddled extremely hard for over an hour, with Verlen hanging on, kicking to stay warm and helping to propel Steve's canoe. Verlen thought he could see people on shore and felt they knew he and Steve were in trouble, but there was nothing they could do to help them. Steve never remembered seeing anyone on shore, because the breaking waves were too high. They were so big as they broke on shore that he felt there was no hope of going through them. They had to stay on the sea-side of the breakers, but that caused Verlen to remain in the fifty-degree water. Both of them knew Verlen was on the edge of hypothermia. He was shaking involuntarily, turning blue, and fading fast. Verlen once said, "I began to think I probably wouldn't make it, but I wouldn't give up. There is always hope and I have never prayed so hard. Then we heard a wonderful sound—the thumping engine of a helicopter. The big chopper came straight at us. It was the Coast Guard. But they flew right over us and kept going. 'Oh no,' I thought. In all the white, foaming water, the spray and turbulence, it looked like they had missed us. But no, in a minute the helicopter reappeared, settled above us, and lowered a basket. I was too weak to climb in. The pilot put it at water level. I rolled in and was pulled up. Saved! The pilot yelled down to Steve, 'Do you need help?' Steve signaled that he would keep paddling. The chopper took off to deliver me to the nearest hospital."

With Verlen rescued and removed from the back of his canoe, Steve was in much better shape. Without the extra weight on the back of the Monarch, the boat behaved as it was designed to. He pushed on another six miles through the big seas until he paddled into Port Orford harbor, their original destination goal for the day. Steve remembered his feelings of that time. "Verlen crawled up on my stern deck. After a long hard look at his Loon I headed for shore a mile and a half away. Although I had little faith in being rescued, it dawned on me to at least turn on the EPIRB distress radio beacon we had just received before we left Coos Bay. Fortunately, I had placed it within easy reach and I was able to activate it with one hand on the paddle. I picked up the stroke and commenced my most demanding race. Verlen's legs created a tremendous drag and his weight forced the bow of my boat higher, which caught the raging wind, making it difficult to stay headed toward shore. It began to look as if we would miss the next point and be blown to sea. The next landfall in that direction was Antarctica, which made me paddle harder! The rudder and kayak paddle proved to be our saving grace. After a ninety-minute struggle, we were just off the breakers. Suddenly, as I paddled down the beach just outside the breakers, looking for a way in through the surf, a Coast Guard helicopter, buffeted about by the winds, dropped to fifty-feet and lowered its basket. At first, Verlen couldn't lift himself to the height of the basket, but they lowered it to allow him to simply roll into it. Verlen was

Verlen once said, "I began to think I probably wouldn't make it, but I wouldn't give up."

severely hypothermic and flopping about involuntarily as the basket went up. Relieved of his weight, I pushed on to Port Orford alone. It took several hours, but I didn't have much trouble making it. Once into the calm harbor water, I stopped paddling, leaned back and took a deep breath, staring out to sea and pondering our faulty strategy and how it could be improved for the future. I knew we would be back out there together soon."

When Verlen arrived at the Coos Bay Hospital, his body temperature was 91 degrees. Hospital personnel immediately recirculated his blood through a blood-warming machine, which brought him back out of his hypothermic condition. Verlen later discovered that the Coast Guard helicopter that had rescued them was the only one on the Oregon Coast within two hundred miles, and had only been moved there two weeks before. They had been lucky and they both knew it. They agreed that they could not put themselves into such danger again, and had to develop a new strategy that would enable them to catamaran on rough water.

Within hours, Verlen was released from the hospital. He rented a plane and searched the waters below Port Orford for his Loon, but to no avail. The Loon had disappeared. He and Steve talked strategy and decided their best plan would be to get their reserve Monarch from Lansing to continue the trip. Within a week, Verlen had arranged for his spare Monarch to be shipped from Lansing to Seattle, and had arrived in Seattle himself via bus from Port Orford. He had arranged to work on the Monarch in a dealer's boat shop to pre-

Verlen and Steve paddling Seattle harbor *(photo from Kruger Archives)*

pare it. Meanwhile, Steve spent a week with Sarah and his mother in Seattle. Verlen said, "In Seattle, the persistent Valerie Fons volunteered to help. She worked in the shop with me and, in exchange, I did some repair work on her damaged wood strip canoe. She kept trying to persuade Steve to let her join, without luck."

When the work on the Monarch was finished, Verlen heard that an Oregon fisherman had found his Loon. Valerie gave Verlen and his Monarch a ride back down to Coos Bay, Oregon. About a week after the capsize off Cape Blanco, the DuPont company had publicized a $2,000 reward for finding the boat. When Verlen's Loon was returned to him, he found that some ID markings had been scraped from it, which led him to conclude that whoever had found it may not have initially intended to return it. Nevertheless, Verlen had his Loon back. After some quick work, it was refitted and ready to continue.

Steve said, "During the few days before we left Port Orford, Verlen and I agreed to test an alternative method of hooking up the catamaran in rougher waters and to explore a self-rescue technique using one catamaran pole and a collapsible water jug as flotation for an outrigger. We did not agree on Verlen's unwillingness to learn a standard paddle brace or use a kayak paddle and knee-braces. He could be as stubborn as I." Steve knew there was no one he'd rather paddle to the sea with than Verlen, but his SEAL training had convinced him to minimize risk through maximizing preparedness. "To add to the tension, Valerie Fons was still there, insisting upon accompanying us for several days and still proposing she join us for the entire trip around the Baja! It seemed incredible to me that, again, I was forced to deal with her obstinate attitude when we should have been solely immersed in planning our own survival." It was also obvious to Steve that during his absence from Seattle, Valerie's persistence had gained some ground in convincing Verlen that she might accompany them down the coast. Steve said, "Verlen could just not say no to Valerie Fons."

Verlen and Steve in a rare television interview, together (photo from Kruger Archives)

"We're over halfway, Steve"

VERLEN KRUGER

On To Tragedy

Paul Hoobyar, a writer from *Canoe* magazine, wanted to accompany Verlen and Steve from Port Orford as far as San Francisco. He was working up an article that later appeared in the June, 1983 issue of *Canoe*, entitled "Paddling with the Possessed." Paul was paddling in a Sea Hawk kayak provided by Easy Rider Kayaks of Seattle.

Verlen, in the UCC book, said, "Coming out of Port Orford, we headed north to Cape Blanco, 6 miles back to the place where I had capsized, to resume the trip from there. We reached the scene of the near-disaster and turned south again, enjoying the scenery this time." Steve did not remember backtracking up to Cape Blanco where Verlen had capsized. Rather, he remembered the three of them turning south to paddle toward San Francisco. Verlen didn't write about the incident until twenty-one years after it had happened; the effects of time on memory, combined with the UCC principle and practice of always backtracking to the place where they left the water and resuming the trip from there, likely accounted for this error.

The first day was, in fact, a forty-mile paddle south before they securely harbored in Gold Beach. The next several days were lengthy, with 3:00 am starts, as Paul discovered the UCC team enjoyed eighteen-hour days of mile-eating paddling. Though an excellent and experienced paddler, Paul was being pushed hard by the UCC duo. A few days later, Paul found himself fiercely paddling his way past a reef to avoid being swept onto it. He did this while watching Verlen and Steve, catamaraned and moving smoothly under two paddlers' power and aided by rudders, which his kayak did not have. After a few days, he began to use one of Verlen's spare single-blade canoe paddles. He found it eased the pain in his arms, and that he could better keep up with the UCC pace. Verlen always felt that more kayakers should discover what he and Steve knew about: single over double paddles for long distance paddling.

Leaving San Francisco under the Golden Gate *(photo from Kruger Archives)*

Verlen held that, over distance, canoe paddles had great advantages over kayak paddles. Steve basically agreed with him and used a canoe paddle himself, but always kept a kayak paddle at the ready for rough water. Verlen wrote in his UCC book, "It is my belief that marathon paddling, the kind of canoe travel where you might stay on the water 18 or 24 straight hours, is best done with a canoe paddle. Constantly switching sides keeps the workload on the various muscles of the body more balanced, and the lower body is more involved in the paddling motion. Both Steve and I normally used canoe paddles on this trip. Paul found, after a few days, when he was sore and looking for relief, that a canoe paddle worked better for him, too, and he began using one as he 'paddled with the possessed.'"

Steve remembered, "Paul was a strong and capable paddler all the way to San Francisco. He was quick to lighten the tension between Verlen and me with his infectious smile and sharp wit. Sea lions were plentiful and we kept an uneasy lookout for their natural enemy, the Great White Shark."

As Verlen and Steve departed Port Orford and the open waters of the Pacific again dripped from their paddles, Valerie drove north to Seattle with Verlen's newly equipped Monarch on the roof of her car. She had agreed to store it at her home while Verlen and Steve continued south. This kept Verlen's Monarch safe, just in case he needed it. Having Valerie store the Monarch naturally made her closer to the Ultimate Canoe Challenge team.

Photo shows hard sea-coverings of the Monarch ready for sea
(photo from Kruger Archives)

The presence of that Monarch she was storing began to haunt Valerie. In her Baja book, she says, "I began taking the new Monarch out for water practice on weekends, working in the surf on the coast and paddling in Puget Sound. I was floating the deluxe cruiser every chance I could get. The more time I spent with the canoe, the more my eagerness for an ocean journey grew. What did I have to lose?" By letter, she again made a formal proposal to the Ultimate Canoe Challenge team to join their expedition. She sent the request to their next mail drop and waited. The answer came within a week: No. The main reason was the commitment of Verlen and Steve to each other for the UCC. No one else could be a part of their team. Not Mark McCorkle, not Paul Hoobyar, not Valerie Fons. Valerie was not really asking to become a member of the team, but just to paddle with them down the coast. Steve repeated it was also her lack of experience that eliminated her. Valerie wrote, "I respected their partnership and knew that Steve was right about my limited experience, but there was something inside me that understood their journey as if it were my own."

Progress down the coast went well and Paul Hoobyar was enjoying the experience. The new strategy Verlen and Steve had adapted to catamaran in rough water was working. When the winds blew, they joined the Monarch and the Loon and pushed on. On August 22, the day before the three of them reached San Francisco, they overnighted at Bodega Head. Verlen said, "On shore at Bodega, I was surprised to see Valerie Fons again. She had a week off from work and had come down from Seattle with her friend to see us. She had my Monarch on top of her car and was hoping to paddle with us for a few days. That didn't happen, but we did loan the Monarch to Paul to use for the next day's run to San Francisco. His kayak had been leaking and a dry boat was needed. I think he also enjoyed his time in a Kruger boat." Valerie Fons went on down to San Francisco and was present during most of the days they were hosted by the Dolphin Swim and Rowing Club of San Francisco. In her book, she said, "What did I have to lose? By letter, I made a formal proposal to the Ultimate Canoe Challenge team to join their expedition."

On August 27, Verlen and Steve pulled out under the Golden Gate Bridge—alone—and headed down the California coast toward Point Conception. The team left San Francisco with more discussions caused by Valerie's persistent proposals. Steve said, "Verlen now seemed more open to the idea of her tagging along. I was not. The tension between us on this issue increased." The faint crack in their partnership and friendship that Steve had first sensed in Seattle seemed to be widening. As they paddled south, Valerie drove north to Seattle, again with Verlen's Monarch.

Progressing south from San Francisco to Long Beach, Verlen and Steve were more than once chased off the seas, even while catamaraned, by some of the fiercest winds they had encountered on the west coast. Verlen spoke of four miles of desperate struggle to keep the catamaraned boats upright. Steve's biggest concern was that they were fighting an off-shore wind, which could blow them all the way to Japan. They both admitted to having been exhausted by the effort it took them to reach the protection of a Coast Guard break-water, which had to be reached to survive.

Verlen and Steve were headed for a two-week vacation with Jenny and Sarah once they reached Long Beach. This gathering had been planned for weeks. Verlen and Steve had been hard pressed on the sea since San Francisco, and they both knew they needed a break. Verlen wrote in *The Ultimate Canoe Challenge*, "It had been 149 days since we put in at Dyea near Skagway and started down the Pacific Coast. We had come 3,809 miles in that time. It had been 149 calendar days, but about 60 of them did not involve paddling, owing to wind and snow, the celebrations in Vancouver, Seattle, and San Francisco, the July vacation, and the regrouping after Cape Blanco. We went 3,809 miles in about 90 days of paddling, or an average of 42 miles a paddling day. At Long Beach I noted in my diary; 'The North American West Coast has been beautiful, but I would not care to paddle it again. The Pacific Ocean is not really canoe country.'"

After reaching Long Beach, Steve immediately flew to Lansing where he met Sarah and their baby, Saba, who was less than three months old. On September 25, 1982, Jenny planned to fly to Long Beach to spend time with Verlen. On the first morning Steve was home, Jenny was in the kitchen stirring up pancake batter before catching her early morn-

Verlen and Steve were more than once chased off the sea by some of the fiercest winds they encountered on the west coast.

ing flight, when Saba was discovered by Steve, dead in her crib, a victim of Sudden Infant Death Syndrome (SIDS). Jenny said she would never forget Sarah's scream from the bedroom, then rushing in to see a stricken Steve holding the still infant in his two hands. Verlen was notified by Jenny and immediately flew home. It was a long and tragic week for the Landick and Kruger families.

After the funeral, Verlen waited a week for Steve to bring up the discussion of the balance of the trip, but Steve did not. He was confused, felt guilt and remorse, and was not sure what to do. Toward the end of their second week in Lansing, Verlen asked, "What do you think about the balance of the UCC, Steve?" According to Verlen, Steve's response was, "You go ahead and do what you want to. I'm through. I'm not going to go on." Verlen said he was both surprised and not surprised. He could understand Steve's quandary; he just never expected Steve to quit. He didn't think it was in him.

Years later, Steve said, "Including prior visits, I had been with Saba only ten days and ten hours of her less-than-three-month life. I couldn't help but blame my excessive ambition for the Ultimate Canoe Challenge for those precious days lost. A week later, in my desperation, I told Verlen I needed time to think and urged him to make his own plans for continuing, if he was going on soon. Almost immediately, he phoned Valerie Fons and asked her to join him on the Baja. I spent the balance of October with Sarah, weighing my decision to continue the trip. In the end, we both agreed the best medicine to ease the pain would most probably be the tangible goal of finishing the trip."

By the time Steve reached that decision, Verlen had already decided he was going on. His modus operandi had always been to select as a partner the individual who most wanted to be there. The likely candidate, who had persistently asked to join the UCC team, was one Valerie Fons. Choosing her was consistent with the way he had always chosen partners—including Steve. He was confident that he could always teach someone the needed skills. Steve and Verlen had discussed the possibility of Valerie joining them at the tip of the Baja. Steve felt the protected inside shore would be a safer place for an intermediate paddler—if she must join them at all. The trauma that Steve was experiencing at this time in his life was the opportunity for Valerie to step into the UCC Team. Verlen called Valerie, asked if she still wanted to go on the ocean, and she responded with an immediate yes. Verlen accepted Valerie's "yes" to his invitation, and the world turned upside down. During later interviews I had with Jenny Kruger, she vividly and specifically remembered Verlen calling Valerie Fons.

Valerie describes things similarly in a book she later wrote. She said Verlen called her in late October to ask her to join him. He explained the Saba tragedy, that Steve had decided to stay home with Sarah and was not going on with the UCC at this time, and that Steve had suggested Verlen go on alone. She said he dramatically described 2,000 miles of paddling the Baja between Long Beach, California, and Yuma, Arizona, at the mouth of the Colorado. And that it seemed impossible to find someone capable of handling the Baja, both mentally and physically, by the end of the month. Valerie quoted in her book, *Keep It Moving*, "I didn't hesitate. I probably could have phoned him back. I should have thought about the consequences, but immediately I said, 'Yes.'"

Steve spent the month of October with Sarah in Lansing, both trying to remake sense out of life and wrestle with decisions that needed making. The week after Saba's funeral, September 28, 1982, Jenny flew back to Long Beach with Verlen, on her originally planned three-week vacation trip. Steve and Sarah stayed behind at the Kruger home. Though by then he and Sarah had agreed that the best course would be for Steve to rejoin and complete the UCC, he was still lacking motivation and having a tough time getting organized again. Finally, he called Verlen in Long Beach and asked his support. He asked Verlen to wait for him so he could rejoin the trip and paddle with Verlen down the open Pacific portion of the coast and then have Valerie join them in the protected waters inside the Baja on the Sea of Cortez. Verlen said it was too late to change their plans. He had asked Valerie to do the Baja portion of the UCC and she had agreed. She found renters for her house, quit her job, and was on the way down to join him. The two of them were moving on! Steve could rejoin Verlen at the mouth of the Colorado, or before, but Valerie was part of the team. Verlen and Valerie left Long Beach together October 25, 1982, as one of what would soon be "two teams on the Baja."

New team loading for launch at Long Beach *(photo by Lloyd Fons)*

This left Steve hanging in the wind, and he later said, "Perhaps unfairly, a part of my grief turned to anger. When Valerie left Long Beach harbor with Verlen, her Monarch was decked out with our UCC stickers and logo, but she had added the names of her own sponsors!" Steve was convinced that Valerie had no business being with Verlen—period—especially on the open Pacific, which had already nearly claimed his and Verlen's lives more than once. Jenny later said that she begged Verlen not to take Valerie on the Baja leg of the journey. She feared for her husband, his safety, and definitely did not give him her blessing on his change in paddling partners.

Verlen had been Steve's Ultimate Canoe Challenge partner for nearly twenty thousand miles. He had been Steve's closest personal friend, his father-in-law and grandfather to Saba. Steve was determined to finish the UCC that he and Verlen had planned for five years.

"The mistake most people make is they fight themselves and each other. If you fight anything, it's got to be the circumstances, as Clint and I did."

VERLEN KRUGER

Two Teams on the Baja

Verlen and Valerie, his new partner for the Baja trip of the UCC, met in Long Beach, California, on October 25, 1982. In *The Ultimate Canoe Challenge*, Verlen said, "She was as prepared as she could be for something she had never done before. Steve had warned me, 'You can't go out there with someone who just started canoeing this spring, who has no experience.' I said that I thought I had enough experience for us both. Valerie had the main thing that my partner needed: a burning desire to make the trip."

Verlen in a teaching pose readying Valerie for Baja *(photo by Lloyd Fons)*

Verlen's confidence in his experience and teaching ability was not misplaced, considering his past achievements. To him, teaching someone to paddle with him was not a monumental task. Steve felt Verlen's judgment was clouded by Valerie's persistence and that he was again counting on faith rather than preparedness. In Steve's mind, there was no way Verlen and Valerie belonged on the open Pacific Ocean between Long Beach and Cabo San Lucas, the area he and Verlen always thought would be the worst conditions of the entire UCC.

There had always been a little imbalance of authority between Verlen and Steve. Verlen's recognition in paddling circles, his military status as an officer and flight instructor, and the fact that he was Steve's father-in-law and thirty years his senior made it easy for Verlen to sometimes champion his decisions over Steve's. At times, according to Steve, Verlen also would try to good naturedly push him around a little. Steve, however, was not easily pushed. Steve felt himself an equal partner to Verlen in critical judgment, military training and paddling ability, if not in age and experience. He had more than held up his end of the first 21,000 miles of the UCC. Steve perceived Verlen's decision to partner up with a beginner on the open Pacific as an unnecessary risk, but Verlen had made up his mind.

Steve sensed dangers in the new partnership, other than those presented by the open Pacific. He regretted his own absence on the Team, but he also feared for Verlen—his father-in-law and best friend—whom he held in high regard. No matter the innocence of intention, or naivete with which this new team set out to sea, Steve knew they were entering dangerous new waters in more than one way.

Before they launched at Long Beach, California, Valerie had decorated her canoe with sponsor logos and goals. She quickly discovered the length of Verlen's shadow. Though she had dressed to look appropriately capable and professional, the press, as usual, posed most of their questions to Verlen. Verlen told her, "They didn't take any notice of me either when I first started," but did so with a smile.

Verlen and Valerie began the Baja stretch, the area Verlen and Steve had always planned on being the most difficult portion of the trip. Both Verlen and Valerie later wrote of episodes of anger, frustration, or of recognizing errors for which they occasionally affixed blame on the other. Verlen also spoke of needing some conversations on attitude adjustment, and of nurturing the development of a good relationship between the new team's members. As early as November 20, just twenty-six days after leaving Long Beach, Verlen commented in his UCC book, "I was moved to comment that Valerie was 'noticeably toughening up,' and developing a good, positive attitude. I regretted that she had had to plunge right into demanding, dangerous paddling. Gradual development of skills would have been better. But she was learning fast." Valerie began to understand the rationale of a team mate in the UCC and discovered she was most often better off to accept Verlen's advice and suggestions for a successful paddling routine, some of which she had earlier resisted.

Almost immediately out of the Long Beach harbor, Verlen's new partner had some disagreements with seasickness. A tough start, which even Verlen had experienced before. Verlen had to paddle both boats as a catamaran the entire first day as Valerie lay in the bottom of her canoe recuperating. Verlen urged her to take anti-sickness pills before leaving shore, but Valerie declared, "I don't take pills." Later, when she took the pills as Verlen suggested, before leaving shore, she overcame the affliction and, after a few days, needed no pills at all.

Seasickness, dousing by waves as they attempted to shore, cold wet nights, 3:00 am starts to avoid afternoon winds: all caused the magnitude of their task to present itself harshly to Valerie as the new partner. Verlen said there were times when she would be mad at him for things that occurred. Most of those things were almost common occurrences to Verlen, but they were new to Valerie. They were extremely fortunate to not be overtaken by severe weather during that first week on the open ocean.

December 6, 1982, found them off Abreojos, in the Baja of California. A nice day launched them at 10:00 am for a paddle through the Bay of Whales to the next safe harbor. In his book, *The Ultimate Canoe Challenge*, Verlen said, "It was twenty-two miles through Bahia Ballenas (Bay of Whales) to Laguna San Ignatio, the famous gray whale calving grounds

Steve knew they were entering dangerous new waters.

and the last harbor before the long unprotected stretch." South winds began to blow, a bad sign of storms in that region, and the waves grew. Verlen said Valerie became uneasy. Her senses were correct. They both agreed a storm was imminent and, by late afternoon, decided to try to run back, with the wind at their backs, to the safe harbor they had left that morning at Abreojos. The wind and waves continually grew behind them and they soon found themselves fighting the waves, which were now trying to pound them onto the breaking surf and the thundering surf ashore. Their only choice was to again renew their struggle for Abreojos harbor, still twenty miles away. This became the most fearsome of nights in the whole Baja paddle for Verlen and Valerie. Though claiming exhaustion, Verlen later said that Valerie had responded to the demands placed upon them by the storm. He could not have accomplished Abreojos without her, nor could he have kept the bows pointed into the waves throughout the night. Daylight found them again off Abreojos harbor, with extreme surf between them and the shoreline. Steve Landick and Ed Gillet, a renowned sea kayaker whom Verlen and Valerie had met in San Diego, had partnered up at Long Beach on November 20, and had easily overtaken the new team.

Steve saw their plight, but could not talk any of the fishermen into launching to their aid. He donned his wetsuit jacket and flippers and swam hard out through the surf. Seeing this, one of the fishermen launched, picked Steve up outside the line of surf and delivered him to Verlen and Valerie's canoes. They were resting just outside, on the ocean side of the breaking surf, when they noticed fishermen on the beach launching a boat. It appeared that those ashore saw their plight and were coming to get them. As the boat drew near, Verlen and Valerie saw Steve Landick sitting with the fishermen in the boat and wearing a wetsuit jacket and fins.

This was the perfect time for an ex-Navy SEAL with a point to prove to arrive on the scene. When the boat was close, Steve jumped back into the water, climbed onto the stern of Valerie's Monarch and said, "I'm taking your place."

A kelp bed is a refuge of safety in bad weather. The sea's waves do not break as they roll through the kelp. (photo by Valerie Fons)

Arrival in San Diego. *(photo from Kruger Archives)*

Product photo for sponsors *(photo by Valerie Fons)*

Verlen later said Valerie, after making it through a brutal night at sea, did not like being replaced in her own boat. Nevertheless, she complied by climbing into the fisherman's boat. Verlen and Steve paddled on in through the breaking surf to the beach without further incident. There was no better way for Steve to drive home his message to Verlen: "You can't go out there with someone who just started canoeing this spring, and who has no experience."

The first meeting of these three since Long Beach was intense and laden with a sort of I-told-you-so finality, though Steve never said a word. Verlen later added, "I was truly impressed by the way Valerie had held up during the long night before. That was a terrifying night at sea! Of course, she didn't want someone else to land her boat, but it was the right thing to do at the time. She was exhausted; Steve was fresh and stronger as well. Once he was aboard, we quickly found our stroke-timing and with our combined strengths had no real problem bringing the boats into shore. Though I knew Valerie felt badly, I have always been grateful to Steve for doing it. I was exhausted as well." Verlen said this had been one of the worst storms to hit that area in years and many boats, including large sailboats, had been driven onto the shore by winds in excess of 70-miles per hour. A catamaraned Loon and Monarch had survived it all. Verlen was grateful for Steve's rescue and he hoped the four of them (he, Valerie, Steve and Ed Gillet) would just continue paddling on down the coast of Baja together. Steve was quoted in Verlen's UCC book as saying, "Send Valerie home and then it'll be ok." Ultimately, Steve and Ed went on alone.

Verlen said, "Valerie was discouraged by the meeting with Steve. She told me that it would be best if she quit and I could go on with my 'real' partner. I wouldn't even think of it. We had made a commitment to the trip when we left Long Beach, I said, and we were going to stick to it. I would join Steve and Ed only if both of us were welcome, and we were not. The conflict between Steve and me was still strong, and it seemed better for us to travel separately at this time. But I was confident that he and I would enter the Grand Canyon together. On December 10, Steve and Ed seized a short interlude of good weather and moved on. We didn't have much to say to each other as they left. I felt pretty low watching the two of them paddle off. He and Ed Gillet set their usual fast pace and moved on."

Verlen and Valerie were no longer in the lead. Steve and Ed were ahead of them. There soon came some discouraging days of being wind-bound, as Steve and Ed continued on down the coast. Verlen and Valerie suffered sickness as well when they were both visited by Montezuma's Revenge, the dreaded dysentery. On the 28th of December, 1982, they broke another longstanding UCC rule, and accepted a forty-eight-hour sailboat ride south, with their canoes on deck. Steve and Ed had already paddled that same 150-mile stretch. Verlen was making some accommodations for speed and comfort.

Verlen paddling near Cabo San Lucas (photo by Valerie Fons)

On New Year's Day of 1983, Verlen and Valerie finally rounded the tip of the Baja and began their ascent of the Sea of Cortez. This would be a thirty-nine day journey from Cabo San Lucas, on the southernmost tip of the Baja, to Yuma, Arizona, at the mouth of the Colorado River. They had come 1,255 miles down the exposed Pacific coast and now had an 1,120-mile paddle back up the inside Baja waters to Yuma. Valerie had become stronger and more skilled as a paddler and Verlen was feeling he had a more capable partner. The weather and big seas that had originally shocked Valerie had now become routine. She had adjusted to the camping, the meals, the 3:00 am starts to avoid the afternoon's normal growing winds, their behavior in weather, and no longer needed someone to blame for the discomforts afforded them on a daily basis. Their daily mileage was also improving. February 1, 1983, a month from Cabo San Lucas, found them at San

Verlen paddling on the Sea of Cortez (photo by Valerie Fons)

Felipe inside the Baja, just days from their goal of Yuma, Arizona. Those days would be spent dragging their boats through the muddy Santa Clara Slough, often knee-deep in mud, then towing them with lines upstream through the currents of the saline canal that paralleled the Colorado River. They had come 500 miles in the last sixteen days and had made it to Yuma on time! Verlen was able to fly to the National Sporting Goods Show in Chicago, as planned, to be with some of the UCC sponsors. Jenny drove to Chicago to be with Verlen during the show. Valerie went home to Seattle.

Shopping time at Cabo San Lucas with campsite in background (photo by Valerie Fons)

Valerie had paddled around the Baja Peninsula with Verlen in 107 days. No small accomplishment. Steve had paddled the same distance, the first half with Ed Gillett, who left him at Cabo, plus the 150-mile stretch Verlen and Valerie had hitchhiked on the deck of a sailboat, in 77 days.

Verlen wrote in his diary, "It is nearly 3,000 miles from Seattle around the southern tip of Baja, California, at Cabo San Lucas. It is scenic, impressive, and quite an experience. When I paddled out of the salt water below Yuma, I was very glad that this was the last for the remainder of the trip. I have no plans for ever tangling with the Pacific ocean area again. Yet, there are some terrific spots I'd love to return to. For me, the Pacific Ocean was the most hazardous part of the entire Ultimate Canoe Challenge."

Thus, the Baja portion of the Ultimate Canoe Challenge ended. The greatest remaining physical and mental challenge lay ahead: America's Grand Canyon, going upstream on the Colorado River.

*"We couldn't imagine a canyon
big enough to stop us."*

VERLEN KRUGER

Up The Grand Canyon

As planned, Verlen attended the NSGA Show in Chicago, where Jenny joined him. Jenny later said that she and Verlen flew to San Diego where Steve and Sarah were meeting after their divorce papers were signed. "We all said goodbye to Sarah there and she flew to Alaska. Steve was at an all-time low. Then Steve, Verlen and I flew to Las Vegas for a sporting goods show." The show helped ease Verlen and Steve through the transition of teaming up again, before tackling their biggest challenge. When they returned to San Diego, Steve, Verlen and Jenny drove to Yuma where Verlen and Steve would resume their trip and go up through the Grand Canyon.

Steve, like Verlen, never quit anything he had started and Verlen knew this about Steve. Despite the fact that Verlen had teamed up with Valerie, Steve had made the descent of the Baja to Cabo San Lucas with Ed Gillett and then solo-paddled back up the Sea of Cortez to Yuma. Steve had to ignore what he considered Verlen's violation of their original agreement that no one else was allowed to join the UCC team, because Verlen was not apologizing or accepting any fault for what had happened to fracture their partnership on the Baja.

Steve said that at the time he resented that Verlen and Valerie seemed to have taken advantage of the circumstance surrounding the death of his daughter. He felt, instead of offering support to his daughter, Sarah, and to Steve, Verlen pressed for a decision too soon after Saba's death. When Steve said he wasn't sure what he was going to do, Verlen and Valerie seemed to take advantage of his grief and temporary inability to make a decision by teaming up earlier at Long Beach. By then, Steve was tired of fighting the lack of teamwork and Valerie Fons's involvement in the UCC; those times made him determined to never paddle with Verlen and Valerie as a team.

This was a complicated time for Verlen and Jenny too. When Verlen and Valerie completed the Baja, Valerie had gone home. By the time Jenny met Verlen at the NSGA Show in Chicago, she knew that her relationship

A team again, Steve and Verlen head for a dam portage! It wasn't even going to slow them down!
(photo from Kruger Archives)

They both knew there was no better team to be fielded for this challenge
(photo from Kruger Archives)

with Verlen was in trouble. She had known it since Long Beach. But Jenny was a fighter. She did not want their marriage to fail and she had not blessed Verlen's involvement in this section of the Baja with Valerie Fons. But it was difficult to deal with the emotional and physical distance that had developed between them. The UCC was coming to an end and Jenny still hoped Verlen would come to his senses. She said, "I knew Verlen had lost his bearings and I realized how I was being treated. I also knew that his behavior was not the same Verlen Kruger I had been married to for thirty-eight years. He was acting crazy and so far away from his normal self. I just wasn't sure how to deal with it all. I was pretty sure when he paddled back into Lansing, surrounded by family and his old reality, he would come back to his senses and see what he had done. I know most people think they would have handled things differently than I did, but they haven't walked a mile in my shoes. I don't know who could have handled the Verlen I was then dealing with." Verlen had trapped himself between two worlds. Jenny's last words to Verlen before she left were, "If this is not an affair, there has never been one. You're going to have to decide."

It was a tough way to start. When they left Yuma, Steve and Verlen paddled together only one day before Steve said he needed to go on for a ways alone to consort with his grief. They would meet up again below Hoover Dam.

Verlen understood Steve's need to be alone and had plenty on his own mind. Verlen said he reached Bullhead City by the 24th and took a few days off with Valerie Fons, who came down from Seattle on her week off.

It added to Steve's low that Valerie Fons was still showing up. He had begun to realize, if he and Verlen were to remain a team for the balance of the UCC, he was going to have to get used to Valerie. At Hoover Dam, she again left, leaving Verlen and Steve alone with the Grand Canyon.

Verlen and Steve began their ascent of the Grand Canyon on April Fool's Day in 1983. They had scarcely paddled together since parting at Long Beach, California. Six months of their UCC partnership had passed while Valerie Fons paddled in Steve's place. Verlen said in his UCC book, "There had been hard times, and hard feelings, going back to the time of the death of baby Saba and even before. But when things settled down we both had the same powerful drive to keep going and to finish the Ultimate Canoe Challenge. The next stage was the Grand Canyon, and there was no question of attempting to paddle it alone. We would have to work together." With their loads of troubles, it was difficult for them to get back together; but swallowing pride, and knowing there was no one else with whom they wanted to tackle the Grand Canyon, they did it.

Steve was ready. He wanted to set the past aside for a while, and tackle the immediate challenge of surviving the turbulent waters of the canyon. Verlen said he could tell by the look in Steve's eyes, the tone of his voice, and the firmness of his handshake at the Hoover Dam that there was an opportunity for renewal of their friendship and their UCC partnership. The Grand Canyon was just what they both needed to make it work: a challenge so great that it demanded their total focus. Besides, everyone told them that their ascent of the Grand Canyon *couldn't be done.*

They portaged... *(photo by Verlen Kruger)*

Steve had a "momentum theory" of their UCC. As an analogy, Steve envisioned what it would take to stop the inertia of a freight train with 23,000 cars in tow. Each of the 23,000 miles of successful challenges behind them represented one train car as they paddled upstream from the Hoover Dam on the highest water Lake Mead had seen in fifty years. What could stop the momentum of such a train? Verlen said, "Quite frankly, I couldn't imagine a canyon big enough to stop us from succeeding."

They had four methods of going upstream through over 200 separate sets of rapids. They could paddle, line, pole, or portage. Sometimes they had to make multiple attempts, but they always made it. Over the entire canyon, they actually paddled most of the rapids, and portaged the rest. While lining and poling were occasionally used, these methods proved to be the least productive. Portaging was

They lined... *(photo by Steve Landick)*

They climbed... *(photo by Steve Landick)*

They paddled... *(photo by Steve Landick)*

And sometimes did the impossible. *(photo by Steve Landick)*

the toughest, because it involved carrying the two boats and more than 200 pounds of gear, which meant double portaging—and sometimes more—on routes that involved precarious positioning on the canyon walls. They found the first few days to be difficult portaging, but later described those first portages as cakewalks. The previous 23,000 miles had primarily been spent paddling while sitting. That did little to strengthen their legs, which were now desperately in demand. As the going got tougher, so did those legs.

Verlen said sometimes Steve's talents with the kayak paddle allowed him to accomplish more than Verlen could with the canoe paddle. At those times Steve would take both boats through a stretch and Verlen would walk. Sometimes Steve could find a successful route through the currents and turbulence and Verlen would follow that same path successfully. They did not take unnecessary risks. Verlen and Steve knew how to minimize the risks involved by working together. Verlen and Steve both had the groomed ability to not panic when something went wrong; they were trained not to. When something went wrong, that was the time for their coolest observation and logical thought to evaluate what kind—and how much—trouble they were in.

While in the Canyon, Steve had gone ahead around a small outcrop in his Monarch. When he came ashore at his landing, he looked back downstream and saw an empty Loon circling in a small eddy farther downstream. He ran back around the outcrop to find Verlen standing on a small rock, surrounded by turbulent waters. While trying to paddle around that rock, Verlen had dumped. He managed to climb up onto the rock shelf, but lost his Loon in the process. He could do nothing but stand there and hope Steve would notice his predicament before his Loon vanished downstream. Verlen said that while he seldom felt fatalistic about things, there was a good chance that without Steve discovering his situation, then paddling out to get him, he might not have survived that one. Steve and Verlen's environment of constant challenge and risk had created a deep friendship similar to that of brothers-in-arms. Verlen and Steve were again as close a team as they had ever been.

It took them twenty-one days, averaging ten miles per day upstream, and 100-vertical-feet per day, to reach Lees Ferry at the top of the Grand Canyon. They had climbed, paddled and portaged 1,907 vertical feet above Lake Mead at Hoover Dam. This upstream Grand Canyon had never been done before. And no one has done it since. Verlen commented, "Twenty-one days is what the Park Service usually allows on permits for the guided rafts, which follow a downstream route."

Verlen wrote in UCC, "Our excitement grew as we drew closer. We had done it. Would there be an official greeting? Media people? We had been alone with the river for three-weeks, and now we were coming back to civilization. There was no one in sight at the landing as we approached. We paddled around the last boulder and—surprise!—Valerie Fons popped out with a big smile and shouted, 'Congratulations!' It turned out that she was on her way to train on a Montana river for the Au Sable race in Michigan and had stopped, hoping to see us. See us she did, as we finished our successful run up the Grand Canyon."

Verlen and Steve were disappointed that no press showed up. According to an article that printed a week later in the Lake Powell Chronicle, "Not since John Wesley Powell's first pioneering journey down the uncharted Colorado River in 1869 has any other river trip been as daring as the one completed on April 27 of this year. Two Michigan men arrived at Lees Ferry Wednesday after successfully paddling and portaging their fiberglass canoes upriver through the Grand Canyon from Lake Mead." But as they stood at the top end of their enormous quest and success, Valerie Fons and John Peterson, a National Park Ranger, were their only greeters.

DuPont and Dow Chemical had partnered up to create a brief movie of the Grand Canyon portion of the UCC, and had agreed to shoulder the responsibility of coordinating press releases and the timing of their twenty-one day trip through the Canyon. They only accomplished some filming above the Hoover Dam, but no press releases were issued and the world was unaware of what had occurred in western America's Grand Canyon involving Verlen Kruger and Steve Landick. While press was never their foremost goal, press was important to sponsors. Ranger John Peterson, at least, appreciated their awesome accomplishment, and afforded them a couple of days' rest in his house trailer.

First the paddlers climb to the top of the latest obstacle... *(photo by Steve Landick)*

Then they would drag their loads over the rocks, which required tough canoes. *(photo by Steve Landick)*

"Take the advice of locals with a grain of salt. They probably aren't paddlers and don't see things the same way we do anyway."

VERLEN KRUGER

Return To The Beginning

From the triumph of the Grand Canyon, on to Canyonlands and into the Wind River region *(photo from Kruger Archives)*

After the Grand Canyon, Steve and Verlen now had another 1,100 miles and 3,000 vertical feet of rivers and canyons to run to get to the Big Sandy River in Wyoming. Many of them were as formidable as those behind them. They planned to follow the Colorado River beyond the Glen Canyon Dam, to the Green River in Canyonlands National Park, and then head north on the Green aimed at South Pass, Wyoming.

They launched again on May Day of 1983 for the twenty-mile paddle to Glen Canyon dam. The next portage would be a doozy! Following their rule of accepting no help, they portaged their canoes 2.5 miles up through a dam tunnel to the top. Returning for their packs, they climbed 710 vertical feet of steel ladders inside the dam, repeatedly refusing elevator rides each time the dam employees stopped to offer a ride.

"What do you think, Steve? Should we walk or run?" Glen Canyon Dam photo
(photo from Kruger Archives)

Then, it was on across Lake Powell, named after John Wesley Powell, forty-nine miles the first day and forty-six the next. Campsites were tough to find, so they slept in their boats at a marina dock one night. They met up with their film crew from Dow Chemical, as pre-arranged, in nearby Cataract Canyon for some filming of whitewater scenes. Using a motorized raft and a helicopter, they shot film multiple days. When combined with earlier film the same team had shot, Verlen expected a full-length film would be produced by them. To his disappointment, it turned out to be only an eleven-minute segment, which was only shown once at the UCC homecoming celebration held in Lansing in December.

Verlen said, "Cataract Canyon was just the first of the 'other' great and demanding canyons we would pass through." Another month of whitewater adventures, daylight to dusk, averaging thirty-mile days, brought them to the Flaming Gorge Dam in Utah on May 28, 1983. Verlen and Steve had not been separated since arriving at Hoover Dam.

On the 29th, Verlen paddled fifty-eight miles, but Steve fell behind. According to Verlen, this was the date that Steve's divorce from Sarah became final. He thought that Steve just wanted to be alone, and expected Steve to catch up before Verlen reached Green River, Wyoming, but he didn't. Steve came in the next day. They played tag, passing each other on different occasions, until they arrived at Farson, Wyoming, on the Big Sandy River. As he came in, Verlen found Steve camped uncharacteristically early and not feeling well. The following morning, Steve was still sick and Verlen urged him to see a local doctor. Steve agreed and hitchhiked into the nearby town of Rock Spring. He stayed the night in a motel and called his father, who was a medical doctor. He and his father decided that Steve should immediately come home for rest and examination. He did, and it was discovered that he was suffering from mononucleosis. Verlen spoke with Steve via phone. Steve thought it could take him up to a month to recoup and was very discouraged. Verlen said there was no way either of them could be sure he would be able to come back at all.

Grand Canyon behind, a team again, they move on to the Wind River region
(photo from Kruger Archives)

It was time again for Verlen to decide whether to go on, or to wait for Steve's return. It was not an easy decision. They had repaired their damaged relationship in the canyons, were together again as a paddling team, and had both intended to finish the UCC together. Knowing that Steve would probably be at least a month getting back, Verlen didn't want to just sit and wait. He told Steve he would go on, hoping for him to join him later, and would store all of Steve's gear in Farson, Wyoming. Then Verlen pushed on.

From Farson, Steve and Verlen had planned a route that went partway to the Popo Agie River on Pacific Creek and the rest of the way from South Pass on the Oregon Trail. But

Verlen found that the Pacific Creek route was too low to paddle. Thus began the longest portage of Verlen Kruger's life: sixty-six-miles and one-thousand vertical feet to Popo Agie. Verlen would do it alone—almost. He began his long portage on June 16, 1983, just two weeks short of his sixty-first birthday.

He used his leap-frog approach, carrying the Loon for fifteen or twenty minutes, then dropping it along the side of the highway and returning for his packs and gear. When he would catch up that gear with the Loon, he would drop the gear, shoulder the Loon and proceed. This process aimed at gaining ten-miles of distance per day, but required nearly thirty-miles of walking due to leap-frogging back and forth. While Verlen sometimes complained of being lonely when his partners were absent, he also enjoyed much of that time. He said, "People used to ask me why I paddle so fast, meaning fifty to sixty-strokes per minute while using the power stroke. What they failed to realize is that while I appeared to be paddling fast, I was only moving at about four miles an hour. How many do you know that go through thousands of miles of beautiful scenery at four miles an hour?" Verlen had greater opportunity to really see what others thought he was missing by going too fast. A sixty-six-mile portage was a similar opportunity and even slower than the paddle pace. He pushed himself at a comfortable speed, loving all that time (eight days and nights) to think, and thoroughly enjoyed the scenery. He was in his element and, as usual, would enjoy every moment of it.

"Country beginning to flatten out, with fewer portages, it's getting easier again." *(photo by Steve Landick)*

About three days into the portage, Verlen spotted a scenic-highway turnoff to a parking area. The signs said it talked about the historic Pony Express. Always a history buff and needing a break, he dropped his Loon along the highway and proceeded to hike into the scenic byway. After a grub-sack lunch, while absorbing history and view, Verlen hiked back out to the highway, which had been out of view from his luncheon area. When he got back to the highway, his Loon was gone. Someone had taken it while he was eating lunch! After flagging down occasional cars from both directions to ask if they had seen his boat, he asked one of them to drop him in the town of Farson. He contacted the local police and explained his loss. They put out a Loon description with an all-points-bulletin, and even the local radio and TV stations began to make news of this strange bulletin of a stolen canoe in the middle of near-dry Wyoming. Apparently, some people had seen the canoe and reported it, but it was still missing the next day. Verlen wrote in UCC, "It looked like my boat was gone, and I would need a replacement. I needed to call Valerie and ask her to bring me the reserve canoe, the Monarch, which she was keeping. Fortunately, she was then in Montana training with her partner, Anne Koblinski, for the Au Sable, Michigan, race. When I told her my problem, she said she would be in Farson the next morning."

According to Verlen's book, *The Ultimate Canoe Challenge*, Valerie arrived the next morning with the white Monarch on top of her car. They agreed that Verlen should take it. She didn't need it because she was training with Anne in a tandem canoe. Before she left, they went on a canoe hunt in Valerie's car. They checked with local police stations and even stopped at some churches, because it was Sunday. Many in the churches had heard of the missing canoe on the news, but none had seen it. At the last church they visited, Verlen and Valerie joined their services, then thanked them and asked them to pray for the Loon's return. As they proceeded up the highway, they saw a small truck loaded with household items approaching them. Verlen's Loon was on top of the load. They turned around, caught up with the truck and, by honking and waving, pulled it over to the side of the road. Verlen approached the driver and demanded his boat back. The driver stepped on the accelerator and left Verlen standing aghast on the side of the highway. He sped off toward the town of Farson.

Siblings Steve and Robin Heth with Verlen and Valerie at Souris River spillway
(photo from Kruger Archives)

They continued the chase, but could not get past the truck and were unsuccessful at making him stop or pull over. They didn't want to lose sight of him, so wrote notes that said "Help! We are chasing my stolen canoe. Notify police!" and dropped them out the window onto the street with a holler at a pedestrian as they passed through Farson. "Give that note to the police! Thanks!" Following the truck, they turned north onto another road. Verlen thought the pedestrians might not react to the notes they had thrown, so he had Valerie pull into a roadside restaurant. He ran in and hollered, "We're chasing my stolen canoe. Please call the police and tell them we're headed north on highway 191!" Verlen and Valerie followed the truck nearly sixty miles, hoping it would stop somewhere along the way.

As they approached Pinedale, Wyoming, they saw several police cars blocking the road. Someone had alerted them and they had responded. The truck had been stopped. After telling the police several lies about the boat, the young man admitted he had taken it. The police gave Verlen the option of taking his boat and pressing charges, or just taking his boat. The young man apologized to Verlen, who in turn gave him an earful of advice and tried to introduce him to religion, probably, "Thou shalt not steal." Then, he loaded his canoe and Valerie drove him back to the Pony Express byway where his portage had been interrupted.

Verlen and Valerie teamed up again, shown here in Westhope, North Dakota, on August 11, 1983. Steve was home recuperating from mono. *(photo from Kruger Archives)*

The UCC between Wyoming and Lansing, Michigan, gets a little confusing. Valerie Fons's book, *Keep It Moving*, in its epilogue, says that Verlen and Steve went on to finish their UCC in Lansing, implying that they paddled and finished together. Verlen and Brand Frentz's book, *The Ultimate Canoe Challenge*, says that Valerie paddled with Verlen for three weeks on the Souris River and on across North Dakota and the Boundary Waters Canoe Area of Minnesota to Lake Superior. After she and Verlen reached Lake Superior, Valerie left. In a later interview, Jenny confirmed this, saying, "Because I was coming to meet Verlen on Lake Superior, Valerie temporarily left." Jenny then left Verlen in Duluth and he continued on alone.

A cold day's arrival in Lansing *(photo from Kruger Archives)*

Verlen paddled on alone; though he and Steve were within a day or two of each other all the way to Lansing, sometimes passing each other in the night, they never paddled together again before reaching Lansing. They had not paddled a stroke together since Farson, Wyoming. Just as on the west coast below Long Beach, California, Steve was not about to paddle with Verlen and Valerie on the UCC. The bad feelings that darkened the Baja stretch may have returned after Valerie again paddled with Verlen when Steve became ill with mono.

On the outskirts of Lansing, Verlen and Steve communicated by phone and after much urging by Verlen, Steve agreed to a coordinated and staged arrival together. Steve agreed it was to the benefit of all involved, especially their sponsors, that they return as a team. Steve had satisfied himself by completing the entire 28,000 miles of the UCC, and arrived a day ahead of Verlen in Lansing, though he never announced that. Valerie Fons paddled among the many other "welcome home" canoe paddlers during the finish ceremony in Lansing.

Except for the 150-mile stretch between Abreojos and Cabo San Lucas, which Verlen and Valerie did on the deck of the sailboat Dorvida, both Verlen Kruger and Steve Landick made every single paddle-stroke of their 28,000-mile Ultimate Canoe Challenge. Though their partnership, relationship and friendship had been severely taxed by a variety of circumstances, no one could take that away from either of them. Their records stand and they carved their names into the annals of canoeing history worldwide with this trip. Most seem to feel those titles, records, and accomplishments are theirs and theirs alone. Valerie Fons laid claim to her own portion of the UCC by writing her book, *Keep It Moving*, and rightly so, for she did paddle all but that 150-mile sailboat ride stretch of the Baja with Verlen. The Ultimate Canoe Challenge homecoming, however, belonged to Verlen and Steve, alone.

28,043 miles from the beginning of the Ultimate Canoe Challenge, Verlen Kruger and Steve Landick are welcomed by the city of Lansing, Michigan. It was done! *(photo from Kruger Archives)*

When Verlen and Steve were planning the UCC, they had only positive anticipation throughout the entire route. Verlen never planned on paddling 8,000 miles by himself. There was no mention of Valerie Fons. Verlen never planned on paddling 3,600 miles with someone other than Steve Landick. Steve never planned on paddling 15,000 miles without Verlen. There had been dramatic changes between the start and finish in Lansing.

Home again, Verlen had some enormous decisions to make. He was in Michigan for the next year, again building boats in his shop. He tried to renew his ties to Jenny and his family, but could not overcome the ties he had developed with Valerie. The Baja and some 1,500 additional miles of paddling with Valerie between Wyoming and Lake Superior had left its mark on him. Though Verlen was home with Jenny, he and Valerie continued to communicate regularly. They wanted to race the Mississippi, more adventure, more dreams to seek, and more of each other. He finally had to admit it to himself, to Jenny, and to his family. He knew things were fragile and that he had caused them to be that way. He had stepped so far out of character while reaching for his dream and following his obsession that he could not re-enter the life he had left behind. He later said, "The problem was I never came home."

One night in Chicago, Verlen announced to his friends during dinner, with Jenny by his side, that he and Valerie Fons would race the Eddie Bauer Mississippi Challenge the following spring. Some of Verlen's longtime friends who attended the dinner couldn't forget Jenny's deeply saddened reaction. She had begun to hope that Verlen was returning to reality, and was shocked by his announcement. Verlen's legendary image took on a selfish and callus taint. Jenny remembered Verlen's statement that ended their marriage: "If you can't accept Valerie in my life, there will have to be a divorce." For the first time, Verlen had found his limits—and exceeded Jenny's. And the person who least wanted to be where she found herself was Jenny. They divorced in December of 1984.

Verlen was no hero, and would never accept that status from anyone, yet was still frequently offered respect in the form of hero-worship. That's part of his legacy. But he also made mistakes, and when he did, they were usually large. Despite the trail of debris left by some of his questionable decisions, friends who have known him the longest describe Verlen as a kind man—kind to everyone. Even those injured by some of his actions tend to describe him the same way. He always had time to help someone who needed it, physically, financially, and with counsel and wisdom when asked. He was humble and admitted that he could offer wise counsel only because he had made so many mistakes. He owned his own poor decisions and would go out of his way to help others avoid making similar errors. He was a man of deep faith. Verlen said he had read the King James Bible at least ten times cover to cover, also the Catholic Bible, and the Qur'an. He didn't wear his religion on his sleeve and avoided evangelizing after his short-lived missionary experience after returning to Lansing from Japan. He would occasionally quote scripture and usually

There had been dramatic changes between the start and finish in Lansing.

autographed books and posters with a scriptural quote or title. More than its religiosity, he seemed inclined to pass on the wisdom of the Bible and scripture.

Some wonder about Verlen's religious convictions. A paradox existed during the years he violated his personal Christian commitments while quoting sacred scripture and praising God for blessing his decisions. How could a man so biblically oriented and such a staunch follower of fundamental Christian philosophy justify his decisions? There are no easy answers, and no final answers. Verlen wasn't exactly pioneering in his behavior with Valerie Fons, but he was way outside his known character. One thing he was always capable of doing, however, was making decisions. A person with the mind and talents of Verlen Kruger, plus the faith and beliefs he generated, could sometimes be confident to a fault.

Steve Landick said, "When Verlen made up his mind about something, no one was likely to change it!" Clint Waddell grinned and said something similar when asked if he and Verlen ever argued about their daily decisions during their six months on the Cross Continent Canoe Safari. "Well, you know how Verlen was when he made his mind up about something!" Verlen never cut himself much slack either. Valerie Fons once said, "Verlen doesn't allow himself any excuses." When he had a schedule to keep, he kept it. When he set a goal, he reached it.

"When Verlen made up his mind about something no one was likely to change it!"

"It's not impossible anymore, Steve."

— Verlen Kruger

Eddie Bauer Challenge

Verlen was back in Lansing, though he never really came home. Though he was living at home, he and Valerie continued to communicate and grow closer. They spent time together whenever they could to plan their assault of the Mississippi Eddie Bauer Challenge Race, which Valerie had helped to organize with sponsors while she was back in Seattle. Valerie had motivated the Eddie Bauer company of Redmond, Washington, to sponsor the Challenge. During the months prior to the race, Valerie lived in Iowa with her brother and sister-in-law, John and Marrianne Fons. Verlen continued to live with Jenny in his home on the Grand River, and work on the canoe design and planning for the Eddie Bauer Challenge Race. Valerie and Verlen wanted the Challenge and preparing for it created the atmosphere they both craved: facing adventure and strenuous challenge together. He and Valerie were challenging the existing Mississippi River Guinness World Record, which was then held by a British Special Air Service (SAS) team that set the Record of 35 days, 11 hours and 27 minutes in 1980.

Training before Eddie Bauer Challenge *(photo by Lloyd Fons)*

Their training and planning began seven months before their departure. Valerie said, "Verlen planned the Eddie Bauer Challenge like a space shot at the moon!" No detail was overlooked. Both Verlen and Valerie were as fit as they had ever been and in the paddling groove. Verlen's rule of maximum efficiency kicked in big time! He insisted the two of them practice everything they would be doing during the race. Valerie said he took it to the level of an art form. They practiced loading the canoe for balance. Their shore crew saw to the needs of replenishing stores. They rehearsed sleeping arrangements by removing the canoe seats, and how to make their moves with efficiency. They practiced attaching and removing their spray cover while underway, so as to be able to do it quickly and safely when weather demanded. Every move was rehearsed until they were convinced that it was the quickest, most efficient, and produced the best result from the least amount of time and effort. Over a thirty-day race, the time saved through efficiency could

Eddie Bauer Challenge underway near Minneapolis *(photo courtesy of Star Tribune/Minneapolis-St. Paul 2006)*

accrue to a winning margin. It was only through practicing the moves that they could discover their inefficiencies. Between Lake Itasca and the Mile Zero Gulf marker, there would be few wasted moves.

Verlen had never attempted the Mississippi in a tandem canoe with a partner, but by then he had paddled over fifty-thousand miles and he knew how this new boat had to be designed and built to accomplish the tasks before it. He called the newly designed tandem canoe the Kruger Super Cruiser. It was 18 feet, 6 inches long and built to Verlen's design by the Mad River Canoe Company, who intended to produce it commercially to Verlen's specs after the race. It had special features such as head-lamps and head-lights for night paddling and an elaborate communications system, which enabled them to talk to barges, the shore-crew, and the Corps or Coast Guard as necessary. Mad River built two so they could carry an identical spare on the shore-party's vehicle, in case something happened to the first one. In addition to a new boat, Verlen and Valerie were outfitted by Eddie Bauer in their special clothing to protect them from the northern to southern elements.

It was to be a round-the-clock effort intended to reduce the existing 35-day Guinness record to less than 30, and it was to be done by a male/female team, which, at that time, Verlen said, "Could have been referred to as a senior citizen in the stern, with a young lady in the bow!" On April 27, 1984, Verlen Kruger, at age 61, and Valerie Fons, age 33, launched from Lake Itasca and headed down the Mississippi after a new record in what was then called the Eddie Bauer Mississippi Challenge Race.

Their support team and shore party consisted of John and Marianne Fons, Valerie's brother and sister-in-law. They provided 24-hour communication, food, water, and assistance as needed, but nothing to do with propulsion or carrying, which was forbidden by the rules established for the Eddie Bauer Challenge Race. The Eddie Bauer news release described John Fons as, "An accomplished handyman, the 34-year old brother of Valerie Fons will provide invaluable service to the canoeists. He is an experienced plumber, electrician, carpenter, auto mechanic and photographer." At that time he was a vice president of Lloyd Fons Exploration, Inc., an oil and gas exploration firm based in Houston. His first support-team experience came when he acted as a bank runner (shore support) for Valerie when she and Anne Koblinski paddled the famous Au Sable race. There had never been a women's division in that race. Another women's team, Truda Gilbert and Donna Buckley, had been the first women to race the Au Sable race marathon; but Valerie and Anne were the first women to finish in qualifying time in 1983. Their finish time, according to Valerie, placed them tenth in the men's division. Verlen Kruger manufactured two medals and presented them to the two of them after the 1983 World Championship Au Sable Race.

At that time, Valerie had even begun to sound a little like Verlen. In one of the Eddie Bauer official news releases, she was quoted as saying, "'We want to show individuals that you really can accomplish what you dream,' said Fons. Verlen added, 'By establishing the record we will prove that out. We're not the combination people would pick to break the record, that's for sure. But we believe we can do it. The idea of a senior citizen and a woman beating the best is inconceivable to most,' said Kruger. 'You expect record setters to be big, strong athletes. But there's more to being the best than age, size and strength—there's spirit. And we've got the spirit. When we set the record, it's going to warm the heart of many senior citizens and tickle the heart of many women,' he added. 'This victory will be shared by everyone.'" At this time there were only four known attempts that had been made for this Mississippi record, and this would be the first that included night-paddling.

"'The idea of a senior citizen and a woman beating the best is inconceivable to most.'"

It was a challenge. On the first day alone they braved high winds, extreme cold, snow, and wind chills of fifteen degrees below zero. Their daily routine was two three-hour sleep shifts a day, with twelve hours of joint paddling and six hours of paddling solo while their partner slept. Equipped with a rudder, and foot-pedals bow and stern, either paddler could steer their Kruger Super Cruiser canoe while the other slept. They had headlights for night paddling, chamber pots for relief until the shoreline became easily accessible for brief stops, food and water, and a great deal of determination aboard. Verlen, having paddled 28,000 miles in the prior three years, and Valerie's 3600-plus miles just the year before, made them a formidable team!

Locking through provides brief rest on the Mississippi *(photo by Lloyd Fons)*

Verlen and Valerie arrived at the Mile Zero marker at the Gulf of Mexico on May 20, 1984, after paddling for 23 days, 10 hours, and 23 minutes. They beat the all-male SAS team's Guinness record by 19 days! What made this an even better record was that it had been set by a man and a woman. Valerie was now an accomplished canoe racer. She and teammate Anne Koblinski had been among the first women to complete the famous Michigan Au Sable race, and she now had a Guinness World Record with Verlen on the Mississippi. Verlen and Steve Landick had already secured the upstream Guinness record, and now Verlen had the distinction of holding the downstream record as well. Adding the Mississippi record, in a tandem, to his well-established tandem canoe marathon racing record made Verlen an accomplished tandem canoe racer.

After successfully gaining the Guinness World Record, they both began serious planning for the Two Continent Canoe Expedition (TCCE) they had dreamed up. These were good times for them both and they were happy with their new life, together when possible, yet unmarried. Valerie said that Verlen had proposed marriage more than once, but that she had resisted. Consequently, she was surprised when Verlen issued the equivalent of an ultimatum just before they were to start the Two Continent Canoe Expedition.

If they weren't married before the Two Continent Canoe Expedition, he wouldn't go.

Valerie said she again resisted for some time, but eventually said yes. They were married on April 3, 1986, by Pastor Dale Boocks of the Delta Mills Methodist Church, near Verlen's home. This was a complete departure from the Baptist environment Verlen and Jenny had practiced for more than thirty years in Lansing. But Valerie was a lifetime Methodist, Verlen had been ousted from the board of Deacons of his church before he left on the UCC, and he possibly did not want to bring Valerie into that old circle of past friends. That would have been an ironic way of admitting they had been right about leaving Jenny for the Ultimate Canoe Challenge.

The Kruger Super Cruiser at a mile-eating pace (photo by Lloyd Fons)

*"Skill and strength are less important than
spirit when facing the unknown."*

VERLEN KRUGER

The Two Continent Canoe Expedition

When Verlen and Valerie began planning the Two Continent trip, they knew it had to be in solo canoes (the new design was called the Sea Wind), not in a tandem, as they had raced the Mississippi. Verlen's past experience had shown the need for space and freedom of choice, provided by single canoes, to be crucial during long-distance tripping. The partnership of Verlen and Valerie for the Two Continent, though man and wife by then, would also need similar space. And, they would need the Sea Wind's ability to catamaran when weather or route dictated. There would be open water crossings of more than 100 miles. There would be times they would be out of sight of land for up to two days at a time in whatever weather came along. Catamaraning provided safety and enabled them to sleep, cook and perform normal housekeeping chores, day or night, wherever they were. When catamaraned, the Sea Winds were great under sail as well.

Their original plan called for them to leave the mouth of the Mackenzie River from Inuvik, Northwest Territories, on June 1, 1986. They planned to paddle for 963 days (roughly 2.6 years), not counting non-travel days, to reach Cape Horn at the tip of South America. They hoped to arrive at Cape Horn by February 1, 1989. Preparation was huge—it took years of planning and preparation to get to the launching of this venture. Verlen always felt it was easier to make the canoe trips than to gather all that was necessary to make them. He was complimentary of Valerie's ability to help round up sponsors, funding, and support for the trip. He said, "She was better at it than I was and I was grateful for that." Besides sponsors and cash donors, they had set up what they called the Two Continent Expedition Newsletter. A friend, Dorothy Webster, would act as editor and coordinate the content of the newsletter monthly, as well as send it out to more then 1,000 friends and supporters who had subscribed. They structured the newsletter as three columns monthly, called "The View

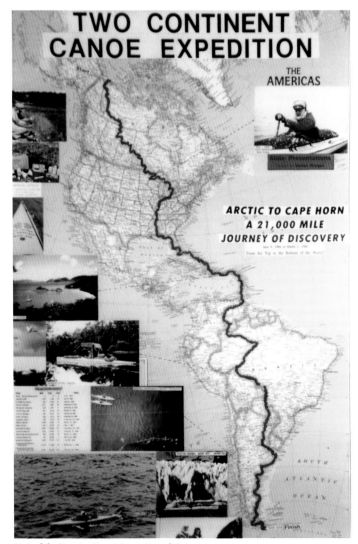

Map of the Two Continent Canoe Expedition *(photo from Kruger Archives)*

from Verlen's Canoe," "The View from Valerie's Canoe," and the "Land Base" by Valerie's brother, John Fons. It was a good concept and provided insight into the daily activities of the trip, as well as different viewpoints and perspectives. Editor Dorothy Webster planned there to be thirty-three newsletters published over the duration of the Expedition.

Verlen and Valerie were on a high, in love and intrigued by the adventure of the Expedition. Their very first edition of the newsletter depicts some of those feelings. She and Verlen were going to explore the Western Hemisphere in canoes and felt they were among the luckiest of people alive. She said they were no more special than others, but she felt especially good because she had discovered her special purpose in life. She claimed to have a special feeling that she was now exactly where she was supposed to be. Verlen said, in the Verlen's View portion of the first TCCE newsletter, "It's true that I have covered this entire length of this first leg of our journey, from the arctic to Lake Superior, twice before. This time we are reversing the direction, going upstream for the first 1,850 miles. Actually, this venture is totally different from anything I've ever done before—the nature, the plans, the purpose, the direction, the strategy—everything is different." And different it was. Verlen had told many in the press that they were embarking on the world's longest honeymoon. It would last for two and one-half years, until they reached Cape Horn.

The following newsletter article, issued by Dorothy Webster, was written by Verlen and Valerie when planning the TCCE. This newsletter was issued in both English and Spanish:

"The Two Continent Canoe Expedition is a story of two people who love one another and love exploration. Together, the team will begin paddling in Eskimo country near the Arctic Ocean. Starting in June, 1986, when the ice breaks at Inuvik, Northwest Territories, they will paddle 1,800 miles up the Mackenzie River, following Alexander Mackenzie's epic journey of discovery (of 1789) to its conclusion at Fort Chipewyan. The team will be reliving a part of the historic far north fur trade route through the Indian settlements of the Northwest Territories and Saskatchewan and will follow the Voyageur's Highway to Grand Portage. Routing through Michigan, the team will be pushing to beat freeze-up and navigating four of the Great Lakes; paddling on the south shore of lake Superior in November, then crossing the Upper Peninsula of Michigan to Lake Michigan, where they will paddle under the Mackinac Bridge and enter Lake Huron. Following the Michigan shoreline will be a highlight of the expedition as the Michigan Sesquicentennial Commission has named the expedition as the number one project of the Sesquicentennial, to celebrate Michigan's 150th birthday with the people of Michigan and throughout the hemisphere. After paddling past Detroit, the team will head into Lake Erie to Toledo, up the Maumee River to Fort Wayne, overland into the Wabash and south across the state of Indiana to the Ohio. Paddling up the Tennessee River, the team will follow the Tennessee-Tombigbee Waterway to Mobile, Alabama. From Mobile, the team will paddle east around the Gulf of Mexico to Miami, Florida.

"This time we are reversing the direction, going upstream for the first 1,850 miles."

Caribbean

At Miami, the nature of the route changes completely as the team heads across 2,300 miles of the Caribbean Sea. In two solo canoes, the team will be stretching their endurance and courage as they cross the open ocean and island-hop the entire Caribbean chain through an international mix of countries and customs, paddling over 100 island crossings, 10 or 12 times being out-of-sight of land which will necessitate overnight paddling. The Caribbean is a sail boater's paradise where the modern history of the western hemisphere began—where Columbus first touched ground in his discovery of the western world.

South America

When the team arrives at Trinidad, they will enter South America and head up the Orinoco River and through the unusual natural canal that connects the Orinoco to the Negro River. Navigating the black waters of Negro, the team will paddle to the modern city of Manaus at the junction of the Amazon. The team will proceed down the Amazon and up the Madeira River, paddling through huge rain forests during the rainy season until this great river diminishes to a mere trickle. At the source of the Madeira, the team will face one of its biggest questions of the expedition, as they attempt to carry two canoes and equipment overland to a small tributary of the Paraguay River. There the team will be entering the middle of the South American continent and the large relatively unknown and uncharted region called the Mato Grosso—a land of countless tribes and frightening stories, where civilization as we imagine has not yet reached. Before they are finished, the team will have explored portions of all three of the major river systems of this southern continent; the Orinoco, the Amazon and the Parana. South America will be a totally different experience as the team paddles through rain forests and among uncounted primitive tribes. This portion of the Two Continent Canoe Expedition will possibly be the most hazardous and probably the most rewarding. The team will follow the Paraguay-Parana River to reach Buenos Aires, Argentina, a major city in South America where Verlen and Valerie will paddle out into the south Atlantic Ocean and down the east coast of South America, into the Strait of Magellan to Punta Arenas, Chile out through the Patagonia island system, around Cape Horn and back to Punta Arenas; 21,000 miles and 2½ years from the beginning of this amazing paddling exploration.

Canoe Explorers

Canoe exploration was not new to Verlen. He had paddled over 65,000 miles, more than any canoeist in history. Verlen, listed in the Who's Who of Michigan, and is known internationally for his boat designing and building skills. News of Verlen's past adventures and accomplishments have circled the globe. He is also an experienced photographer, writer and lecturer.

Valerie is a long distance canoe touring and racing enthusiast who has paddled and

"He had paddled over 65,000 miles, more than any canoeist in history."

portaged over twelve thousand miles in North America before beginning the Two Continent Canoe Expedition. She has developed a unique perspective as a woman explorer in the wilderness and is a published writer and experienced lecturer who regards sharing the story as the blessing of adventure.

Verlen and Valerie have a history of successful canoe adventures, including the World Record for racing the entire 2,348-mile length of the Mississippi River in 23 days, 10 hours, and 20 minutes. Their teamship developed into a romance and the two were married on April 3, 1986. Their combined energy, love and dreams created the Two Continent Canoe Expedition; the most exciting and challenging of all the adventures they had achieved in the past!

The Canoes

The team has chosen the canoe as a vehicle because the canoe opened up North America. There is a special romance about a canoe. The canoe puts an explorer as close as possible to the natural world. The canoe is a personal vehicle powered by effort and is an unthreatening presence in any language. Verlen designed and built the two solo canoes that will be used on the Two Continent Canoe Expedition. These two, 17'-long, partially decked boats, are built for comfort and efficiency and have many special features including a unique catamaran system used to add stability during the ocean portions of the route."

Verlen said the outline of the Land Base article of the planned trip was done from his and Valerie's detailed planning pages. It outlines much of the next 21,000 miles of the intended lives of Verlen Kruger and Valerie Fons. Enthusiasm was bursting from the team. After months and months of preparation, Verlen and Valerie were thrilled to finally be paddling. Dorothy was anxious to get on with the newsletters. Valerie's older brother, John Fons, who was to help coordinate the flow of information from the paddlers to the subscribers of the newsletter, wondered, "What's that zany kid sister of mine and the greatest living canoeist in the world doing all the way from the Northwest Territories to Cape Horn." The Two Continent Canoe Expedition had begun.

Tuktoyyaktuk in Northwest Territories' frozen Arctic (photo by Valerie Fons)

After the first month on the Mackenzie River, Verlen said, "We are putting in long, hard days of 12 to 15 hours of paddling and the first two weeks nearly killed us!" He went on, "The lifestyle of living in a canoe and experiencing a big river has become comfortable and we are at home. This is where we belong. It is great that we both enjoy the same things. We seem to complement and inspire each other in what we are doing and what we are experiencing. We are both totally involved and think we make a great team."

It was a good beginning. They liked the Sea Winds Verlen had built specifically for this trip. They felt they were the perfect boats for this adventure. Verlen had only one complaint at this time. He felt that because of the roominess and capacity of the boats, they were more heavily loaded than on any trip he had ever made. Already famous for a tendency to carry too much, Verlen was surprising even himself. They had more comforts, luxuries, and the best array of foods ever. In addition, they carried five still-cameras, a movie camera and film, their water testing gear, and a variety of "Valerie things" he had not carried in the past. To equalize the differences in strength between himself and Valerie, Verlen tried to pack most of the heavy gear in his boat. Olympic canoe trainers had once said that adding approximately sixty-pounds of weight to the men's canoes would tend to equalize the male and female paddlers in a race, so he sort of targeted that approximation when they loaded their canoes.

Flew to Inuvik to get past Mackenzie River ice *(photo by Verlen Kruger)*

At the end of her article in this 2nd newsletter Valerie said, "It seems to me that in a way our expedition will be measured by these newsletters. This is number 2 and there are 31 ahead. The newsletters, these wonderful opportunities to share our journey, will be my measurement of the months and miles ahead."

The Two Continent Team cleverly used the monthly newsletters to thank those who had helped them along the way in the past month, and also to list the planned mail-drop addresses they had not yet reached. This enabled friends and supporters to send their letters to wait for the team's arrival at the drop they chose. This technique had been used on most of Verlen's previous trips—they always loved arriving at a mail-drop.

The twin articles, Valerie's and Verlen's views, were always entertaining. They were both good writers. Valerie's would be more detailed, have a little more drama, and would describe weather, challenges, and happenings differently than Verlen. Verlen's were more tied to actualities, with less flavoring, perhaps because he had another 50,000 miles of similar experiences under his belt that Valerie didn't. But, they were always interesting and readers enjoyed them. Many of them would write letters back, and Dorothy and John Fons would sometimes include brief messages from them in the next newsletters. Verlen and Valerie refueled on the abundance of letters at each mail-drop. Valerie ended her article in Issue

Measuring river acidity *(photo by Valerie Fons)*

Two Continent Canoe Expedition Newsletter

NUMBER 2   AUGUST 1986 ©

Bulletin: Verlen injured

Editor's note:
A late-night telephone call from Valerie tells us Verlen has been injured while trying to pole his canoe around floating logs in a rapids. Not once, she explained, but twice during a 12-hour period.

She managed to get the canoes onto a riverbank and they are seeking medical attention for Verlen, who is in a lot of pain from what they think are torn muscles in his back.

The paddlers are determined to keep to their schedule (in order to brave the Great Lakes in November) and we'll have full details in the next newsletter.

—Dorothy Webster

Paddlers mark first 30 days of Expedition on Mackenzie

The View From **Verlen's Canoe**   Inuvik to Wrigley, Northwest Territories - 658 miles

A month has gone by since the day Valerie and I put our brand new Sea Wind canoes into the ice cold water of the East Channel of the Mackenzie River at Inuvik. We have come over 600 miles upstream and it has been a tremendous experience. This much of the river could be a significant trip in itself, but we've only scratched the surface! We can still hardly believe our good fortune at being here and the exciting anticipation that the best is yet to come!

Today finds us sitting on the west bank of the river at Mile 401 of our navigation charts. We are about 30 feet above the water, sitting on a rock with our sleeping bags for a back rest. There is a small babbling brook beside us that spills water into the big river. (We've filled our water canteens from it - using our Katadyn water filters). We have a grand view from here and are watching the fascinating display of the process of nature.

The river is at its seasonal high and there's an enormous amount of logs and debris rushing by. Some of the logs are huge, having come from hundreds of miles upstream, from above the permafrost. Some are freshly fallen trees, washed into the river by eroding banks. It will be years before some of them make it to the Arctic Ocean, and by then they will have changed size and shape considerably.

We paddled hard this morning against a strong
(Continued next page)

TCCE newsletter, the View from Verlen's Canoe *(photo from Kruger Archives)*

---

6 with, "I would also like to share with our readers that I love my husband very much. Without his vision, we never would have attempted this expedition and without his love it wouldn't be worth doing."

High water and swift downstream currents fought their upstream progress. On the cover of Issue 2 was the announcement: "Bulletin: Verlen injured." While trying to pole his canoe around a mess of floating logs, Verlen had torn muscles in his back by falling onto the canoe's cockpit combing. He managed to stay aboard and upright, but he knew he had injuries. Then, about twelve hours later, while doing some extremely hard upstream paddling in a severe current around a point of land, Verlen felt something snap in his back. The pain was so excruciating that he was immobilized. Valerie managed to get the canoes ashore, but Verlen was in such pain it took him an hour to get out of the canoe and into a prone position in the tent she had pitched. Flat on his back on his mattress seemed to be the most comfortable position for him. They definitely had a problem.

The next morning, having decided to try to reach a visible cabin downstream, Valerie launched the boats as a catamaran. Verlen could get into the canoe, but couldn't paddle. Valerie said, "I paddled upstream at a snail's pace for more than two miles until I could be assured of ferrying across to the cabin and actually reaching it. It worked!" She had paddled far enough upstream so the downstream current didn't sweep them past the cabin before she reached the other side. They found a friendly Indian family in the cabin. They agreed to take Valerie and Verlen the thirty-three miles upstream to Fort Simpson where Verlen found a doctor who diagnosed his affliction as a "massive muscle-tear." Verlen was still in so much pain and he could barely walk. There was no way he could paddle, and his injuries were going to take some time to heal. They had to make some decisions that would enable them to maintain their time and distance schedule, or they would be caught in the freeze-up of the Great Lakes. They either had to maintain their pace or figure out how to make up the time lost while Verlen healed.

On most of Verlen's trips, he had followed the rules of accepting no help of any kind. Injury was the first thing to cause this trip to be different. They purchased a six-horse outboard motor and, with the help of a local fellow, modified their catamaraned Sea Winds into an outboard-powered craft that would take them the next three weeks and 1,000 miles to Fort

McMurray. There was no other choice—Verlen could not paddle and had to heal to continue the journey. The outboard, of course, produced its own form of adventure. When it quit, Verlen was an adequate mechanic to get it going again, but it slowed their pace. Valerie said that stress and strain between them increased and that Verlen was not a good patient. He sort of resented her words of caution that seemed to him to accompany each physical move he made. Valerie said they had become comfortable with the division of expedition labor they had established and now she had to pick up all of Verlen's physical chores, as well as her own. They went on to Fort McMurray at nearly five miles an hour.

Verlen healed, and they left Fort McMurray nearly two months after starting the trip at the mouth of the Mackenzie River, under paddle again. In "The View from Verlen's Canoe" in this same Issue #2 Verlen wrote, "We sold the outboard motor to the Bernard Jean family of Fort McMurray. They were very good friends from the previous two times I'd paddled through the area. After three weeks of rest and healing, I felt great! I could hardly wait to get my hands on the canoe paddle. God Bless. All things are possible!" That was Verlen Kruger, after an incapacitating injury and three weeks of fifteen-hour days in a motorized canoe.

By September 9, 1986, Verlen and Valerie left The Pas, Manitoba, and were paddling down the Saskatchewan River. In the first 5,000 miles of the Expedition they paddled, less than 300 of those had been downstream. They now had about a day and a half of downstream paddling to enjoy. They would see no more until they reached Fort Wayne, Indiana, near where Verlen had lived as a child. That would be about Christmas time. It took them 10½ days to paddle across Lake Winnipeg, Verlen's fourth crossing of that lake. Then, on September 24, they started up the Winnipeg River. They

Ghosting past Mackinac Bridge *(photo by Dorothy Webster, courtesy of Kruger Archives)*

reached International Falls, Minnesota, on Rainy Lake, to find Dorothy Webster waiting for them for a reunion. Then it was on down through the BWCA and onto Lake Superior in late October, the second time they had paddled through the region together. Lake Superior is famous for its "Gales of November" and the sinking of many ships during its fall seasons throughout history. It took Verlen and Valerie 26 days to transit Lake Superior, much of it in winter weather.

Valerie and Verlen should receive a good deal of recognition for having transited the Great Lakes of Lake Superior and Lake Michigan during the winter season. This route they were on, and the season in which they paddled through Superior, is far beyond what might be considered "normal" paddling. Most people who live near any of the Great Lakes will not go near them in the winter season, no matter what the size of their boats, and certainly not in a canoe. To be out there in wind and weather, during the storm months of November

They'll thaw in a minute! *(photo by Valerie Fons)*

and December, is considered foolhardy by most. But Valerie had caught some of Verlen's determination, and they weren't about to stop their journey.

Dorothy had this to say of winter paddling in Newsletter Issue #5 in November of 1986: "Verlen and Valerie had arrived in Marquette, Michigan, on the shores of Lake Superior. The paddlers rounded the break wall next to the Marquette Lighthouse and paddled the 600–700 yards to a sandy beach near the U.S. Coast Guard boat-house. It seemed to take them forever. Small whitecaps broke the lake's surface and the spray formed a thin film of ice over the paddlers, their canoe and their clothing. Beaching the canoes was difficult—no one wanted to get wet feet in those conditions—so the paddlers backed off, gathered up steam and paddled those craft right onto the beach with a mighty effort. Everybody cheered!" Dorothy continued, "The press conference was short. Most of the news people were so cold they had probably forgotten the questions they wanted to ask, and the wind was howling enough to drown out sounds for the microphones anyway. It was cold."

The next morning they found the waters of the harbor iced over. Valerie wondered if the TCCE might be over. But it didn't even slow Verlen down. He had been up against ice before and it would not stop him from launching this day. He took his paddle and fractured the ice around the dock. Using his paddle he broke the ice around the edge of the dock, making a wide enough channel to launch the two canoes. He dragged his Sea Wind over the snow and onto the ice. Loaded, the weight of the canoe fractured the thin ice. Then, like a miniature ice breaker, he paddled forward, sliding the front half of the canoe far enough up onto the ice so the weight would break it, and the canoe would settle into the water with the ice chunks rattling against the hull. Then he would do it again, and again, until he reached the edge of the shore ice and the open water beyond its edge. Occasionally, he would have to back up to have enough paddling distance to gain adequate speed to slide up onto the ice sheet.

This practice is seldom performed by most who paddle, especially on the Great Lakes. Valerie had good reason to feel some fear while paddling the Great Lakes in winter. There is no margin for error when ice breaking, and Verlen and Valerie were not wearing the survival or dry suits of today's technology. If they were to dump into this water, they would likely not survive. Despite her fear, Valerie, launched her canoe as she had watched Verlen do it, and paddled out the same channel he had broken to the open water. Valerie's concerns were legitimate. Once the harbors of refuge froze, it would be next to impossible to come ashore when the weather kicked up waves. She was right in being concerned about icing harbors during the early and severe cold of the winter of 1986.

Reloading after portage (photo by Valerie Fons)

Verlen and Valerie were soon back in their home turf and the people of Michigan welcomed them soundly. There was what Valerie described as a whirlwind of media activities and schedule of interviews, school presentations, and gatherings. They replenished supplies, and as the weather allowed, continued to paddle on into Lake Huron, paddling during the days and making presentations during the evenings. There was a high energy level shared between these two paddlers. Verlen's View from Issue #7 provides another insight into the Two Continent. He said, "The Two Continent Canoe Expedition is not an endurance event, although it may seem like it at times! We are making no macho claims, although we may accidentally break a few records. We are not playing games—pretending to be Columbus or Lewis and Clark. We are not trying to do this trip as old-time voyageurs, or as Indians, either. We are not reenacting history—we are making history.

Underway again (photo from Kruger Archives)

A little heat won't hurt *(photo by Valerie Fons)*

"We are modern day explorers with purposes and projects of observing and documenting the water quality, the land, and the people, of the Western hemisphere. We are ambassadors of goodwill for the State of Michigan's 150 birthday celebration. We are carrying the Michigan flag and the Explorer's Club flag from the Arctic to Cape Horn. We are Verlen and Valerie—doing our own thing, in our own way, in our own time. We are living off the land—as it is today. The canoe is our home. We are fully equipped and prepared to camp wherever nightfall finds us, whether it's in some remote wilderness shore, a sand beach, or a rain forest—or to camp in some luxurious home with hot food, a soft bed, and warm hospitality. We will make use of whatever the land has to offer for the length of the hemisphere—whether it's a McDonald's hamburger in Paducah or monkey meat in South America." He went on to say, "We were once asked, 'Isn't it cheating to take assistance?' No. Not unless we are making a claim to something we didn't do. Did Lewis and Clark cheat or was their image tarnished by hiring Indians and guides or using horses for overland travel? Did Alexander Mackenzie cheat by not paddling his own canoe, but by hiring it done? As far as we know, our journey has no precedence. It is our personal preference to paddle and portage every mile without any assistance. But not at the expense of jeopardizing the expedition. The expedition must go on. You cannot explore a hemisphere by canoe without some hard spots. Some of our toughest moments and our most hazardous, up to date, we've had to do alone—no one was there—we had no options. We kept going without assistance. But when we began running out of time to beat freeze-up, we took help—but only enough to keep it moving.

"We are not wild-eyed adventurers. We are not going to bull it through come hell or high water. If a revolution breaks out in some country along our route and it becomes a battleground we will try to find some way around it and keep our expedition going—even if it means using a helicopter! But we sure hope it won't come to that."

"We are going to Cape Horn by canoe by the grace of God. We are going 100% pure if we can."

"One thing you can be sure of: We are having a fantastic experience and the best is yet to come!"

"Come along with us... God bless, in love and friendship, Verlen. Math: 6:33"

That's the best explanation of the Expedition, by Verlen, I've ever found to date.

Verlen and Valerie continued south throughout the winter. By March 13, 1987, they were in Mobile, Alabama, 7,000 miles south of their starting point at the mouth of the Mackenzie River and one-third of the way through their 21,000-mile Expedition. Their spirits remained high; they had renewed enthusiasm for the upcoming Caribbean portion of the route, and they both continued to believe the best was yet to come. They had come through the seven locks of the Tombigbee Waterway, and been introduced to parts of the country and its people that neither had seen or met before. They were enjoying it and continually expressed their appreciation of the treatment they received from these people. Hearing of Verlen and Valerie's approach on the radio, television, or in newspaper articles about the Expedition, people would watch for them downstream. They knew the Krugers were coming and wanted to see

Verlen was usually on a first name basis with Coast Guard *(photo from Kruger Archives)*

them. Their frequent press exposure and the newsletters kept supporters up- and downstream informed. This provided them with a great deal of support they never planned on having. Unless they had prearranged something, they never knew quite what to expect, but seemed to be met with nice surprises. Those surprises varied from enthusiastic welcomes to being hailed in the dark from shore by someone shouting, " Krugers?" Sometimes people would bring food to share, offer lodging and showers in their homes, and drive them to and from stores to replenish their supplies. Verlen and Valerie shared an equal enthusiasm in their religious practices and would even sometimes end up in church services with someone they hadn't known a few hours before. They both thrived in this environment and seemed to revel in the newness of each day.

Another day, about to launch *(photo from Kruger Archives)*

These two were now paddling more populated regions of North America and their newsletter articles changed from discussions of challenging weather, dangers, animals, Indian friends and thousands of miles of upstream hardships, to discussions of people, places, crowds of well wishers, media, and presentations. They were through the primary winter weather as they drew south and their daily activities, while still strenuous, were nothing like they had been for the last several months. Verlen modified their Sea Winds into the sea-going versions with hard spray covers in preparation for the Caribbean adventures ahead. Mobile, Alabama, was not too far from Florida. The Bahamas and island-hopping was not far off.

"There is satisfaction in getting to where you want to go."

VERLEN KRUGER

The Caribbean

Progress continued across the bottom of North America, down the inland waterway toward Florida. They planned to be in Miami just after May 1, and to then prepare for 2,463 miles of island-hopping across the Caribbean to Venezuela and into South America. Issue #10 of the newsletter placed Verlen and Valerie on the inland waterway of the Gulf of Mexico. Wardrobes had changed from cold weather garments and footwear to hot weather wear. Verlen's candy bars were melting on the deck of his Sea Wind, and the sea life was rapidly changing from those of the colder climate to more of what they were destined to find in South America. Valerie's View was lamenting the fact that Verlen and the press were touting the Two Continent Expedition as the longest honeymoon. She said that Verlen was an incurable romantic and that they were on an elongated honeymoon was Verlen's misconception. She said she felt, "The proposals I was writing were a matter of business and not pleasure," and went on to say, "During our first months of paddling I knew I was right.

Though we were together 24 hours a day, our concentration and efforts toward our goal of Cape Horn left little time for each other." She said if they didn't enjoy it, they wouldn't be out there. The only thing that caused them to take a day off was weather and, even if wind-bound for a day or two, they would stay busy writing in their journals, writing the views for their newsletters, letters needing answers and planning the next day. She felt they had been paddling daylight till dusk for months, and though they had married shortly before the beginning to the Two Continent Expedition, this trip certainly was not a honeymoon. Though she and Verlen avoided, when talking to the media, use of the word honeymoon, many in the media continued to refer to the Expedition as the longest honeymoon. Even Canoe magazine introduced a story about the Two Continent as The

Catamaraned and under sail between Bahama Cays (photo from Kruger Archives)

Longest Honeymoon, and Outside magazine did something similar. This was a real issue, because Valerie said she was incensed. Later, she said the term "honeymoon" made the TCCE seem soft and easy. She wanted readers to know, "This ain't no picnic!"

Later in her article, Valerie sounded like Verlen when she wrote of the reasons many expeditions fail. She said, "Many expeditions fail not because of miscalculations of strategy, injury, illness, or inadequate gear. What tears expeditions apart is psychological tension among the group." She explained that marriages were made up of two people and that the normal strains and anxieties of everyday living are amplified between them when the marriage partners are physically under stress. She was explaining what was happening to the two of them on the Expedition. Valerie's energy was waning, and she was feeling new strains in her relationship with Verlen. She provided the example of how exhausted they would be after spending a daylight to dark day of paddling some 30 miles and then making a new campsite on a muddied riverbank during a rainstorm, or even in snow. She said, "I tried to tell Verlen that we had more stress in our marriage while en route than if we were living a more normal life at home. He never allows himself any excuses. 'The canoe is our home,' he remarks."

Key West before Gulf Stream crossing (photo from Kruger Archives)

Valerie went on to explain that she felt, whether at home or at sea, it was love that was making their expedition successful, and though the Expedition's demands took most of their energy, it was also essential that they each expend additional energy into their relationship and commitment to each other as well. Their first wedding anniversary was approaching, April 3, and they had been paddling for all but one month of their married life. Among the myriad other stickers on her canoe, Valerie had attached a bumper sticker that said, "Married and loves it!" But, she went on to say she felt they were growing closer throughout the Expedition days. She also felt she may have contracted some dread South American disease, which was turning her too into an incurable romantic!

Verlen related an afternoon of thunderstorm-racing. After a night of continuous thunderstorms, it appeared to be clearing, so they launched to cross a six-mile opening between points of land. As they progressed out onto the open water, another storm loomed behind them. As thunder and lightening rolled in behind them Valerie said, "Dear, are you sure we're doing the right thing?" What she meant was, is trying to cross this open sea, with a storm brewing on our heels, a wise thing to be doing right now? Verlen said, "I didn't want to say what I thought, so I said, 'Only fools are positive.' What should we do? Do we cower in camp waiting to see if the storm is coming our way—or do we act like brave and sure expeditioners and keep it moving? I have learned that in a disagreeable situation, it is sometimes hard to distinguish whether I am motivated by wisdom or by fear. Sometimes it is wise to have a little fear, but not too much, for fear can be a miserable taskmaster." Verlen went on, "We paddled less than a mile while the weather was developing surprisingly fast behind us. The thunder was getting louder, the lightning flashes were closer and brighter, the clouds were getting big and black and were slowly darkening the sky. As we talked, Valerie's voice had risen about two octaves. Suddenly, there was a very bright flash and a loud crash as lightning struck the water nearby. This was followed immediately by a loud report from Valerie. She had looked quickly back at the boiling black clouds bearing down on us and yelled, 'Verlen,' (her voice had raised another octave!) 'Look at that! We are not going to make it!' I was already looking, and she was right, it did look bad. This storm was heading right for us. Furthermore, it was moving so fast that there was no way we could beat it to shore before it hit us. I tried to be calm. 'Yes honey, you're right; we are doomed!'" They did make it to shore and spent the afternoon watching more storms approach and pass. In a later interview, Verlen laughed, saying he could sometimes predict the degree of approaching weather by the octaves used by Valerie.

Verlen and Valerie met Dr. Forgey, who had flown down to Miami to consult with them before they departed for the Caribbean and South America. He ultimately declared them both fit for departure, but not before discovering an irregular heartbeat in Verlen, which required more tests before Dr. Forgey released him to the Southern Hemisphere. In Florida, he gave them needed inoculations: among them, according to Valerie, were shots for typhoid, polio, tetanus, diphtheria, and yellow fever. Both Verlen and Valerie's level of enthusiasm seemed to continue to build as they neared the launching into Caribbean waters.

Verlen's View in Issue #12 listed the safety gear they would carry as they headed for island-hopping and the Bahamas:

Life jackets: The very best hi-flotation from Extrasport Co.
Compass: A large, lighted navigation compass plus many pocket compasses.
RDF: Our Radio Direction Finder is a small hand-held radio compass that points toward whatever station you turn it to—up to a 200- mile range.
VHF: A compact, handheld unit that can transmit and receive any marine traffic a short distance (5-10 miles) on a line of sight.
AM/FM Radio: Transistor radio for weather reports and news.
Weather Band Radio: Receives weather information only—continuously 24-hours a day.
Barometer: To do our own weather checking. A drop in barometric pressure is almost always a sign of bad weather coming.

Sextant: To locate wherever we are when all else fails—if we can read it accurately from a bouncing canoe!

Radar Reflector: Mostly for shipping traffic.

Strobe Light: An emergency signaling and navigation light.

Waterproof Flashlight: For use in signaling and for navigation lights.

Extra Everready batteries: It's very important to have the very best with all this electronic equipment etc.

Flare Gun: For emergency signaling, perhaps as a shark deterrent and for big mosquitoes!

Anchor: In case we have to anchor offshore to sleep or rest.

Sea Anchor: To help fight out a storm if waves get so big and steep as to flip the catamaran. We'd head into the waves, and the sea parachute, tied off the bow on a long rope would help hold the canoes into the wind. It also would help hold the bow down so really huge waves would not cause the canoes to flip over backwards. Can also be used on the stern when running with the wind to act as a drag to prevent broaching.

EPIRB: An emergency SOS signal that can be received by any aircraft or bounced off a satellite. Ours is provided by ACR Electronics.

Swim Fins: Work best with goggles and snorkel in case of sunken or swamped canoes or getting through surf.

Hand Pump: For pumping water out of the canoes. We also use a bailer and sponges.

Desalinization Unit: A compact five pound device to convert salt water into drinking water. We also carry a funnel and plastic tarp to catch rainwater.

Wetsuit: Likely to be used most when we are drenched by breaking waves."

Verlen explained, "In addition, our best flotation is the canoe itself with its stern bulkhead and watertight stern compartment. We carry tether ropes to tie ourselves to the canoes so we won't get separated from them. Our heavy duty fiberglass connector poles to make the two canoes into a catamaran also give us maximum stability and make it better for sailing when needed on the long crossings when the wind is favorable. We will also carry extra food and water for the long crossings—up to 10 gallons of water. And, when all is said and done, the most important safety device we can have—the one that will make the difference—your prayers." (What a difference between equipment available to them in 1986 versus what's available today—how much a GPS would have simplified their gear!)

All of the fund-raising efforts, to date, by their Land Base had been unable to raise enough funds for them to complete their journey to Cape Horn. Verlen discussed how funding was beginning to affect the Two Continent Expedition. "Perhaps a brief review of our financial situation would help explain where we are. We started this big venture on our own financing, and during the two years of planning and preparation we cashed in every stock and

"Sextant: to locate wherever we are when all else fails..."

bond and every insurance policy, finally mortgaging our home. Then, through the generous grants of Canadian Hunter Explorations Ltd. and General Motors Environmental Research Labs, and a few personal contributions, we have received enough to get us this far. (They were now in Florida). By the time we have paid for this expensive safety equipment, and this month's telephone bill, we will be right at a zero bank balance. In December 1987, the Michigan Sesquicentennial Commission voted to try and raise $50,000 for the Two Continent Canoe Expedition as a part of their 150th year celebration. Earlier, we had been named Goodwill Ambassadors for the state by the Governor, James Blanchard. In December, Joe Muer and Freda Fenner put on a fundraising dinner and raised a little over $3000 for us. Apparently the wheels of government move slowly. It has cost us considerable out of our own funds to fulfill our obligations as Michigan's goodwill ambassadors. We are expecting the first payment of $7,500 any day now. At any rate, we find ourselves in the unhappy state of financial uncertainty at the critical time of departing homeland shores. Nevertheless, we are proceeding at full steam with our plans and preparations."

It was a gutsy move to continue on faith that the money would be coming as planned. At this time, they also had to make a big decision about transit to the Bahamas. Verlen went on, "We have conceded that the advice to have an escort across the Gulf Stream is wise, so we are looking and waiting. Right now we are ready to make the crossing, but we are practicing our strategy of patience. For the past two weeks the weather has been unstable. Hopefully within the next couple of days we will find both calm weather and an escort."

Those who have crossed the Gulf Stream will appreciate the wisdom of that decision. The Gulf Stream has carved its name in history through the records of sailors who have dealt with it. Many call it the weather-maker, for it tends to make its own. The Gulf Stream, sometimes called the North Atlantic Drift, is a powerful river of warm water from the Caribbean Ocean and the Gulf of Mexico that flows north up the coast of the eastern U.S. and on to Europe. This warm-water river of strong currents meanders its way north in an always-changing serpentine fashion, which tends to make it unpredictable. The evaporation of some of its warm waters as the Gulf Stream flows north into colder waters tends to make its weather patterns. Its northward flow, combined with tidal currents, winds, and other local weather phenomena, can produce weather found humbling by boats of all sizes. Squall after squall, gully-washer downpours, some of the strangest, billowing cloud scenes, accompanied by brief, but sometimes fierce winds are the norm.

John Fons, in his View from the Shore in Issue #12, thanked a number of Michigan people that had been working hard in support of the Caribbean portion of the Expedition: "Congressman Bill Broomfield and his assistant, Helen Lomax, of the 18th Michigan District have achieved wonders. They have obtained letters of diplomatic recognition from virtually every South American country for the expedition and when it was learned that Caribbean islands permit no camping on their perfect beaches, the Congressman's staff

It was a gutsy move to continue on faith that the money would be coming as planned.

began requesting permission for Verlen and Valerie in the form of letters to each island on which they will land."

It was this type of support that continually allowed Verlen and Valerie to pass through their South American routes within an almost ever-present, welcoming atmosphere. These letters could not only be presented by them whenever and wherever needed, but they also initiated the expectance of their predicted arrival times. Rural residents and townspeople always welcomed them. It was the National Guard that needed to see their official letters from the government in the language of the countries they were in. That degree of preparation not only took a tremendous amount of support effort from their Land Base, but it proved invaluable to their routine progress. Verlen related, "I could never figure out how people like Starkel (author of the book *Paddle to the Amazon*) had so many problems with local soldiers and others. It's pretty simple to figure out that, if they know you're coming, when they see you, you wag your tail, and then they wag theirs!" Verlen said this approach never failed to work for him and Valerie.

At about 8,000 miles into their 21,000-mile Expedition, and after paddling from June 1, 1986, to March 26, 1987, the tone of some of the Land Base comments began to flatten a little. In some ways, Land Base tasks were more demanding and less forgiving than those of Verlen and Valerie. Land Base tasks were the sometimes unrewarding and routine work of behind-the-scenes labor. Soliciting funds was never easy. Failing to solicit adequate funds was disappointing, because others involved in the expedition were counting on success. Coordinating the management aspects of the Expedition back in the mid-eighties was not as easy as it would be today. John used snail mail, not e-mail. He had to count on mail-drops working. He counted on what they mailed actually reaching someone, and having the desired effects. Sometimes, the mail didn't reach its destination, and when it didn't, planned communications failed, as well as their planned results. John couldn't make quick, casual, phone calls to somewhere on a river in South America. Bigger than that, Land Base had to continually make all of this happen, and never got to enjoy the daily wonders and satisfactions Verlen and Valerie faced. It was one thing to make a pledge to these support tasks, but another to maintain them over a two-and-one-half-year period of time. It took a lot of fortitude and dedication to maintain the level of support that Verlen and Valerie counted on.

The Land Base of the Two Continent Canoe Expedition deserved a lot of credit for Verlen's and Valerie's accomplishments. Verlen and Valerie always expressed that. But, by March of 1986, the Land Base was beginning to stray from the usual enthusiastic praise of the V-team's progress and to voice new concerns about inadequate funds to complete the Expedition. John talked of the need to produce a smaller newsletter with fewer photos to save money and to encourage anyone and everyone to help with more funding. It appeared he was becoming increasingly worried about Verlen and Valerie making it to the Horn.

"...you wag your tail, and then they wag theirs!"

Meanwhile, Verlen and Valerie moved on. After waiting for weeks for good weather and a proper escort, they headed for the Gulf Stream on June 12, accompanied by Larry and Miriam Otera and their sailboat, LUNA as their companion boat for crossing the Gulf Stream. The weather did not cooperate, nor the wind and waves. When it became too rough to continue, Verlen and Valerie went aboard the boat and fell victim to severe sea-sickness due to the strange rolling motion of the boat, in comparison to that of the canoes they were used to. The LUNA, towed two Sea Winds behind her for 146-miles to Gun Cay, in the Bahamas, while Verlen and Valerie slept, ill, on her deck. They remained in Gun Cay, however, for less than 24 hours.

Ahead was a 74-mile crossing from Cat Cay to Andros Island over the Bahama banks, an open-ocean, but shallow water stretch. This was the first crossing they had to make out of sight of land during their months of island-hopping to Venezuela.

A high percentage of small-boat sailors will tell you, "Your worst crossing is your first crossing," when referring to open water passages like the one Verlen and Valerie were about to begin. Adjusting to being out of sight of land would take a trip or two. While boats are generally safer out there than near land, there is a false sense of security attained from being able to see land. The vast majority of shipwrecks occur where sea meets land. These facts, however, have little to do with canoes at sea. In weather, canoes have little business being out there at all. Still, oceans have been repeatedly crossed in kayaks, Kleppers (a sort of folding canvas kayak), row boats, and a variety of other small craft—even wind surfers.

Verlen said it was not a long night, but two long nights. He had paddled through many nights alone, with Clint, Jerry Cesar, Steve Landick, and with Valerie on the Baja, but had never been this far at sea between landfalls. They used paddles and sails for progress, and an anchor while they fixed and ate meals in the shallow waters of the Bahama Banks. Verlen did the navigation with his radio-direction-finder and made the mid-course corrections to compensate for the current through the nights. Valerie ticked off the hours by announcing each as, "Only five more hours until daylight.... Only four more hours.... Only three...." Then the gray dawn in the east would welcome them to the new day's relief.

Caribbean traffic (photo from Kruger Archives)

They were covered with salt spray, which irritated the skin and caused festering little sores if not washed off within hours. But with stinging eyes and lips they pressed on. An ocean rain shower eased the sting of salt and refreshed them on their way.

Verlen had some additional insight to their first crossing. Verlen's View said, "Valerie has a 'thing' about clouds. Some people can make mountains out of mole hills. Valerie can make a storm out of the most innocent little cloud! And if there is lightning (as in this case) her imagination flares with each flash! (This one went by without hitting us.)" Verlen had been trained on weather and flown with most imaginable cloud formations, even using them to hide in occasionally during flight and combat training.

Under sail (photo from Kruger Archives)

The differences in the levels of experience between Verlen and Valerie were big, and those differences were also amplified by Verlen's additional thirty years of age, his military experience and training. He had also had another fifty-thousand miles or so of paddling experience, which she did not. They seemed to handle those differences, however, and Valerie admitted, more than once, that it was Verlen's experience she counted on. Verlen was pleased with how well Valerie managed the newly discovered raw nerves of open ocean travel at night while island hopping. He said, "What does it feel like to be out in the ocean in a canoe? Just to think about it seems to scare Valerie the most. Once into the mindset of it, she handles it like a trooper and seems to grow with the experience. There is satisfaction in getting to where you want to go. The hardship itself is not something I want to do, but neither do I believe in letting hardships prevent me from accomplishing my purpose. What does it feel like to be out in the ocean in a canoe surrounded by nothing by endless horizon? Words can never tell. You would have to be there to really know."

Verlen continued, "The Bahama Banks between Bimini and Andros are quite shallow in spots. Most of the time you can see the bottom in the clear emerald water. At 6:30 am just at sun-up I threw out the anchor off the bow on 100 feet of rope in 20 feet of water. The canoes swung around into the wind and rode fairly comfortably. I detected about one mph of northerly current, about as I had suspected. We took down our sails and put them away. Valerie took out her seat, made herself a nest and promptly went to sleep. I got out our

Radio Direction Finder (RDF) and spent nearly two-hours trying to figure out where we were. I was getting a good strong signal from Bimini radio tower nearly 70 miles away, but unfortunately my first reading was incorrect. I had to take about six more readings to restore my confidence that I was getting an accurate reading. I was not able to get a good clear reading from any other radio station to give me a good triangulation. So I drew a line on my map from Bimini, the direction the RDF indicated and I knew were on that line. After some calculations, I determined that we had been blown and drifted over 12 miles off course and were still 10 to 20 miles from land at Andros Island. We took up a new heading of 120 degrees nearly head-on into the wind."

They dealt with tailwinds, headwinds, strong winds and no winds for forty-three hours before Andros Island was in sight. Sight of land is an eons-old balm for the strained senses of those seeking terra firma. It was the same for Verlen and Valerie. They approached Andros with newfound excitement of another successful stride in their journey from the north end of the world to the south end of the world.

It took the rest of June, July, and August to finish island-hopping to Venezuela. The Michigan Food Dealers Association flew Verlen and Valerie back to Traverse City, Michigan, to put on a slide presentation for them on September 14, 1987. Sponsor funds and presentation payments bolstered funds and raised their enthusiasm for the rest of the trip. After spending thirty-eight days at home, raising money, putting on presentations about the Expedition, and sending out more proposals for funding, they returned to Puerto Rico in the middle of October, 1987. It was what we, today, call hurricane season. They could not make headway against some of the weather and current conditions of the waters they were in, and had to hitch a ride on a larger boat. On one such occasion, aboard the 67-foot Tempesta, between Crooked Island to Provo, the water was so rough the boat started to come apart. Valerie said, "The refrigerator came out from the wall. The marble top of the counter cracked and fell on the floor. Cabinet doors ripped off at the hinges and a can of paint leaped over the guard rail of a shelf and spilled into the storage area, painting the deck orange. Verlen and I were so seasick that our guts ached for a week and it hurt too much to laugh. I sure was glad we weren't paddling on that crossing. We barely made it as it was."

Another time, they hitched a ride on an old and beat-up freighter to the Dominican Republic. While there, they were surrounded and escorted by soldiers during their entire stay. Hitchhiking was something Verlen Kruger had never done on his other journeys with Clint Waddell and Steve Landick. He

Clean is good! A South American bath (photo by Valerie Fons)

was careful to explain, however, that they had set no such firm parameters for the TCCE as he had on those other journeys.

Verlen's view, in Issue #16, spoke of visiting Grenada. "Grenada, the 'spice island' of the West Indies, is a small independent nation with a total population of 110,000. Counting the so-called 'out-islands,' this population is over 95 percent Negro or mixed. St. George's, the capital city, is an exceptionally beautiful city built along a fantastic deep-water harbor that is actually the crater of an extinct volcano. The city is framed by a beautiful green mountain range. It all blends together. Several sailors had told us that St. Georges was the most beautiful city in the Caribbean."

He went on to say, "We talked to fisherman, dock workers and people on the street. We went to their churches. You will be happy to know that not once did we find anyone that didn't think the United States was the greatest. Our President Reagan is their hero. Some are still wearing Reagan T-shirts. His picture and poster were up all over town. Everyone was quick to tell us that it was not an 'invasion,' but an intervention, a rescue.

"The people of Grenada were caught by surprise and didn't really believe what was going on until it was too late. In 1979, a man named Bishop, identified as a deceptive liberal Communist, got the military to back him. There was only a handful in those days. They illegally took over the government by force and Bishop proclaimed himself in charge. He placed the President of Grenada under house arrest, jailed the newspaper editor and his staff and seized the radio station. He told the people that he was doing this for their own good and kept promising them an election that never happened. Slowly Mr. Bishop built a heavily armed military force to 5000 men, which was more than all the rest of the Organization of Eastern Caribbean States (OECS) combined. A steady flow of arms from Communist countries was being sneaked into the country at night or under camouflage and stockpiled, hundreds of 'technicians, advisors and workers' from Cuba, Russia, East Germany and North Korea were quietly coming into the country. Cuba began building an airport large enough for long range bombers and heavy freight.

"A man named Coard who was a hard-line Communist was Bishop's Lt. Governor. In three and one-half years of slowly growing Communism under Bishop, Coard began to get impatient for power and wanted to move fast and forcefully. Bishop advised going slowly, hoping to dupe the people into believing that Communism wasn't all that bad. In the power struggle it was Communist against Communist.

"In October, 1983, Coard brutally murdered Bishop and some of his friends and burned their bodies in the garbage dump. In his six-day reign of terror, Coard tried to keep tight control by ordering a 'shoot on sight,' curfew. Anyone caught outside their homes after 6:00 p.m. until 6:00 a.m. was to be shot on sight. To the peaceful, freedom-loving people of Grenada, this was a great shock and an outrage. Many courageously tried to speak out, or to resist in some way. About 30 people were killed. What could be done? All the arms were in the hands of the Communists. The people were caught totally unprepared and defenseless. The OECS had also become alarmed, now that the truth was out. The Governor General and the OECS sent out an urgent appeal for help to the United States, the United Nations and the rest of the world.

"Only President Reagan responded. (He had known something of what was going on). Reagan acted quickly and courageously. Within days the U.S. Navy arrived and the Marines landed. There were a few small skirmishes. Bombs were dropped and shots were fired. (Although we never did see any evidence of either). We were told about 30 some people were killed. The Grenadian military would not fight for Communism. (I'm trying to keep this story short, so it's rather condensed). Within a week, most of the foreign Communists were on their way home and the U.S. Marines had departed, leaving Grenada once again a happy, free nation. There was great rejoicing and a truly sincere gratitude for a neighbor who had come to help them out when they needed it." There was no doubt in Verlen's mind that the people of Grenada were extremely grateful to the U.S. for restoring their freedom. He never understood why the American press was so negative about the U.S. intervention in Grenada.

In that same issue #16, the View from the Land Base article was getting longer than the articles of Verlen and Valerie's Views, and becoming more negative. Dwindling funds, extravagant spending on a camera (as they put it) and a slowing of donations was making Land Base functions more difficult. There is no question that Valerie's brother, John, was becoming worried about Verlen and Valerie entering the vast jungles of South America, and doing so with the problem of inadequate funding for the balance of the trip. One of Verlen and Valerie's miracles popped up on December 18, 1987, when Alex Tilley, of the company Tilley Endurables (maker of one of the world's most recognized hats), called the Land Base to announce he was mailing a $200 check, and would continue to do so weekly for the balance of the Two Continent Canoe Expedition. Many can vouch that they have never seen Verlen within five feet of a floating Sea Wind without his Tilley Hat! The Tilley contributions were truly one of the saving graces of the Two Continent Canoe Expedition.

Many can vouch that they have never seen Verlen within five feet of a floating Sea Wind without his Tilley Hat!

"I'm a traveling man. I'm happiest when I'm moving."

VERLEN KRUGER

South America

The Orinoco River would now swallow Verlen and Valerie for the next 1,350 miles, again upstream, until they reached the Negro River where they were 11,000 miles into the Two Continent Canoe Expedition. Contrary to the manner that Verlen and Steve had paddled the Ultimate Canoe Challenge, Verlen and Valerie almost never separated. While they would not always have their two Sea Winds in catamaran formation, they were seldom far apart. Verlen always tried to stay close enough to help Valerie in an emergency, and Valerie always tried to stay close enough to help and/or be helped. Verlen and Valerie had been together almost nonstop since their marriage. They had also been nonstop on the Expedition for nearly seventeen months and eleven-thousand miles.

For years, Verlen Kruger had been saying, "Wherever I am, when I stop paddling for the day, is my home. I can lie down for a sound night's sleep where I am." Verlen firmly believed that and had been doing it for some years and thousands of miles. As he evolved into the canoe-tripping life, he no longer noticed the discomfort, the strangeness, the dangers, and the constant stress of being out of his comfort zone. He *was* in his comfort zone.

Verlen's sun bimini did not interfere with paddling *(photo by Valerie Fons)*

Some 1,300 miles up the Orinoco River, Verlen and Valerie entered the Rio Casiquiare. In the first three days paddling downstream, the river's level rose more than four feet. The first three days, they had been able to camp on sand bars and shoreline. By the fourth day there was no place to camp. Later, they learned that they were participating in the worst flooding in nearly fifty years.

Verlen's View, in Issue #18 said, "About the fourth night, we could find no place to camp. Finally, we just anchored about two canoe lengths off shore and had our first experience sleeping in our canoes. We tried out our new canopy and mosquito netting system. We found we needed to iron out a few wrinkles, but it worked, even when a rain storm hit us that night. We had apparently anchored near a colony of monkeys and they were disturbed. All night long we could hear them scurrying around in the trees and breaking off branches to throw at us. There were all kinds of strange jungle noises. We also contended with the splashing of water creatures and exotic smells, being only a few inches above water. We felt very vulnerable and slept lightly that first night in the canoes."

There were always adventures of some nature. Verlen describes one: "While I was cooking supper on our MSR gas stove in our campsite on land, quite a few honey bees came buzzing around. They were very bold and getting in my way. Down on the farm in Indiana, we had several bee hives, so I was used to bees. Generally, if you don't bother them, they won't bother you. And don't panic. The bees kept getting thicker. It must have been the delicious smell of the Alpine Aire chicken noodle stew I was cooking. Just at sundown when the stew was done to perfection, a wave of bees arrived and began buzzing me aggressively. I hollered to Valerie, 'Better get inside the tent, I'll bring the food to you.' For once she listened to me, with a little help from the bees! I divided up the stew into two equal portions and took them to the tent. Then I went back to put things away and put on my cockpit weather cover.

Into the rivers of South America (photo from Kruger Archives)

"Just then a bigger swarm of bees arrived and began buzzing me frantically, working themselves into a frenzy. I knew I was in trouble and with my weather cover in hand, I began backing slowly away towards our tent. A bee got under my shirt sleeve and when the sleeve crowded him, he stung me. I instinctively slapped him dead, and that seemed to be the signal for the others to attack. They began hitting and stinging. The bees peppered my shirt like hail. The shirt kept most of them from me. By now, I was swinging the spray cover, batting off bees as if my life depended on it. I ran for the tent. I outran the bees. It is surprising how fast a person can move when they are highly motivated. Once inside, I quickly took off my shirt and Valerie pulled out the stingers.

"If it is any consolation, every bee that stings you dooms itself to death, by the loss of the stinger, which rips away part of the abdomen. I was surprised to find I'd only been stung five times. It felt like much more out there in the thick of the fight. Valerie found a dead bee in my shirt which she taped into her diary. Later, at Manaus, Brazil, it was identified by an expert as one of the infamous "killer bees." At this stage, Verlen referred to their daily camping this way: "We ended up sleeping in our canoes. By then we had learned how to make ourselves fairly comfortable. It was not exactly Holiday Inn, but we were getting a good night's sleep."

On the Rio Negro they were paddling downstream while catamaraned a good deal of the time. The current expedited their progress; in the first twenty-two days they averaged some thirty-eight miles per day. Verlen gave Valerie a break by paddling much of the time alone. She responded by reading aloud from the Bible and shooting photos, and enjoyed the needed rest.

Flooded village in the Mato Grosso region (photo by Valerie Fons)

Verlen did most of the cooking, when they had to cook in their canoes. Valerie said she didn't want to be responsible for losing any of their precious equipment overboard. Valerie adjusted to the southern continent travel mode, developing more confidence as they paddled deeper into the jungle. It took a good deal of courage for these two to penetrate the wilds with no communication to the outside world. Should emergencies arise, they were on their own.

They spent almost five weeks of frustration in Manaus while awaiting gear shipped from the States to reach them. They were nearly out of film and did not want to proceed without an adequate supply.

The photo of Verlen displayed on the front page of Issue #19 (May-June 1988), titled "A Far Horizon," is one of the most striking photos of Verlen. Unless Verlen was wrestling with something, he almost always smiled in photos. There is true fatigue, concern, and strain showing on Verlen's face and in his eyes. Including their time in Manaus, they had been paddling for twenty-three months since leaving the Arctic. They were now some 4,000 miles into South America.

Issue #20 of their newsletter spoke of some trouble for the paddlers near Santa Teresita in Argentina. It was then, in the month of September, when they had trouble reaching shore. Their canoes, which had been in catamaran formation, were broken apart by the heavy surf as they tried to land. The Land Base portion of the article said the connector pole had broken and resulted in what could be serious injury to Valerie. The article intimated a pos-

Ready in the nests for nightfall *(photo from Kruger Archives)*

sible concussion and several massive blows to her legs, and later talked of a "massive contusion of her thigh." A camera and some equipment was lost overboard.

In a later interview, Verlen said "I always felt that incident was blown out of proportion by Valerie and her brother, John. There is no question that it was scary, and that Valerie was scared when it happened, but I never believed that she was seriously injured in that incident. It was sure not the first time a Sea Wind had been dumped either landing or leaving shore." Verlen described the dumping. He said they had had a good day of paddling that day and the winds had been moderate. They were about to face several thousand miles of open Atlantic ocean and he felt that was weighing heavily on Valerie. Most of the day, they watched surf rolling ashore—more surf than they had expected to be there. He said the paddling was easy, as long as they stayed away from the shoreline where the surf would break. Watching that surf for hours began to make Valerie nervous. Verlen would normally have just kept going until he found a break in the surf, which presented a landing opportunity, but Valerie kept saying she wanted to land. From their position, a few hundred yards offshore, the surf looked manageable, but as they got closer in, it looked more challenging.

Verlen's normal approach to a surf landing was to paddle toward the shore, timing their position between the waves to keep them riding in on the backside of a wave. This approach kept enough water beneath the canoes to float them onto the sand beach beyond the surf. There was a lot of potential for trouble if the boat got ahead of the wave, because as the wave comes in, the front surface of the wave becomes steeper as the bottom rises beneath the shore-bound wave. There is less and less water immediately in front of that surging wave. Verlen knew that a boat on the front of a wave would accelerate down that steep slope due to gravity, just like a surfboard. The bow would plunge into the shallower water (or the bottom) at the base and stop moving forward. Then, the rushing wave behind would lift the stern of the boat and try to push it to the left or right into a broach. When the boat was broached it was no longer aimed at the shoreline, but became parallel to it; it would have less forward momentum, and no steerage. Then, the next onrushing wave would roll the boat over and over in the breaking surf.

They had many breaking waves to negotiate to get to the sand beach beyond. Because of that, Verlen and Valerie agreed to catamaran their Sea Winds for the beaching. As they approached their selected landing spot Verlen wanted to time their approach in their normal fashion, riding the back of a wave onto the beach. He kept saying to Valerie, "Wait, wait," meaning for her to paddle backward until they were properly positioned on the back of the chosen wave. But as he said, "Wait," Valerie shouted, "Hurry, hurry!" and paddled forward. In Verlen's View, in Issue #22, he said, "I kept saying, 'Wait, wait! Even though it didn't look bad, I wanted study the wave pattern first. We headed in too fast. We got caught by an unexpectedly large wave that picked up our sterns and pushed us even faster, surging us ahead of it and then broached us sideways." The bow of Valerie's Sea Wind swung a few feet ahead of the bow of Verlen's and rammed into the sand at the bottom of the wave.

The full weight of Verlen's loaded Sea Wind was now on the two carbon fiber poles that catamaraned the two boats. The shock of the sudden stop and the weight of Verlen's boat broke both connector poles off at the point where they entered the sleeves on both boats. This left one pole protruding from each boat. Valerie's boat rolled over and dumped her into the onrushing water of the surf. Verlen stayed upright, and grabbed the broken pole of Valerie's boat, which he could reach. They next oncoming wave, however, ripped the boat from his grasp, tearing the palm of his hand on the jagged edges of the broken pole. Then, all of a sudden, Valerie stood up, finding the water to be only waist deep and several men on shore waded out to help them both ashore.

Verlen beached his boat and turned to help Valerie, but found that she had already been brought ashore by the helping hands. Verlen went on, "Valerie was very wet, cold, and unhappy!" He said that he asked her if she was ok and that she responded with an, "I think so." Later that day, he asked again if she thought she was injured, but she didn't think so. In the newsletter, he wrote, "The next day, she seemed emotionally low. We discussed how she felt. She had the sniffles. She had been fighting a persistent head cold for over a week. She had found a bruise on one thigh. It disappeared in a few days. But Valerie still thought she must have banged her head, because it felt as though the top of her head had been iced. The rest of the outcome of this incident was described in Verlen's View. Verlen continued, "In analyzing the spill in the surf at Santa Teresita, I realized we had made several mistakes. But we still would have come through the surf safely if we had been back paddling, instead of going forward when that big wave hit us. It might have climbed up our sterns and gotten us wet, but it would have gone on under us and then we could have followed it in."

Verlen and Valerie reached Buenos Aires about the same time they heard Valerie's father had been taken ill in Houston. Verlen said Valerie was bushed and when she heard her father was ill and hospitalized, it proved the weight to tip the scales in her own mind, and she flew back to Houston for two weeks, August 21 through September 3. Verlen stayed in Buenos Aires to work on the boats and garner the full measure of hospitality from Ricardo Kruszewski, a newfound friend.

Verlen's gravest photo. A combination of fatigue and problems. (photo by Valerie Fons)

While Valerie was in Houston, Verlen stayed with Kruszewski in his apartment, which was above the kayak factory he owned in Buenos Aires. Ricardo had manufactured over 5,000 sea kayaks over the past years, but because of the ongoing recession at the time was currently experiencing near zero production. Verlen said Ricardo was a gracious host. In Issue #22, he commented, "My time in Buenos Aires was very busy, meeting people, doing travelogs, doing minor repairs, giving the canoes their 18,000-mile checkups. And a complete rethinking of the planning and preparations for the final leg of our journey. It was almost like planning a whole new trip." Through the Argentine Canoe Federation they were finally able to access some very good maps covering their remaining route to Cape Horn.

Buenos Aires seemed to be a turning point for Verlen and Valerie. Change is guaranteed in life and 20,000 miles in a canoe can cause some too. (Issue #22 was a catch up issue for the editors and four different articles of Verlen's View appeared in that single issue. The following quote was from the last paragraph of the first article). Verlen wrote, "What are our feelings at this stage? We have talked a lot about this—pro and con. Even though Valerie's enthusiasm for the rigors and hardships of the expedition, have dampened considerably over the last two years, we both are agreed—Cape Horn had become a magic word that we cannot resist. The attraction has become too strong. We must go on by whatever means best fulfills our goals and opportunities." Verlen always sounded more positive about the remainder of the trip.

"...Cape Horn had become a magic word that we cannot resist."

Some days later, on the shores of Golfo San Jose in Patagonia, Verlen and Valerie had a serendipitous meeting with Roger Payne, Ph.D., famous in the study of whales and the books and movies he has produced on the subject. Dr. Payne was living with his family in a house he had designed and built on the shore, while doing a 22-month study of whales in that location. During an interview he told me, "Of all places for Verlen and Valerie to end up it was on that shore. It was the only dwelling on the shores of the bay. There were a couple of fishing shacks and a large barn elsewhere along the coast, but when Verlen and Valerie came through both of those areas were empty. So they landed their canoes at the only place where people were visible, and we turned out to be those people.

"At that time the population of the Peninsula, a sheep-growing area bigger than Rhode Island, was about 90 people. Verlen and Valerie had recently been through a traumatic landing in high surf in which Valerie suffered serious injury. They lingered for several days, camping near us in an arroyo as they rested and allowed Valerie's injuries to mend (and I suppose, so that she could recover her nerve after such a trauma).

"I remember that we had several meals together around our fugon, an outdoor fire pit surrounded by bushes that affords protection from the strong Patagonian winds—an invention of the indigenous Patagonian people, the Tehuelches (now extinct). Fugons are wonderful inventions: your back is protected from the wind, the fire that is cooking your food before

Right Whale swimming with Verlen and Valerie *(photo by whale biologist, Roger Payne, Ph.D., who was studying whales in Patagonia)*

you is warm (and gives you a place to throw the bones), and there is an unparalleled view of the southern stars above. Some of those meals lasted far into the night and I recall Verlen describing some of his adventures, and that my young children were enthralled.

"During the time Verlen and Valerie were camped with us I made an aerial census of the right whales in Golfo San Jose, something we have done every year since. Because the whales are very numerous in Golfo San Jose I suggested to Verlen and Valerie, who planned to do a bit of kayaking, that if they turned out to be near a whale when the plane was overhead, that I would try to get a shot of them with a whale nearby. As it turned out they didn't know just where the whale was at the moment I shot the picture, but I could see it."

What Verlen and Valerie had already accomplished was incredible. Valerie had paddled over 25,000 miles to this point, and all but 1,700 of those miles were with Verlen. It is no wonder that, as she now faced the remaining 3,850 miles of open Atlantic Ocean between Buenos Aires and Cape Horn, the fatigue, exhaustion, fear, and need for space escaped suppression. She talked of times when she had suppressed her feelings by denying she had been cold, hungry, tired and scared. While Verlen always said, "the best was yet to come," and Valerie normally supported that view, in Issue #22, Valerie said, "I began to realize that we had saved the most horrendous portion of the journey for the last. The Atlantic Ocean and Cape Horn were terrifying." She added, "The other kayakers had no trouble understanding. They knew that the expedition was inconceivable and that we had set out to do the impossible."

More of Verlen's philosophy surfaced in Issue #22, in Verlen's View. He wrote: "To move efficiently in one direction you may have to forego many others. For us to get this far has taken a real commitment and willingness to deny certain other things of normal life, but also a courage and willingness of spirit to live a full life.

"It does take courage to live fully. Obedient life requires effort. It is not always a bed of roses without thorns. Ask the mother who has nine children all of school age or less. Ask the president of the USA. Ask the two canoeists who are paddling from the Arctic to Cape Horn! What may cause a weaker spirit to break down may be just what is the needed exercise to cause another to grow and develop. The choice is largely our own. The biggest difference is in the mind. Exceptional things do not happen by themselves. Someone or something has to be the catalyst, the spark to make it happen, and to keep it moving through thick and thin. Even at times you may have to stand alone."

Verlen's View, in Issue #22, tells of the time they were camped in the whale breeding grounds of Puerto Madryn. He wrote, "One night I was restless, I couldn't get to sleep (domestic problems), so about 4:00 am, I got up, got dressed and went outside into a bright moonlit night. I climbed a nearby high bald-top hill and stood there for over an hour, looking out over our campsite below me." He said that while he was up on that hill, he began to think

South American rivers, like the Paraguay shown here, can be big *(photo by Valerie Fons)*

of the great price that had been paid by him and those affected by his decisions. He said he thought of his family, so dear to him, of his children, grandchildren, and great-grand-children. He talked of his mother, who had tried to dissuade him from leaving Jenny after the UCC, and of divorcing her to be with Valerie. He thought of his brothers and sisters, many of whom felt he was doing wrong, as his mother had. He continued in the newsletter, "A wave of homesickness mixed with love and sadness came over me and I realized afresh the emotional, traumatic and difficult price they too had paid. It takes a lot of energy, emotions, pain and determination to push the limits of horizons—even a little bit. I am afraid that it can not be done without some hard spots. Yet, I have this unexplainable feeling that this is where I was supposed to be right now—right here on this hilltop in Argentina. For a moment, I felt rather small and alone, standing there in the cool night on this remote desert hill." Verlen said, "I sometimes wondered if I was reaching too far, and in too many directions on this expedition, but then, as I stood there on that hill, I remembered that I wasn't alone. God was always near and whenever I prayed I found warmth and comfort and new strength." He added, "While I was at it, I prayed for each of my family, naming them one by one." The one name that was not mentioned in that reflection on homesickness was Jenny. Jenny Kruger, the ultimate rock of the Kruger family, paid a higher price than anyone. When I asked him about that omission later, Verlen said, "I always prayed for Jenny—always."

Cooking while underway on the river (photo by Valerie Fons)

In Valerie's View, Issue #22, she said, "When Verlen and I landed on the southeast corner of Golfo San Jose, I didn't want to be there. I was burned out and there was not one more ounce of adrenaline left inside me to use on any more adventure. I stared at the walls of our yellow tent and wondered how I was going to work my way out of a depression that had been accumulating for several months. My husband was no help. 'Compared to my other journeys,' he said, 'this one is easy. We have had no physical exertion to speak of,' he insisted. This only made me feel worse." Nevertheless, she appeared to bounce back with renewed vigor and said, "I have no doubt that we will reach our goal of Cape Horn," as she ended Valerie's View, Issue #22. Verlen was always pleased at her rebounds and wanted her to reach the Horn.

Verlen said there was never a time when he and Valerie paddled at the pace he had paddled with Clint Waddell or Steve Landick. This did not bother him, because he had known what pace he and Valerie could travel on the Two Continent, from their experience paddling together on the Baja and the Mississippi Challenge. He knew they would be slower, but he was happy with that. "Though our relationship changed during the last months of the TCCE, you have to give her credit for the fact that she did participate in all of those Arctic to Cape Horn miles."

"To stretch your horizon will sometimes mean reaching beyond what we can see or what is rational."

Verlen Kruger

Cape Horn

It was in Buenos Aires that they had some big decisions to make. How would they travel the remaining 6,198 km to Cape Horn? Most new friends advised Verlen against attempting the Atlantic coast via canoe. While some portions had been accomplished by kayak, they could find no record of anyone paddling the whole distance. There were other issues as well. Valerie admittedly was "terrified" at the thought of paddling on the open Atlantic Ocean again. Verlen knew she was exhausted when she left for Houston, and the recent weeks had taken a severe toll on her reserves. While he was quite sure she would bounce back to some degree, he was not sure she could handle the balance of the trip, because of the open ocean. In Issue #22 of Verlen's View, he put it this way, "Arriving in Buenos Aires was a very big thing to us. It was the main accomplishment of our route. We could stop here and not feel defeated. It has always been an option that we could be happy to make it this far if finances, health, or personal problems became too much. Or even if the Atlantic Ocean was not navigable for a canoe expedition in a practical sense." He appeared to be seriously considering alternative options to paddling the final part of the remaining route. Later, he said, "I did consider it, but not for long."

He summarized the distance of his accrued paddling exploits in that same issue: "It could still be that the best is yet to come! In bringing the figures up to date at Buenos Aires, I also find that I have paddled an accumulated lifetime total of 126,828 km or 79,361 miles. This does not include many, many unrecorded miles of short pleasure paddling and race training that would be difficult to verify, without a speedometer on my canoe. Nor does it include any miles by motor or sail. Furthermore, did you know that Valerie Ann has accumulated a lifetime total of 40,303 km or 25,033 miles? All but 1,706 of those miles have been with me!" He went on, "That has got to be a husband and wife record. Amazing, isn't it? These strange but true statistics have heretofore been revealed only to TCCE newsletter readers. There is no doubt but that Valerie has already paddled a lifetime total of more miles than any woman in history. The last time I read a Guinness Book of World Records, it stated that the all-time, lifetime total record for any man was 55,000 miles."

Drifting among Victoria-Hazig waterlilies of Manaus, Brazil (photo by Lloyd Fons)

Surf launch. Without a brace or roll, he managed 100,000 miles. *(photo by Lloyd Fons)*

Valerie returned from Houston to Buenos Aires on September 3. She had used the time in Houston to do some of her own recuperating. On September 13, 1987, she and Verlen launched again onto the waters aimed for the Atlantic Ocean and Cape Horn. In that same issue, Verlen said, "When we departed Buenos Aires, it was with a bag of mixed feelings that we too were about to enter the ocean (Hopefully not to be recycled.)" Four days later, as they sought a campsite along the coast, they were challenged by four riders on horses, carrying firearms, who thought they might be smugglers or horse thieves. Verlen and Valerie were greatly relieved when the man in charge spoke fluent English. They wound up as house guests, with gracious hosts, and a good meal. Two days farther down the coast, they were blown ashore by strong winds. High tide enabled them to avoid dragging their canoes through miles of mud, but they were then stranded in their low-lying camp for the next four days by high winds. Some of the things they had feared were happening. The 92-hour storm tormented all in the region and did much damage. While Verlen and Valerie huddled in their mud-bound tent for three days, roofs were being blown off houses and roads were made unusable by drifting sand. Other than having to listen to the high winds and the discomfort it included, they came through it fine and were surprised that the local coast guard authorities were out looking for them after the storm.

Verlen experimented with ways to negotiate the surf they frequently encountered most of the way down the coast. Members of local kayak clubs made suggestions like, "Don't try to canoe the coast," and "Try a sea anchor astern as you paddle in." Verlen did try sea anchors, as did some of the club members, but they didn't work unless surf, currents and winds all cooperated by going in the same directions. When wind fought current, their sea anchors tangled or cast their canoes at such an angle to the incoming surf that they rolled in the tumbling waves. Verlen laughed, "After having my head mashed into the bottom by my boat I had to repeatedly wash my hair just to get all the sand out!" Verlen never rolled his canoe on purpose, and was aware that Valerie wouldn't either. Verlen said, "One friend named Tony, another new South American acquaintance commented, 'I can see that you have to think for two, not for one only.' He was right. All the time that I was test-

A South American school presentation on the Two Continent (photo from Kruger Archives)

ing for the surf, I was always keenly aware of Valerie—would she be comfortable and safe doing this? The answer was a very obvious no!"

Verlen said nearly everyone urged them to do this portion of the coast by car, paddling the easier stretches they found, but reverting to wheeled transport when the surf was severe. They finally agreed to do that. They traveled via car, truck and bus, with canoes on top, and their gear in the vehicles. At one point, they boarded an oil tanker with canoes and gear and steamed to Bahia Blanca and spent several days there. They felt good about it and said it enabled them to meet more people and see sights they would have missed while paddling. In issue #22, Valerie said, "Verlen and I have so much expedition equipment, water test paraphernalia, cameras, personal gear and 'stuff' that we are overweight and dangerous tumbling in the surf. Also, our large volume Sea Wind canoes are not built for Eskimo rolling." She later added, "We paddle on the ocean in areas where the surf is reduced. In dangerous surf areas, we hitch a ride on a freighter or truck."

They proceeded south, trying to find ways to use more of the rivers instead of the coast. That was a good approach, which enabled some progress. Verlen wrote of an incident on the Rio Chubut while paddling with friends in two additional kayaks and one canoe. "I had just come around a sharp bend with a sweeper below it, when I heard Valerie yell 'Verlen!' The tone of her voice spelled trouble. I whirled around and

The kids hated to see them leave (photo by Valerie Fons)

there was the 16-foot canoe in the brush up against a tree trunk. The paddlers were hanging onto the brush in a death grip, barely managing to keep the canoe from rolling over. I yelled to them to lean down stream into the brush and raced back to pull cautiously upstream beside their canoe and clamped the two canoes together with our hands, stabilizing them into a raft. I found that it was the first time in a canoe for one of the paddlers. He was immobilized by fear. It took a little while to convince him that he was safe. I am not sure that he was ever totally convinced. He got out at the first road we came to and hitch-hiked home!"

A river campsite in South America *(photo by Verlen Kruger)*

Verlen loved the river approach they used. He said, "In looking at the maps in our planning stages, the big attraction was the river. I love rivers. If I were to live long enough, I would probably paddle every one of them. I have never ceased to thrill at the prospect of experiencing a new river. Especially to go from its source to the ocean, which is the common meeting ground of all rivers, where they eventually interchange, regroup and start all over again. You can feel the life in a river, in the moving water against the bottom of your canoe. And, it is great to watch it grow day by day and slowly develop a character and distinct personality all its own." He said, "I think everyone, at some time, should be able to paddle a river. Not just a part of a river, but from its very source to its end. If you watch closely, you can see how rivers mimic life. The part you are currently paddling in will never, ever, be there again. You are unique with that part of the river. It is yours and as it grows, you grow with it. You will never be the same again. Everyone should sometime have that experience." Verlen went on to say the most exciting South American river they paddled was the Rio Santa Cruz, almost from ocean to ocean across lower South America.

Verlen felt they should detour from their planned route long enough to paddle Lake Argentina to see its famous glaciers. December 9, 1988 found them camped at the foot of the Andes mountains, watching huge blocks of ice fall from the Perito Moreno Glacier into Lake Argentina. Valerie took some excellent photos of Verlen paddling among the ice, and she said in Issue #23, "We crossed some of the biggest waves we have experienced during our entire journey." Lake Argentina turned out to be one of the biggest adventures of the TCCE, featuring 100 mph winds, flying canoes, and courage supported by scripture read aloud by Valerie. They wondered if they might not have been better off on the open ocean.

Verlen met a young man where they first camped on Lake Argentina. He saw the man looking at him. The man suddenly ran over saying, "I know you and I know your daughter in Alaska. You're Verlen Kruger!" Verlen couldn't believe it. He expected no one on Lake Argentina in South America to know him. It turned out that the man, Rich Abramson, had spent some time with Verlen's daughter Sarah, her husband, and two children where they lived in Fairbanks, Alaska. "We talked awhile before he left," Verlen added. "It made me feel a little closer, and the world a little smaller."

To summarize Lake Argentina, Verlen said, "Everything you do in this region must be planned around the winds. They are more extreme than anything I have faced elsewhere. Everything must be tied down . . . everything! Canoes and packs must be tied to rocks or Caliphate bushes and there can be no loose items or they are gone! It is noisy and active, but if you don't listen to it, it won't bother you so much. Extra tent ropes keep the tent secure, although it still behaves as though it is leaving at any second. The wind can be so unending that it can wear you down. Even people who have lived with it for years say they hate it." In the same Issue #23, Verlen spoke almost casually about their experience with the winds on the lake and of how he actually aimed their catamaraned Sea Winds into a wind-caused whirlpool to see how well the canoes would handle it. He said, "The first one that came close to us, I sort of steered for, when Valerie wasn't looking. I wanted to test the effects on our catamaran system. It gave us a thrill, but it wasn't quite able to pick our heavy catamaran off the water, let alone turn it over. My confidence in our system remained firm." This was reminiscent of Verlen's piloting days, again testing his and his craft's limits. They were paddling on ice-laden Lake Argentina, whose waters were colder than Lake Superior and the Bering Sea. From Lake Argentina they paddled the Rio Chubut south towards the Atlantic.

Always a friendly welcome ashore (photo by Verlen Kruger)

As they proceeded south, people seemed to expect them and seemed more aware of their presence in the vicinity. Verlen was always amazed at the welcomes, the love, and the support that people freely offered them.

In Punta Arenas, Verlen visited an eye doctor because of a blurring vision, which he had been experiencing since the Amazon River. The doctor told Verlen not to finish the expedition, but to return immediately to the U.S. for further treatment. He added that the result of not doing so could be hemorrhaging and possible loss of sight. With Valerie championing the cause

Anaconda meets Sea Wind via Krugers *(photo from Kruger Archives)*

Verlen was on his way back to the U.S. within twenty-four hours.

Valerie stayed in Punta Arenas with their gear. In Issue #23, she wrote, "I got permission from the Chilean Navy to board a ship bound for the Antarctic. It was an opportunity I couldn't pass up. I didn't need another adventure but I was jumping-up-and-down excited about the prospect of visiting a third continent. Instead of waiting in Punta Arenas and worrying about Verlen, I got on the ship with my pack, tent and plenty of film." The ship went on down the coast and passed within thirty miles of Cape Horn. Valerie wrote, "I remember thinking as I stood on the bridge and stared in the direction of Cape Horn, that the rock of the Horn in the midst of the ocean was only a rock; the place we had quested for so many years and miles of passing. The people of the journey and the lessons learned were so much more important than us standing on a piece of stone and calling ourselves satisfied."

As the ship moved on out into the seas of Drake Passage, Valerie became seasick. She vomited and lost fluid from her nose. This bothered her enough that she mentioned her condition to an English-speaking passenger, so that someone aboard would be aware of her deteriorating condition. She thought it might be connected to her prior beach-surf crash with Verlen and the damage she had done to her head. Valerie had experienced seasickness, so knew what it felt like. She felt this was different enough to arouse more concern. That passenger notified the ship's doctor, who immediately notified the ship's captain, who turned the ship around.

Valerie was evacuated by life raft, transferred to a faster boat, then an ambulance, then a wheelchair and airplane to Punta Arenas. She stayed five days, recuperating in Punta Arenas, after what she described as more nausea and headaches. She decided to return to the U.S. for more conclusive tests. She flew home to Houston where Verlen already was, where she underwent a full nasal scan and head x-rays. Valerie was told she was well, but was strongly advised to cancel the rest of the trip. The doctor reminded her that all have limits. Valerie listened to the advice, but, in her newsletter, said the relief she needed was in the conclusion of the journey.

Meanwhile, Verlen was contending with his blurred vision. After seeing the South American eye doctor, he did not feel he had a serious problem, but Valerie and her mother, who had heard about the problem via phone from Valerie, insisted that he come to the States for further tests. In Issue #23, he wrote, "Valerie would not rest, she consulted with her mother and found it easy to believe the worst. Next thing I knew I was reluctantly in Houston being checked out at a top-notch eye clinic. After extensive examinations and a lot of expenses, I received the good news that there was no emergency and that I did not need a laser operation. In fact, it would have done more harm than good. They said I had a wrinkled membrane (macular pucker) over the cornea, but that it appeared stabilized. The doctor advised taking vitamins (stress tabs with zinc) and to keep a close watch on the eye. In the meantime, Valerie was having problems that concerned me much more. She arrived in Houston by plane and wheelchair the day I was going to leave!

"She went to a neurological doctor considered to be the best in Houston. He was very thorough and very knowledgeable. He listened patiently to her story and symptoms and asked some questions and from that office call said he was 90 percent convinced nothing physically serious had happened to her. But for Valerie's peace of mind we asked for a complete examination. Which he did. With the results that once again came in a dark hour we had good news. He could find no evidence of physical damage of past or present. For which I greatly praised the Lord." Verlen was grateful to all who had supported them during this difficult time. He said the doctor had a long talk with Valerie on the last visit. He wanted to give her some tranquilizers, but she refused. "He said, 'don't kid yourself, you are shot. If this keeps on, you will need professional help.' I always wished she had taken the tranquilizers, because there have been times when I would have used them if she wouldn't. The doctor also advised her not to go on with the expedition, but to stay home to rest and heal."

Verlen concluded his article in Issue #23: "Valerie has a lot of resilience and things have improved considerably all the way around since that day. When I left Valerie behind at Houston to come back to the canoes and to the journey, I did not know whether she would be coming back to this end of the world or not. Or whether I would be going alone. We had talked it over. She was going to stay in Houston a couple of weeks before deciding what she would do. We had agreed that having come this far, somehow the expedition should fly the Explorer's Club flag and fly the Michigan State flag at Cape Horn.

"The past few weeks I have been doing a lot of serious thinking and praying about going on to Cape Horn. Looking deep within myself, how I feel. What is wisest? What is best for all concerned? What is best for Valerie? What is best for the expedition? What is best for

That passenger notified the ship's doctor, who notified the ship's captain, who immediately turned the ship around.

me? How to make the most of this unique moment, this rare opportunity and not make a decision I would regret the rest of my life? I wanted urgently with all my heart for Valerie to be there, to share that special moment at Cape Horn. But under the circumstances I did not dare say anything except take the doctor's advice. It is no secret that I love her very much. Her welfare means more to me than a dozen Cape Horns.

"I agree with Valerie 100% when she says 'I can't wait to get home.' But at the moment, here in Puerto Williams, I am 100% still headed for Cape Horn. I would not want to miss these last days, nor miss the feeling of paddling those last miles.

"I've heard so much about the treacherous, infamous Cape Horn. I've been mesmerized by the awesome stories we heard. Totally changed by the forces of nature, utterly fascinated by the rugged beauty of the area, but somewhat humbled by fear and respect. I want to savor every moment. I must see and touch and smell and taste for myself to be satisfied. I have come a long way for this. I hope and pray that I am not to be denied this most rare opportunity. Strangely, a situation becomes more interesting as it becomes more impossible. 'Lo, I am with you always,' God said. And He has been. We still are not stopped. We are still moving on. God Bless."

Verlen returned to Punta Arenas and, two weeks later, Valerie arrived. Valerie's decision to return and continue on to Cape Horn took great courage. She returned to Punta Arena, Chile, filled with resolve to reach the Horn together. They were headed south again. This time they were both on a Chilean Navy vessel (not headed for Antarctica), which offered to deliver them, their gear and their Sea Winds to Puerto Williams for $24. The ship followed the same route they had intended to paddle, but their paddles stayed dry. They focused on scenery, photography, and the miles shortened to the Horn. Verlen said that he and Valerie had each taken about 10,000 photos on the TCCE. His background in photography went back some forty-three years and he had long been developing his own film for reproduction. When he met Valerie in Seattle she was just entering the field of canoeing, but by the time they reached the southern tip of the Baja, he had also introduced her to the fascinations of photography. He said that when they reached Chile she was an accomplished photographer. Aboard this Chilean naval vessel, they shot more film.

Once in Puerto Williams, Valerie and Verlen Kruger were 105 miles from Cape Horn. Leaving there, they paddled to Cape Ross Naval Weather Station where they waited for the right weather to continue the 37 miles to Cape Horn. On March 1, 1989, in response to their question, "How does the weather look today?" they were told by those manning the weather station, "Bueno Tiempo!" "Good weather" was the reply they had been waiting for. They were into their last day of paddling, closely watching the weather, and after a 34-mile day, at 4:44 pm, reached Hershell Island, only three miles from Cape Horn. They crossed from Hershell to Cape Horn in 52 minutes and Valerie began to weep with happiness and relief. "Don't fall apart on me now," Verlen yelled. Within minutes, Chilean Naval men were down at the beach helping them ashore. "This is the only day you would have made it this week," the captain told them, referring to the weather the week had seen. Verlen and Valerie were at Cape Horn.

A solo 10-mile paddle around the totally unprotected south end of Cape Horn, past the lighthouse and witnessed by Chilean navy personnel at the Cape Horn weather base (photo page 184) qualified Verlen Kruger for an official Cape Horn Certificate.

Verlen summarized the arrival at Cape Horn in his final full segment of Issue #23:

> "Something hidden. Go and find it.
> Go and look beyond the ranges—
> Something lost behind the ranges.
> Lost and waiting for you. Go!"
> –Rudyard Kipling, 1898

Displaying Michigan flag above a nest of U.S. flags at Cape Horn (photo from Kruger Archives)

Verlen's Last View of the Two Continent Canoe Expedition

"In nearly every one of us, there is a little bit of Christopher Columbus, Lewis and Clark, or Alexander McKenzie. There is a spirit of adventure that urges us to reach out beyond ourselves. The magic of exploration and discovery has changed the world and it continues to do so as long as there are those who are willing to push the horizons. This same spirit has changed my life also.

"Exploration today may lack for new lands and people to discover but the unquenchable explorer spirit shall never lack for something to explore. The greater object may not always be the struggle to obtain a goal but to discover a goal worthy of the struggle.

"Out of 10,000 people with bright and shining dreams, only one may be pursuing it. Why? The answer is very simple. Because only ONE is willing to pay the price and you can be sure that there is a price.

"If my big dream in life is hidden behind an excuse, then the dream isn't big enough. But there came a time when the big dream of the Two Continent Canoe Expedition became big enough and worth the struggle. And, we found the courage to go with it.

"When I was a boy down on the farm in Indiana, the story was: 'Go north young man, go north.' North was always the direction of greatest attraction. But something strange hap-

pened. The call of the north got reversed. Our compass needle of attraction got turned around and the call that came to us was 'Go south, Verlen and Valerie, go south!'

"We have followed that call through thick and thin, winter and summer, year after year. From the Arctic, through the tropics, into the Antarctic, across North America, across the ocean, across South America. Like an invisible, irritable, migration instinct that was telling us, 'You are the ones that can do it! You have the unique combination of abilities and talents to spark and spirit, that is just right to make it happen. In spite of the absurdity of being an old man and a woman.'

"By some strange chemistry, when together, we seemed to provoke each other to greater life and venture than we could ever be apart. The sum of what we are together is greater than the total sum of what we could ever be apart. It makes us more vulnerable in some ways because a part of what we are is dependent on the other. It may be fragile, but it is also beautiful.

"Everyone asks, 'Why are you doing this journey?' That sounds like an easy question, but I am still asking myself the same thing. There is no simple answer. I still seem to grope for a good satisfactory explanation. There is an element of unfathomable mystery about it that is still only slowly being revealed. The eagle must soar—we too have soared. The wild goose must fly north in the spring—we must go south. The Arctic tern must go from the top to the bottom of this hemisphere—we must do likewise. There seemed to be something 'waiting for us, something hidden,' that we must 'go and find.' 'Go and look behind the ranges.' We must go and we went. All the way. To the ends of the earth.

"It has been an extraordinary, fantastic experience. But it was not always easy. It was not all downstream. We had to give a lot of our vital self, a lot of valuable time and a lot of real energy.

"What did we find? Something tangible and something intangible. The visible and the obvious we hope to be sharing with you soon, through our slide shows, lectures and reports. The intangible is a part of the mystery and will take a little longer to understand.

"In two years and nine months, we have traveled 21,000 miles. We have spent nearly all of our married life in a canoe! (April 3, 1989 will be our third wedding anniversary).

"The canoe has been our home. The only home we have known together. As you can imagine, we are eagerly, with great anticipation, looking forward to making a more normal life in a normal home if such a thing will ever be possible.

"For the past nine years, I've lived most of the time in a canoe. Way back, in the early spring of 1980, I packed up my canoe and gear and went looking for the head waters of

OPPOSITE: One of Verlen's favorite photos. Rounding Cape Horn!
(photo by Valerie Fons)

CAPE HORN **189**

the Missouri River, up in the mountains of Montana. I found a place where the river was still a new born mountain stream entering a broad valley. Here I put my shiny new solo canoe into its joyful dancing waters and I began paddling.

"Since that momentous day, I have treasured and traversed over 49,000 more miles. One can not travel that far and not have some hard spots. But, overall, it has been a most extraordinary experience. In these nine years, I have been home briefly only a few times but never to stay.

"Our strategy was to be very cautious and watch the weather closely."

"This time there is a different feel about it. I think I can be happy with a change. There are many exciting things to do. It's not that I have grown tired or lost interest in this way of life, or that the explorer spirit has diminished in anyway. It's just that a greater, more important purpose has grown of all this, one that needs to be fulfilled. The life and drive are still there, but it is now directed towards the challenges of writing the books. For me, that task could demand a greater commitment and be a bigger job that the journey itself!

"Puerto Williams, Chile, has a population of nearly 2,000. It is no longer just a Chilean navy base. It has its own local civilian government and is growing into a key tourist stopover. It is now the southern most town in the world.

"Captain Bonnafos, the Commander of the Chilean Navy here was one of the kindest, most helpful people we've ever met. And with the best smile. He seemed to be smiling all the time. He spoke excellent English. Besides being a ship captain, he was a military pilot and flew helicopters. He had graduated from the U.S. Navy SEALs program and the UDT (Underwater Demolition team) in San Diego, California.

"After two days in Houston, Valerie was feeling a lot better and to my great joy insisted on coming back on the route to join me in paddling those last miles.

"The final leg of our journey from Puerto Williams to Cape Horn is only about 110 canoe miles. But due to this area's bad weather reputation, and all the stories we've heard, and all that we recently had been through, this was our anxious anticipation; the most intense moment of our entire long journey. After much talk and prayer, we departed Puerto Williams early in the afternoon on the 22nd of February, 1989. Our strategy was to be very cautious and watch the weather closely.

"In the middle of the afternoon of the third day, we landed our canoes at Guanaco Point of Navarino Island. The country side here was low and without much protection from the wind. We made camp in the shelter of a clump of severely wind-swept scruffy trees. To my surprise, I found that we had settled very near a beaver dam. Beaver are not native to South America. They had been imported many years ago and had adopted quite well. We didn't know it then, but this was to be our last wilderness campfire of the journey. The next day we arrived at a Chilean radio and weather base at Cabo Ross.

"At Cabo Ross, radio and weather base, on the north end of Wollaston island, we got there just ahead of a cold front and heavy winds and were stranded there for four days as wave after wave of strong winds and rain battered the island. But, we were secure and warm inside the radio station, basking in the hospitality and friendship of three navy men. We were treated as royal guests. Usually no one ever stops here, except to bring supplies, for the entire three-month duty period. Valerie may be the first woman to ever grace this base.

"They had two large dogs with a litter of seven, fat, toddler puppies one month old, apparently part Siberian Husky and a few other parts. They urged us to take one, or all. We picked out the one most different. He was tan with dark streaks and strange eyes. We named him 'Cabo.' His full name is Cabo de Bonnafos. In honor of Captain de Bonnafos who did the impossible and arranged it so we could take him home with us. That is a long story in itself. It is too long to tell in this letter.

"Early in the morning on the first day of March, the weather had moderated. There were soft, slow moving clouds in the sky and light variable winds. We started out willing to go only two miles, or all day. From here it was 37 miles to Cape Horn, if we followed the shoreline fairly close. We would be happy if we could make it in three days to the finish.

"All day long, we kept expecting a sudden change in the weather, but the weather pattern seemed to be standing still. To our happy surprise, by 1:00 p.m., we had come 19 miles. Valerie celebrated by getting out and photographing an old abandoned weather base with a dilapidated church. Valerie did an excellent job of paddling hard and steady all day. We didn't even stop for a hot meal. We were going with the conditions.

"When we rounded Punta Duble, we got our first look at Isla Hornos (Cape Horn Island), only about six miles away. It was a bare rocky, mountainous island about five miles long by three miles wide. The end of our long journey was in sight! At 4:44 p.m., we were in the right place at the right time in position for the shortest crossing from land to land. This was only a short crossing of about one hour of hard paddling. But the most treacherous and unpredictable of our entire journey.

"We could hardly believe our luck, there was only a light cross wind out of the west. Still we hesitated. This was supposed to be one of the roughest, meanest spots on earth. But the tiger was asleep.

"While I studied the clouds and double checked the maps, Valerie soothed her fears by surrounding herself with all her safety and emergency equipment. She put on her wet suit,

"This was supposed to be one of the roughest, meanest spots on earth. But the tiger was asleep."

her life jacket, emergency vest with its flares, strobe light, radio beacon and assorted and sundry other safety articles. Then zipped up her spray cover and was ready to go. She was so safe, she could hardly paddle. But she did a good job of it as we raced across the channel in 52 minutes.

"We were elated, we were past the last bad spot. It was a little over a half hour down the shore to the navy weather and radio base at the southeast tip of the Cape Horn Island.

"While I was on the radio, communicating with the navy personnel on Cape Horn Island, a strong north wind suddenly sprang up and began pounding big waves into the rock shore. We had a rough, wet landing on a small cobblestone beach of a small inlet harbor that was unprotected from the north wind. In her anxiety, Valerie jumped out too quick and unpleasantly found herself in waist deep water when a big wave surged in and splashed around her. But it didn't dampen her enthusiasm. This was it! We were at Cape Horn at 6:30 p.m. on the first of March, 1989. One day behind our schedule that had been written up over three years before. All praise and glory to the Lord!

"Our arrival did not happen suddenly. The actual moment of landing was only a small part of a tremendous growing feeling of a most rare experience that had been ours alone. All afternoon with every paddle stroke, the feeling had been growing that we were almost there. Cape Horn was within sight. That feeling will continue to grow as we slowly digest what has happened. All along the route, we have absorbed special moments, observed more than we could comprehend, soaked up great emotions, gobbled up unusual experiences. It may take us months, years, or the rest of our lives to digest it all.

"At Puerto Williams, by rare coincidence, we had met a young man, Howard Rice, from Greathart, Michigan, who had paddled solo from Puerto Williams to Cape Horn, about a month ahead of us. In sharing our stories, Valerie was telling about some of the tough spots. He listened but he was looking at a larger picture when he said, 'Yes, but do you know what you have done?' I am sure that the full realization has not yet hit us.

"There are three Chilean navy men at the Cape Horn weather base. We were there for four days. I was surprised to find out that they issue a special Cape Horn certificate. But only if they witness the event and only if you paddle around the totally unprotected south end of the island past the light house. Certificate or not, I like the idea. The next day, the second of March was another good day. The time was right. From the weather base it was about 10 miles round trip to paddle out past the light house and back. It took about two and a half hours. There were some very big ocean swells and large breakers crashing against the rocky shore. It was a good experience. I got some good photos, and we now have a signed certificate.

"This was it! We were at Cape Horn at 6:30 p.m. on the first of March, 1989."

"We owe special heartfelt thanks to a lot of special people. We can not begin to name them. This letter is already too long. But, we would especially like to thank our sponsors who had the vision and the generosity to support the expedition. Without them the dream could never have become a reality.

"We thank our newsletter editors; all three of them. We thank the newsletter subscribers, all 800 of them. You were a big encouragement to us. We are very sorry the letters came so slow. We never received a penny of the subscription fee, it all went to the editors for the cost of printing. The last six newsletters, Valerie is rolling together and doing in order to get this responsibility wrapped up.

"We also want to thank our family and friends and those who so earnestly prayed and those who wrote letters. We must have received 5000 letters during our journey.

"Especially we thank Lloyd and Venita Fons who endured much inconvenience and anguish, who handled our personal affairs while we were gone. Lloyd handled over 20,000 35mm slides and kept them for us, sending us duplications and kept us informed if our cameras were working. There is no way we can adequately thank all those dear people along the way who helped us when we needed it.

"I will probably also design and build a limited number of canoes for special people with special dreams. As I paddled along the last two years, I have designed a couple of new solo canoes in my head. One of them, the SUPER SEA will be a sea kayak.

"'Delight yourself in the Lord, and he will give you the desires of your heart.' Psalm 37:4. God bless you richly. Always love and friendship. We hope to see you at the HOMECOMING IN MICHIGAN ON MAY 20, 1989."

Resupply of dehydrated foods shipped from U.S. (photo by Valerie Fons)

The Two Continent Canoe Expedition was over, some 21,000 miles south of its beginning.

Author's Note

According to Valerie, three different editors were involved in the newsletters: Dorothy Webster, John Barton and John Fons. Valerie completed the last three at home.

"Rivers are the arteries of the world.
We have to keep them clean."

Verlen Kruger

Grand River Expedition 90

Back from the Two Continent Canoe Expedition and living in Lansing, Verlen and Valerie were very busy with presentations after their big Lansing homecoming of May 20, 1989, at the Wharton Center for the Performing Arts at Michigan State University. Having displayed the flags of Michigan and the Explorer's Club at Cape Horn, they had reached celebrity status in Michigan. They had often talked of the Grand River. On his three previous passages of the Grand by canoe, from its source to Lake Michigan, Verlen had seen sad accumulation of waste along its shores and always felt it should be cleaned up. Through a questionnaire process, he and Valerie discovered most Michigan residents who lived along its banks did not know where it began or ended. They decided to use the clout of their current fame to attempt to do something about it. In spite of their time demands, they agreed to take on the Grand River project and to make it happen in 1990.

Expedition '90 camped along shore off the Grand River *(photo from Kruger Archives)*

The Grand River Expedition '90 was conceptualized by them with the help of many Michigan citizens. Valerie became the chairperson of the event, spending over a full year's time on coordination and promotion, as well as seeking sponsors to support it. As always, Verlen was complimentary of the manner in which Valerie chaired the promotional and coordinating committee for this event.

Verlen said, "One of the things I didn't like about the environmental movement was so much of it was based on doom and gloom. We wanted the Grand River cleanup event to be based on progress already made and what we could muster the people of Michigan to add to it. We had

A lonesome Kruger Loon among Expedition '90 canoes *(photo from Kruger Archives)*

no desire to blame anyone for the circumstances. We wanted to show them how to cooperate to make it better." With the help of their committee and Michigan residents, they raised over $50,000 in cash and another $100,000 of in-kind services to support the event.

Expedition '90 was to be a thirteen-day canoe trip, the full length of the Grand River, paddled by all who wished to be there. Verlen added, "We wanted people to paddle the river with us, to experience the river, so they would later appreciate it as a resource and care for it as they should." Initially, they had hoped to get at least 35 to 40 canoeists involved. They wound up with over 125 paddlers in 55 canoes. Verlen said the State of Michigan had printed out hundreds of copies of a 70-page booklet on the Grand River's history, which they distributed along the way. The communities and towns along the Grand opened their parks for places the canoeist could camp at night. Some had hot meals awaiting their arrival in the evenings, and others promoted the attendance of their town's residents to listen to an Expedition '90 presentation in the evenings. They attracted some exciting crowds along the way and media throughout Michigan picked up on Expedition '90.

Jerry Link wrote in an article, "The first Grand River Expedition took place in August of 1990, celebrating the history, culture, and the environment of the watershed of Michigan's longest river, the Grand. Together with friends, fellow paddlers, Lansing Oar and Paddle Club members, Boy Scouts, Girl Scouts and their leaders, civic leaders, fur trade-era re-enactors, educators, industry representatives, historians, Michigan State University and Grand Valley State University student researchers and their professors, and employees of General Motors Lansing Division, the expedition came together in several months. This amazing effort resulted in a 13-day paddling event from the dead waters of the Grand River in Jackson County to its mouth at Grand Haven on Lake Michigan. The expedition camped at pre-arranged public and private campgrounds each night in a different city, town or village on the banks of the river, displaying interactive water quality assessment demonstrations and exhibits along with watershed information.

Grand River campsite in city park *(photo from Kruger Archives)*

"Central to Grand River Expedition 1990 was learning of the existing water quality of the river after more than a century and a half of farming operations along the river's banks and the stream banks of its tributaries. The Grand River flows through some of the most productive farmland in Michigan's lower peninsula where annual crops of corn, soybeans, and alfalfa assist in feeding the states dairy and beef cattle herds. With the advent of commercial herbicides, pesticides, fertilizers and other chemicals over the past fifty years, it was clear to the expedition's planners that a baseline study of concentrations of the residual toxins in the water and sediments were important information if similar expeditions were to be repeated periodically, comparing future findings with the earlier studies. With that intent, students and faculty from Michigan State university designed and outfitted a canoe that would pump river water into a series of testing devices, perform the tests (a monitor would record the test results), and then pump the water back into the river. Girl Scouts were charged with recording the sightings and locations of birds, mammals, reptiles and amphibians along the course of the river. Michigan Department of natural Resources personnel performed river bottom and sediment inventories of insect larvae and fresh-water invertebrates. The fisher persons on the expedition

Paddling through one of the Grand River's towns during Expedition '90 (photo from Kruger Archives)

caught a variety of piscine species that were examined for fresh water parasites and residual concentrations of toxic chemicals. Others located abandoned trash sites, old tires and debris that had been deposited on the banks or into the river. An attending road crew was assigned to help restore the littered site to as natural as possible in the time they were on that section of the river. Each canoe team had an assigned job to do during the expedition. There were no 'free-loaders' on the two-week river trip. It was not a 'vacation,' although many folks took a vacation from their day jobs in order to participate in GREx'90. A rented U-haul van carried the participants gear after they broke camp at dawn and transported all manner of tents, sleeping bags, and personal backpacks to the next evening's camp location. Usually the paddlers would arrive to the next campsite by late afternoon in time to pitch their tents and relax before the evening meal. Averaging about six hours on the river each day, nearly everyone was heading for a good night's sleep soon after the evening meal's dessert was served."

Expo down the Grand (photo from Kruger Archives)

Jerry added, "The result and viable extension of Grand River Expedition 1990, was the renewed energy that invigorated existing watershed stewardship groups like Jackson County's upper Grand River Environmental Action Team (G.R.E.A.T.), as well as the formation of several new groups formed by local concerned citizenry on the tributaries: the Flat, the Looking Glass, the Thornapple, and the Rogue Rivers."

Truly a "Grand" sight with a noble cause *(photo from Kruger Archives)*

What Expedition '90 accomplished was dear to Verlen's philosophy on the environment. He hated the negative tone and downward spiral of so many environmental forecasts. He said, "So few pay attention to the things we can still do to make it better and turn it around. If all you can see is a sad ending, what motivation is there to fix it?" He wanted environmental groups to paint an honest picture of existing conditions, show what could be done to fix it, and then make those things happen. He wanted ordinary people to believe, and to see how they could do extraordinary things to make it right. That is why he always endorsed and donated time to protecting the waters of the world.

Verlen loved this event, especially what it accomplished. A renewed vigor came over Michigan, especially among paddlers who had discovered, through this event, that there was something they could do. Expedition '90 was a huge success by Michigan's standards. The event triggered lots of media coverage, which helped make Michigan residents aware of how important the rivers of Michigan were and how they must be cared for as a resource. Some of the communities kept Expedition '90 displays up long after the event.

With the success that the Grand River Expedition '90 garnered, other water conservation groups gathered steam. Verlen participated in other environmental events.

About five years later, Verlen Kruger was asked to help inspire and promote the formation of Michigan's now-famous Quiet Water Symposium planning committee. He served on that committee, attended meetings, and presented one of his adventures each of the next eight years. Jerry added, "With his trademark Tilley hat, he was always ready and willing to share his knowledge and experience of time on the water, small watercraft design and construction with others, either during a formal color slide presentation or informally at his 'Kruger Canoes' booth in the MSU Agriculture Pavilion."

In 1996, Verlen was asked to become involved in the Great Lakes Water Trails organization to lend all the support he could to their cause. Jerry Link added a comment, "After three days of meetings several carloads of Symposium attendees, with an assortment of kayaks and canoes drove north to the eastern shore of Lake Superior to Agawa Bay for a morning paddle to the pictographs on the lake's granite walls. This was the first time I had paddled in another watercraft anywhere near Mr. Kruger. I paddled my kayak with a double-bladed wooden paddle and he paddled his Kruger Canoe with a single blade, bent shaft, graphite canoe paddle. Paddling for all I was worth that day, I could not keep up with the 74-year-old master."

Next came Expedition 2000. It was similar to Expo '90, and many of the Expo '90 participants showed up again. Valerie Fons and her son, Steven Ervin, paddled during the Grand River Expedition 2000 from the beginning of the journey to Charlotte. Of course, Verlen was involved. Verlen was then 78 years old, proving, as Jerry put it, "That a person has value at any age and is never too old to support something they're passionate about." (A 2010 Grand River Expedition is currently in the planning stages.)

Another canoe load coming in (photo from Kruger Archives)

In 2003, the first annual "Quiet Water Symposium 'Verlen Kruger' Award" was presented to Verlen. The plaque, which now hangs in Verlen's home says:

The River Guardian
Presented to Verlen Kruger in recognition of his outstanding
Achievements and records in paddle sports
Be it further recognized that he has brought international
awareness to our environmentally sensitive waterways and
fostered stewardship of our treasured water resources.
Presented at the 2003 Quiet Water Symposium
by the Mid-Michigan Paddling Community

When presented with the River Guardian Award, Verlen quickly shed the cape of pride again with, "As always, I pass this recognition and your love onto my Lord and guide. You know I believe all things are possible with God."

(The Quiet Water Symposium will celebrate it's eleventh year event in 2006, and the Verlen Kruger River Guardian Award is now given to a worthy recipient annually.)

Verlen was always quick to say, "If there is any way to put things into my story that will show the good work these clean water efforts are producing, let's do it. Michigan has made great progress over the years in protecting their waters, but this type of effort should be nationwide, worldwide!"

"*The canoe is my home. All of America is my home.*
Wherever I am, I'm comfortable and happy.
It isn't just a canoe trip anymore, it's my life."

VERLEN KRUGER

Readjustment Again

Over the next two years Verlen and Valerie gave presentations, sometimes together, sometimes individually. Their presentations brought in more money than either of them had seen before. Valerie also began to write articles about the TCCE. But later, many of Verlen's friends described those two years as troubled times for both of them. They watched Valerie give more independent presentations and said they were sometimes even better than Verlen's. She was in her element speaking to an audience. Verlen continued speaking engagements, but also involved himself in building his canoes and training additional apprentice help.

Dan Smith, a longtime paddler and friend of Verlen's said, "I give Valerie credit for accomplishing what she did with Verlen, but she would never have done it without him. She wrote her Baja book, and spoke in some of the presentations she and Verlen put on, as though she was sort of equal stature to Verlen in ability. There's no way that was true."

Verlen was getting tired of presentations and thought he and Valerie should get on with their next canoe trip. In the past, he had given presentations of trips until he raised enough money for the next trip. He would always rather do the trips than talk or write about them. A group of U.S. canoeists and kayakers was working on an exchange program with some paddlers from Russia. This was at the time of pere-

Dow Chemical sponsored the Michigan Shore to Shore race featuring Verlen *(photo from Kruger Archives)*

stroika and glasnost in Russia under Gorbachev, which opened new doors of opportunity. The Baikal exchange of paddlers was arranged by private citizens of both countries, without the help of their governments. They asked Verlen to become involved, which he readily did. The plan was to have the U.S. participants go to Russia to circumnavigate Russia's Lake Baikal first. In surface area, Lake Baikal is nearly the size of Lake Superior, but is actually deeper and contains more volume of fresh water. Then the U.S. paddlers would bring the Russians to the U.S. the following year and circumnavigate Lake Superior.

Valerie didn't want to go. Verlen was fired up over the Lake Baikal plan and definitely wanted to go, but his participation kind of fizzled because of domestic problems. It seemed that after the last 21,000 miles on the TCCE, Valerie had had enough of canoe tripping. In an article that mentioned the Lake Baikal event, Valerie Fons said, "First, however, there is domestic business to tend to. We have to retrench a bit after being away from home for nearly 10 years." Domestic was becoming a favorite term for each of them when they referred to their marriage. Though they found some potential sponsors and Verlen did considerable planning for Baikal, he never went with the group. He said, "Our marriage was coming apart and I knew it wouldn't help for me to go alone." Verlen thought Valerie Fons still shared his spirit of exploration and adventure and would continue to be his tripping partner, but that was not to be. By this time, Valerie felt she had spent the bulk of her married life with Verlen fulfilling and helping *his* dreams come true. But, she too had dreams, of becoming a mother, and training for and becoming a minister. Verlen, in fact, did want to do more canoe trips, Lake Baikal among them. These were some of the issues which eventually caused them to separate, and then divorce. The Lake Baikal trip took place in 1993 without Verlen Kruger.

Promoting past trips never enthused Verlen as much as doing the next one
(photo from Kruger Archives)

Over the remaining months of their marriage, Verlen and Valerie drifted further apart. Soon, issues filled more of the space between them than what had drawn them together. They separated first. Verlen came home from a brief Canadian canoe trip with some friends to find Valerie had gone to Seattle on an unannounced trip. He always suspected she left him for a younger man. Later, Valerie said Verlen was wrong. Verlen, however, never changed his mind. They divorced on May 13, 1992. They didn't fight over the spoils. Their parting was amicable and each got on with their own life in their own way. Valerie did eventually remarry, became an ordained Methodist minister, and she and her husband adopted six children they continue to raise.

Verlen said, "It is easy for some of my friends to feel badly about Valerie and how our relationship appeared and disappeared. I appreciate their concerns and any sympathy they might have for me. But, I caused my own problems and some for others as well. They still must admit, however, to Valerie's accomplishments. She has paddled farther than any woman on earth." Verlen always wanted people to get their due. He had nothing bad to say about Valerie.

During one of my last interviews with Verlen, I asked him why neither he nor Valerie had ever written a book on the Two Continent Canoe Expedition. He said, "I started mine, but never got beyond the outline." He likened the writing of that book to "having another Cape Horn to round" and the magnitude of the task seemed overwhelming to him. Verlen was consistent: he would always rather do it than write or talk about it. He went on, "The medicine I was taking then began to effect my concentration and I developed a problem with bad headaches. I just never got back to it after that." I asked, "What about Valerie's book?" He said, "I know she wrote her book, because she asked me to write a forward for it. I might have considered it, as I had on her first book, but not unless she let me read it. She didn't seem to want to do that." I asked him why, and he laughed and said, "I suspect she forgot she wasn't out there alone. She tends to do that."

Valerie is a complex woman and has led a complex life of her own choosing. "Persistent" was her word of choice when I again asked her why she had so vigorously attached herself to the UCC team of Verlen Kruger and Steve Landick in Seattle and beyond, during June through October, 1982, when she and Verlen left Steve behind. Valerie told me she intends to write her own stories, especially on the TCCE, and when she does, I am sure it will be well done.

Verlen said he felt Valerie's leaving was the 2x4 blow alongside the head that began to slowly return him to his senses. He began to awaken to what he had actually done to Jenny. It had never fully hit him until it happened to him. Verlen was now acutely aware of what that had felt like to Jenny. He could no longer bury those feelings beneath a 21,000-mile canoe trip, or ignore them behind the love adventure with Valerie. After his second marriage, he was now alone and had to deal with the reality he had helped create.

Years later, it is difficult to attempt to make sense of what had occurred in Verlen's, Jenny's and Valerie's lives during the UCC. People who love Verlen fondly still scratch their heads when they review those times. I believe Verlen was no innocent bystander, or victim, in the relationship he developed with Valerie Fons. Nor do I believe Valerie Fons was simply bystander or victim. It takes two to tango. But those details belong to Verlen and Valerie and those impacted by the resulting changes triggered by their relationship. It all happened as part of Verlen's life. He paid a price of enormous proportions and caused others to pay as well. But, he also spoke and wrote openly of the many good years of adventure and marriage he shared with Valerie before they, too, separated. I believe he did not realize until years later the degree to which his behavior impacted so many others. Some will justify his behavior, some will not. But Verlen Kruger always marched to the beat of his own drum. The only redeeming factor—if it can be called that—is that he admitted to and accepted responsibility for problems he caused. He never blamed them on others.

Perhaps Verlen said it best, when he volunteered in his book on the Ultimate Canoe Challenge, "But I have to say that, in my obsession with continuing the trip, I did not see the personal ramifications of taking on Valerie, who had been unacceptable to my partner

But Verlen Kruger always marched to the beat of his own drum.

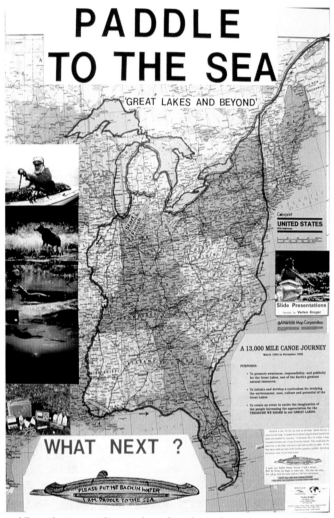

PADDLE TO THE SEA

'GREAT LAKES AND BEYOND'

A 13,000 MILE CANOE JOURNEY

WHAT NEXT ?

Paddle-to-the-Sea was the next planned trip that Verlen Kruger never made
(photo from Kruger Archives)

Steve from the first time they met. Personally, I say, this was the worst decision of my life. My dear, faithful, long-suffering wife Jenny divorced me in 1984, and the trip with Valerie was a large part of the reason. The whole thing was wrong. I knew better. But the trip was warping my judgement. And that was the biggest mistake I ever made. Valerie was an excellent partner and it was an outstanding experience, but it wasn't right. And there is no way I would ever have agreed to do something that would separate Jenny and me. Yet I allowed it to happen. I was very lucky that Jenny later took me back and we remarried." Verlen literally paddled out of Jenny's and his family's lives for those years. He later said, "I just never came home from the Ultimate Canoe Challenge."

After his divorce from Valerie, Verlen began planning the Paddle-to-the-Sea venture he had long thought of. He needed something to take his mind off how he had ended up. What better way than a lengthy canoe trip? In typical Kruger fashion, he made detailed plans of the trip. He was well into planning it as a solo trip when, according to Verlen, there came a knock at his door. The young lady knocking had heard that Verlen was again single and was planning his Paddle-to-the-Sea venture. She had met Verlen during the Grand River Expedition '90 and had heard him discuss the Paddle-to-the-Sea venture then. She was an elementary teacher and wanted to become involved with Verlen in this venture. After a few discussions, Verlen realized that she could bring her talents to bear using the trip in grade school social studies curriculums when students studied the Great Lakes. This would be another way to find sponsors to help finance the trip. Soon, Verlen was again planning the trip, but not as a solo. They would do it together! Neither was he going to again go canoeing into the sunset with a young woman to whom he was not married. They rather quickly agreed to marry and did so in 1992.

Verlen's friend, Dan Smith, said, "When I saw the other lady show up in his life I was really surprised. When he told me they were going to marry before going on the Paddle-to-the-Sea trip, I couldn't believe it. Then, out of the blue, he asked me to be his best man at the wedding in Florida. I didn't know how to say no to him. I did it, but later I felt like I should have tried to talk him out of that marriage and felt guilty about not doing it. I just knew it wouldn't last."

Verlen and bride participated in a canoe race from Chicago to New York, called the 1993 Finlandia Clean Water Challenge. "Placing mid-range, with half the racers ahead of us and half behind, we decided to do a final trial-run of about 1,000 miles on the Great Lakes before attempting the Paddle-to-the-Sea," said Verlen. "During that first trial paddle, she decided she just wasn't cut out for the canoeing life. We both realized early on that we had married for all the wrong reasons and that it had been a mistake. It was just after that not-too-successful trial run of paddling that we stopped canoeing and had a serious conversation." He said there were no hard feelings between them, but they just knew they shouldn't have married. They agreed to divorce and abandoned the venture. Verlen said, "Don't elaborate on my third marriage. It was another part of my 'crazy' time. We're still friends." They remained friends after their divorce and Jenny remembered Verlen doing some boat work for her in his shop years later. The Paddle-to-the-Sea trip went into a state of suspended animation. For the rest of his life, Verlen occasionally talked of wanting to do that trip, but it wasn't to be.

Thanks for building the
best canoes!
Ft. McMurray to Tuk
Summer 98

~ Beafort Sea ~

Your Friend
Norm
Miller

"*Happy are those that dream dreams, and have the courage to make them come true.*"

🦋 VERLEN'S RENDITION OF A QUOTE FROM CARDINAL LEON J. SUENENS

Back to the Future

Verlen abandoned his efforts on the Paddle-to-the-Sea venture and went back to boat building. His canoes were selling well. It was all he, Dan Smith and Scot Smith could do to keep up. Mark Przedwojewski later joined Verlen's canoe building team by accident. Mark and his friend, Matt Garrish, had planned to go on a canoe trip. When they went shopping for a canoe in Michigan, someone told them to call Verlen Kruger. Receiving his phone call, Verlen readily offered to talk with him and invited him over to his shop. Verlen put both Mark and Matt in Sea Winds on the Grand River and they were sold on his craft. Mark said, "We both knew immediately that we were sitting in the best canoes we had ever seen!" Though he had never heard of Verlen Kruger before that meeting, Mark had grown up only six miles from Verlen's home on the Grand River.

They quickly formed a friendship and Mark and Matt bought canoes from Verlen on an installment basis. Though they were not paid for by the time they were to leave on their canoe trip, Verlen allowed them to take the boats and pay him later. In the spring of 1996, Mark and Matt left on the planned 700-mile trip on Michigan rivers and Lake Michigan. Verlen even paddled with them for a short distance. Soon after that trip, Mark became a full-time employee of Verlen's, trained under him for the next two years, and became the heir apparent to take over the business as Verlen phased out. Mark took over two years later and Verlen moved into an advisory capacity.

Mark said, "Verlen was very patient and very encouraging and he always had good things to say about whatever we were doing. His wisdom is so deep. He just knew so much about designing and building canoes so I didn't really question the things he taught me. I just did it the way he wanted it done. He was never critical, always encouraging, and

Verlen training Mark Przedwojewski in the art of Kruger canoes *(photo from Kruger Archives)*

he really inspired you to do it right. I worked part-time with him for a couple of years and then joined him full-time in 2000. At that time, Verlen's knees were giving him so much trouble he was having trouble working full days in the shop."

As he settled into boat building, Verlen took a hard look at his situation. He said, "After I'd had my third divorce, I realized I had to straighten my head out. I had made such serious and bad judgments and had hurt others along the way. I was so crazy then, and so many paid a price for it. I began to realize how much I had missed Jenny and my family during that time. I never fell out of love with her, and when I was alone again, it really hit me."

In discussions of Verlen's experiences, as well as in the three published books about Verlen's canoe trips (*One Incredible Journey*, *The Ultimate Canoe Challenge*, and Valerie's Baja book, *Keep It Moving*), Genevieve Seavolt Kruger sometimes was invisible. When she did show up, it was as less than the engaging, active woman she was and continues to be.

A winter cruise on the Grand River, one of Jenny's favorite photos (photo from Kruger Archives)

Jenny's love and commitment to their family is still rich and enduring and her game sense of humor and joy in life is fun to be around. She came from a small family, but shared Verlen's dream of a large family, which in those days was not unusual, especially for farm families. Verlen wanted to raise the kids on a farm as he had been raised and Jenny agreed with that approach. This former eighteen-year-old World War II bride had her ninth child before she was thirty-three years old! She was as surprised as anyone to be the mother of nine children and laughed as she remembered gathering that young, robust family for dinner. She remembered one dinner when they were waiting for Verlen to finish a business phone call. The tease of the family, their son David, was elbowing his sister, Nancy, and getting her riled up. Jenny told him to calm down while off-handedly flipping a small butter-knife down the table to get their attention. The innocent little butter-knife morphed into a ninja weapon as it cleanly clipped off the top of a gallon milk bottle. Milk poured out over the bottle onto the table as nine big-eyed children stared in silence. Jenny, shocked, burst out laughing and they all collapsed in hilarious hoots, laughing and hollering. There are plenty of Kruger family stories retold by the kids that recall Jenny always on an equal footing with Verlen, both sharing the joys of their family lives.

During the World War II years, Verlen was away for special combat skills training and for a longer time in Korea and Japan. He and Jenny were accustomed to being apart from the very outset of their marriage. Following discharge, he and Jenny shared the adventures of building their new life together within the structure of their church congregation. In Verlen's 40s, when he discovered canoe racing and canoe tripping, she joined him in races with the kids. They were the bank runners and cheering squad from start to finish, and Verlen liked having them with him. Jenny supported his six-month Cross Continent Canoe Safari with Clint Waddell across Canada. She knew it would be hard on them, despite frequent visits en route. Even as he paddled out of their life, their marriage bond remained tight.

Then came the UCC, which started out small and grew into a three-and-a-half-year trip as Verlen and Steve Landick discovered and plotted river connections. In April 1980, Verlen paddled out of their lives again, but planned on prearranged visits en route. Jenny ignored warning advice from friends in order to give Verlen his treasured adventure. They had weathered, then celebrated, the six-month CCCS. She believed in him, trusted their deep love, saved her vacation days to join him and gave him her blessing.

She later said, "While home alone all these times Verlen was gone, I had read of men his age entering a kind of mid-life crisis. Back in those days, these things were just being discovered, or at least studied and written about." Jenny went on, "I knew Verlen was vulnerable out there and I was becoming more aware all the time that long-distance relationships often didn't work out. I was watching Steve and Sarah fall apart as well. I had been married to Verlen Kruger longer than Ms. Fons had been alive. I wasn't naive. I just didn't know what to do about it. I had given him my blessing to go."

He and Jenny were accustomed to being apart from the very outset of their marriage.

Jenny was strong and wasn't about to let a woman half Verlen's age give him forty letters, lots of attention and pour out her troubled life for counseling from him. She told Verlen after the Baja portion of the UCC, in which he and Valerie had paddled 3,600 miles together, "Everything is more important to you than me. When you broke our marriage vows, you broke my heart. I cry every day about us, but these tears will dry up. You are acting crazy! You are not the Verlen Kruger I've known all these years. If this is not an affair you're having, there has never been one. I have been studying mid-life crises in men. You are ripe for the picking! Wake up!"

Newspaper articles, published after the Lansing homecoming of the UCC, made it appear that Verlen had paddled home to be served divorce papers by Jenny, which was not the case. Jenny never asked Verlen for a divorce. She thought and hoped he would come to his senses when he returned home. Eventually, Verlen told Jenny, "If there can be no room in our lives for Valerie, then I think we must divorce." Jenny said, "No. There is no room." They separated and then divorced in December 1984. Verlen and Valerie then continued to race, canoe trip, and present their journeys to the public for the next several years, while professing how right and how blessed their relationship seemed to them.

Verlen said that as he returned to his more normal, less obsessed paddling state, his thought processes changed. He was again alone, was not on a lengthy canoe trip with someone else, and was spending most of his time at home building canoes. Within that environment, he said he began to remember his past life with Jenny and family and to realize how he was missing it. He knew the magnitude of his mistakes and what they had cost him, Jenny, and the family. He knew he wanted to again see and talk to her, but never dared to think she might be willing to allow him into her life again. He said the more he thought about it, the more he wanted to see her. "I didn't know what to do. I never dreamed I would ever be able to approach Jenny again. Then it dawned on me that I had little more to lose by trying." He said he still held off for a while longer. He didn't want to hear her say no.

Jenny said, "I had never stopped loving Verlen, but I never dreamed we'd ever get together again. I had seen him on a variety of occasions during the twelve years we were apart. I had attended family gatherings, like holiday occasions; once, I even went to a Thanksgiving gathering at Verlen's home and I would hear about him sometimes from the kids, or read about him in the newspapers. When I did see him, I would occasionally ask him if the old Verlen Kruger was back yet. I wasn't paying much attention to him. Then I heard he had married again and couldn't believe it! I heard about it when Clint and Bev Waddell stopped by to see me in Michigan. They said they had stopped to say hello to Verlen and a strange person opened the door. It was his third wife! Nobody seemed to have heard anything about him marrying again. I certainly hadn't!" That was a bit of another shock. In less than a year, she heard that marriage had also ended.

It was nearly a year after his third divorce when Verlen called Jenny.

It was nearly a year after Verlen's third divorce when Verlen called Jenny.

Within the next month, they were talking more often. He gradually decided she didn't hate him and began to think of actually renewing their relationship to some degree. He said he couldn't make himself believe she would ever have him back permanently, but grew more confident from the nice way she talked with him and treated him. Finally, Verlen asked Jenny to casually date him again. She said no. She continued saying no for some time before finally accepting an offer to have lunch with him. The old spark began to glow again between them and soon they were dating again, kind of secretly. No one else seemed to know about it.

Mark Przedwojewski said he began to recognize changes in Verlen during this same time period. He said, "We'd all be working on canoes every day together. Then, one day about 5:00 pm, Verlen looked at his watch and said, 'Oh man! I've got to go; I'm late,' and ran out the door. The next day he was back and didn't say anything about where he had gone. The next day he quit about 4:30 and left again. During the next two weeks, it happened several times. Then one morning, he came into the shop with a big bag of homemade cookies to share with the crew. That

Verlen gaming with great-grandson Caleb Jessup *(photo by Jenny Kruger)*

happened again a few days later, but it was fresh bread instead of cookies. We all knew Verlen wasn't baking. We were dying of curiosity, but didn't want to ask him what was going on. Then about a week later, in the afternoon, in walked Jenny with a bag of cookies! Verlen laughed, 'Now you know where I've been going!' It was such a breath of fresh air to have Jenny there!"

According to the canoe crew, Verlen went through a genuine transformation during those times. "I'd never seen him so happy!" said Dan Smith, who was then part of the canoe crew. He said, "I always suspected they might get back together again. Verlen often talked

I want
to run away with you
to a secret place
where the world will never find us,
a beautiful place where our hearts,
minds, and bodies
can know each other again
for the first time.

I want to search with you
and rediscover you.
I want to begin again with you...
I want to open the door
to your deepest thoughts and feelings
and make you happier
than you've ever been before.

"I love you..."
and I always will.

YES!

John 15:12,13
Ephesians 5:28-33

of it and I knew that would be his choice if he had the opportunity. But, he never thought he would get that chance. I was so glad when I found out they were actually dating again. It took some time, though. I think Jenny had to make sure Verlen was really back, and you couldn't blame her for being cautious."

After a month of dating, Verlen actually asked Jenny twice to consider marrying again. Jenny told Verlen, "Give me time to think about it." He did. Jenny later said she wasn't too surprised by Verlen's behavior. It appeared to her that Verlen really was back and that he wanted to stay. She knew she had to be cautious. She had been through so much during that twelve year absence, as had her family. She counseled with her pastor, but kept it quiet from her family. She freely admitted that, while she had been furious at his behavior, she had never stopped loving him. Jenny felt she had to come up with a final "yes" or "no" and once she did, there was no turning back. She could not be selective, forgiving him for some things and not for others. Anything unforgiven would constantly haunt her with bits and pieces that would call up old and powerful emotions. For it to be "yes" she would have to forgive Verlen—totally—for everything he had done immediately before and during his twelve years of absence. That was the only way it would work for her. She had courage!

" I WILL MARRY YOU! "
I Love ♥ you!
Forever and always.

Jenny

Jenny's response (photo from Kruger Archives)

Jenny made her decision and sent Verlen the card shown in the photos. She wrote on it, "Yes! I will marry you!." As soon as he received it, Verlen called her and said, "Yippee, we are engaged! We need to go out and buy an engagement ring!" Verlen was ecstatic. He picked her up, they went out and he bought her an engagement ring, then they celebrated at dinner. Then she began to tell their children and grandchildren.

Verlen Kruger and Genevieve May Seavolt Kruger remarried on June 7, 1997. Verlen was 75 years old, and Jenny was 70. They decided on a small, family wedding, which was held in their daughter's church and officiated by the pastor with whom Jenny had counseled. There is no photo of Verlen and Jenny with happier expressions on their faces than in that wedding picture. They are the smiles that never seemed to leave them for the remainder of their time together. The wedding ceremony was actually larger than the first time they married June 30, 1945, in McAllen, Texas, where Verlen was then stationed in the Air Force. That had been a simple ceremony of Verlen and Jenny with Pastor T.E. Howard performing the ceremony and two of Verlen's military friends as witnesses.

With hands upon the Bible of their faith *(photo from Kruger Archives)*

No better smiles than these! *(photo from Kruger Archives)*

Verlen and Jenny and family were together again! In later interviews, I asked Jenny if it was difficult to handle the publicity that Verlen still received from his accomplishments with Valerie Fons, such as the Mississippi Eddie Bauer Race or the TCCE. She said, "It would have been, had I not truly believed in the forgiveness I pledged myself to when I remarried. Doing it that way enabled me to make the best of the years yet to come and Verlen did the same. I could always tell when he was having a guilt-ridden moment about the past, but when I would remind him that was forgiven he would ease up on himself. That was a real decision I made and it helped to take much of the old hurt away for both of us. Verlen made some big mistakes, but I don't believe he ever stopped loving me. Most won't understand the way we put our lives back together, but it was very good. I was very well loved in our remaining years and I love him still."

The Kruger family grandchildren in 2002; (fourth row top l to r) Seth Kelly, Angela Kelly, Dana Davis, Sarah Schomp, Jon Grisham, Andrea Grisham; (third row) Kevin Kruger, Melissa Norris, Beth Sparkes, Stephanie Prout, Jessica Sparkes; (second row) Zackary Schomp, Caleb Lynch, Verlen and Jenny, Jacob Kelly; (front row) Devin Kruger, Nicole Kruger, Kayla Kelly, Samantha Sparkes, Melinda Kruger. *(photo from Kruger Archives)*

"On the water, the fastest way to a point is sometimes not what it seems. Wind, current and speed all have to be considered when you navigate. "

VERLEN KRUGER

Mississippi Challenges

During an interview with a local newspaper, Verlen once said, "I don't think the average person has much concept of the effort involved in racing one of the biggest rivers in the world." While describing his feelings about the Mississippi River he added, "Of all the rivers I've traveled, I think it's the most interesting because of all the activity on it and its history. The effort it takes to plan a Mississippi trip is a little hard to grasp, and even the ones who get into it find out it's a little more than they expected." Verlen credited his planning and navigation efforts as having much to do with winning races and marathons.

He planned every race as he would have an air combat mission. He scoured the maps, the Corps of Engineers water information, and most everything he could get his hands on about the route he was taking. He immersed himself in the history of the Mississippi, and he wrote detailed accounts of what he expected to see on a daily, sometimes hourly basis. He knew when each lock would be open and accessible, or when he would have to portage, and he watched the weather intensely. He used to say things like, "Well, the race doesn't really get started until down around St. Louis." He knew the impact of time and distance on racing teams. "Microscopic movements of maximized efficiency, though invisible to the untrained eye, can become victory margins over time and distance," was one of the ways he put it. His rule of maximum efficiency, getting the most from the least, was an active ingredient of every race he ever entered.

Verlen on the Grand River at Kruger Base *(photo from Kruger Archives)*

Verlen always said that a paddler must understand the race, the environment, the route, their partner, and how to pace to survive a marathon attempt. Without a clear understanding of each of those pieces, they had small likelihood of even finishing, let alone winning. He proved this again and again, which is why he has held, and holds, so many marathon records. Verlen finished the Au Sable marathon eleven times, which is one of the reasons his name is on the bronze plaque of the Michigan Canoe Monument on the Au Sable River near Oscoda, Michigan.

A writer for Canoeing magazine once called Verlen the King of Pain. Verlen said, "Nothing could be further from the truth. Pain is to be avoided whenever possible. Comfort is key to successful marathon paddling! The confining cockpits of racing kayaks work against their occupants the entire length of a race. You need the luxurious space of an elongated cockpit, which allows you to reach whatever it is you need at the time and allows you to stretch out kinks and change to a more comfortable position when needed. You need room to lie down for a nap while your partner paddles, or to discreetly take care of personal needs as nature calls. Your canoe must allow you to remain dry, warm, and comfortable. Otherwise, you will be fighting yourself as well as the circumstances of the event."

His canoe designs, which evolved throughout his 100,000 miles of paddling experience, bore out his beliefs. Nothing in all of Verlen Kruger's canoe designs came from tradition. He copied no Eskimo or Greenland shapes, curves, scantlings or cool images to make his boats. What he did was build the first model, then paddle it a few thousand miles, then begin to refine it into exactly what his pilot training, paddling experience, and understanding of canoe environment told him it should be. Verlen said, "It took 42 mold changes to get the Sea Wind and the Cruiser where I felt they needed to be." Perhaps this is one of the reasons the Kruger Cruiser still holds the Mississippi record, twenty-four-years after its first win of that record in 1984.

A Mississippi practice paddle leaves the flooded dock of Kruger Base *(photo from Kruger Archives)*

A marathon race along the entire Mississippi River is a different sort of challenge. It takes a complete team of both paddlers and shore support to accomplish it. The paddlers must be experienced, fit and prepared, both physically and mentally. Also, according to Verlen Kruger, "They must understand their goal and have a proper plan to accomplish it, without which they are already licked at the start." Verlen felt some paddlers tend to undertake trips that might be bigger than they are. They perhaps don't yet fully understand what they are up against and, consequently, cannot properly plan for it. "Many think a marathon race is simply a matter of being tough enough, but it's much more than that," said Verlen. "It's usually a matter of survival." He generally didn't race a marathon in sprints, and when he did invoke a sprint it was either to reach the finish line, or for some psychological advantage along the marathon route. He was famous for welcoming those behind him ashore at the rest stops and then immediately jumping into his canoe and taking off! On one of the later

Mississippi challenges, Clark Eid, paddling the Double Helix racing kayak said, "Do you know how frustrating it is to come ashore for a break and see a 78-year-old man jump into his canoe and take off ahead of you, again?!"

The paddlers on the team need to be able to cope with being with each other twenty-four hours a day, for a month or so. They must eat, sleep, go to the bathroom (often in the canoe's chamber pot—without tipping over!), and paddle together. In addition, they must deal with bugs, weather, danger from water currents, wind, tug boats and barges. Nowadays, they may also have to deal with local authorities, Homeland Security restrictions and the Coast Guard to gain passage through and over dams and flooded locks. The team also must work with the shore support team.

When his teammate wasn't there, he'd train alone in his Sea Wind on the Grand
(photo by Jenny Kruger)

The shore team must provide 24-hour communications, scout the river ahead of the paddlers and alert them to anticipated problems and contact points for the dispersal of food, water, clothing, batteries, waste removal, camaraderie and support. They also must take care of repairs or replacement of all gear, clothing, and electronics—including the canoe. They are the ones who must adequately prepare witnessed-documentation, which might later be submitted to an entity like Guinness when asking for recognition of a new World Record.

The shore team also orchestrates media contacts, and schedules those media occasions so they are not a detriment to the progress of the paddlers. If interviews can be done during the racers' normal time ashore for eating, it does not slow down their progress. The shore team also has the task of having hot food ready at each of the rendezvous. One more thing: the team is also supposed to make sure they get at least as much sleep as the paddling team. While doing all of these things—and each must be done—they drive their support vehicles along the shore routes of highways, dirt roads, and trails to make it to the next rendezvous point (which may not be there due to flood conditions). The canoe travels in the nearest to a straight-line-route as possible, while the autos and vans must follow circuitous routes. The shore crew vehicles are often required to travel more than twice the distance of the canoe. One shore team lost three members in three different vehicles for hours due to poor maps and flood conditions. The only way they eventually found each other was through GPS coordinates and cell phones! Stan Hanson, his wife, Dana, and John Young, members of Team Kruger on the Mississippi races, all said they could not remember doing anything more difficult than shore crew duty.

"Verlen, that's a kayak ahead of us."

"Not for long, Bob."

BOB BRADFORD AND VERLEN KRUGER

The Great Mississippi River Race For Rett Syndrome, May 2001

Clark Eid, Ph.D, a research scientist, and Mary Potter, whose young daughter, Amanda, suffers from Rett Syndrome, organized the Great Mississippi River Race. This race down the Mississippi took place in May of 2001, and was dedicated to all the little girls and young women afflicted with Rett Syndrome. It was the longest canoe/kayak ultra-marathon ever held: 2,348 miles from the Mississippi's source at Lake Itasca in northern Minnesota, to the Mile Zero marker in the Gulf of Mexico. This was a free-for-all of entries, with no restrictions on the type of craft used, as long as they were paddled by two people. It was open to kayaks or canoes. To stimulate participation, considerable freedom was granted as to the types of craft entered and variety of paddling style (canoe, kayak, relay). Attached to those freedoms, however, were strict rules on safety. One of these required paddlers to wear a personal flotation device (PFD) at all times, even when underway and sleeping in the canoe. Clark Eid thought it funny that Verlen Kruger, of all people, couldn't swim! The sole purpose was not simply to race, but to call attention to Rett Syndrome and raise funds for research into this devastating disease. All proceeds were distributed equally between the Rett Syndrome Research Foundation and the International Rett Syndrome Association's Permanent Research Fund.

Rett Angels provide send-off for race teams (photo by Kent Spading, courtesy of dreamkeeper.org)

Clark said, "I first came up with the idea of having the longest race in history in the summer of 1999. I had never heard of Verlen at the time. I began to dig into the idea and contacted the United States Canoe Association and they referred me to Verlen. I called Verlen to ask him for ideas, and much to my surprise, he said, 'Count me in!'" Verlen helped Clark and others organize and plan the race. By providing them with the detailed documentation from the 1984 Eddie Bauer Challenge info, for which Guinness had granted a World Record to Verlen and Valerie, the organizers were able to put together a rational race scenario.

Verlen talks at prep meeting at Lake Itasca *(photo by Stan Hanson)*

Team Amazon paddles the start from Lake Itasca
(photo by Mark Albertson, courtesy of dreamkeeper.org)

Team Rebel headed south
(photo by Mark Albertson, courtesy of dreamkeeper.org)

The Great Mississippi River Race for Rett Syndrome was endorsed by the Governor John G. Rowland of Connecticut, Minnesota's Governor Jesse Ventura, the United States Canoe Association and the American Canoe Association. The Cousteau Society provided support and donated pieces of its famous flagships *Calypso* and *Alcyone* for incorporation into a 23-foot wood-strip racing kayak built by Clark Eid for this race. The diversity of craft and teams made the race exciting. There were five teams entered.

Team Double Helix was Clark Eid and Kurt Zimmermann. Clark, who grew up in Minnesota and had canoed all his life, was chairman of the race. Dr. Eid is a Sr. Research Investigator in Central Nervous System Chemistry at Bristol-Meyers Squibb Company in Wallingford, Connecticut. Clark and his wife Mary (Potter) have two children, Amanda and Noah, and live in Connecticut. Amanda has Rett Syndrome. Clark's partner, Kurt Zimmermann, is from Austria. He moved to the U.S. in 1996 to become a research chemist in the anti-cancer department at Bristol-Meyers Squibb in Wallingford, CT, where he now lives. He fell in love with canoeing as soon as he entered the U.S. Their support team was made up of Mary Potter, who built and maintained their event website (www.dreamkeeper.org), Kenton Spading, Tony Swenson, Andrew Gribble, Jeff Romine, William Schmitz, Eric Marshall, Johann Fembek, Edith Paule, Bill Evans, Stephen Bertenshaw, Ed Lisk, Kevin Gendron, Martin German and Jan White.

Team Kruger was comprised of paddlers Bob Bradford and Verlen Kruger, paddling in the renowned Kruger Cruiser tandem expedition canoe. Their support team consisted of Stan Hanson, team captain, Dana Hanson, Chuck Hasenkamp, Mick Wood and Jon Young.

In 2001, Verlen's friend, Mick Wood, was helping him retrieve some planning info on the Mississippi. He had seen Stan Hanson's name in paddlingnet.com, a chat room for paddlers, and asked Stan what the Mississippi River was like around St. Louis, near the Chain of Rocks bridge. Verlen's knees were in bad shape by then, so they were seeking local info as to how tough it would be to portage around that bridge. After Stan answered, Mick told Stan that Verlen needed a shore crew for the Great Mississippi Race and suggested Stan

Verlen and Bob during the first fifteen minutes *(photo by Mark Albertson, courtesy of dreamkeeper.org)*

Clark Eid, Kurt Zimmermann and Double Helix at end-of-day break
(photo by Kent Spading, courtesy of dreamkeeper.org)

call Verlen. He did, and thus began a lengthy relationship between Stan Hanson and Verlen Kruger. Stan captained two different Kruger Teams, and others too, on several occasions. Verlen said, "Stan Hanson, retired from a military career of 13 years active duty, and 17 years as an Air National Guard air-traffic controller, had retired at age 53, as GM13 and Captain in the reserves. Those career choices made enough free time available to him, so I asked him to become the captain of my shore team. After a brief conversation and a day of thought, Stan agreed and immediately went to work finding sponsors."

Team Amazons of the Mississippi consisted of paddlers Cynthia Belbin, who had been a member of the Canadian National Development Team in 1991 and 1992, and Megan Duffy, a former member of the U.S. National Kayak team. They would paddle another tandem kayak. Their road team captain, Tony Mate, and others were to join them after the start, but didn't because the team withdrew early due to injury.

Pre-race meeting of part of Team Kruger, sporting "Tilleys;" (l to r) Stan Hanson, Bob Bradford, Mick Wood, Jon Young and Verlen.
(photo by Janet Hanson, courtesy of Kruger Archives)

Team Alaska-MSC, from Matanuska-Susitna College, had relay paddlers. Will Miles and Tony Degange were the starting paddlers supported by a road crew of David Hoffman, Bud Bourn and Kermit Ketchum. They paddled a tandem kayak.

Team Rebels with a Cause was made up of paddlers Carl Johnson, Al Levine and Eric Kocher. They paddled a kayak but disbanded near Minneapolis due to disagreements among the team. When that occurred Al Levine and Eric Kocher continued the race by joining Team Alaska-MSC.

Beautiful wood marquetry made with more than 3,000 pieces of 63 types of wood wraps around the entire Double Helix kayak, traveling a distance of over thirty feet on the deck and bottom surfaces *(photos by Clark Eid)*

The flagship of the event was the Double Helix, a racing kayak built by Clark Eid, whose purpose was first to capture attention for Rett Syndrome through its design, performance, and beauty. All of the materials for her construction were donated by a unique list of sources. Some of the woods used for the ring around the compass were from the reconstruction of the *La Amistad*, made famous by the 2001 movie, *Amistad*. Materials from Costeau's *Calypso* and *Alcyone* were used for the navigation console. The rose vine pattern set into the polished wooden deck mimicked DNA and encoded the message, "Amanda's DreamKeeper" in honor of Clark Eid's daughter. The pattern was made from over 3,000 pieces of wood, including some from *Calypso* and *Alcyone*. Nobel Laureates James Watson and Francis Crick, who discovered the structure of DNA, signed their names on the deck of the Double Helix. She was truly the most unique kayak ever launched upon Mississippi waters and she was fast. While the Double Helix did not win the race, she did set a new Mississippi tandem-kayak record of 26 days, 6 hours and 41 minutes.

Verlen Kruger and Bob Bradford, in their Kruger Cruiser canoe, were aiming to get back the Mississippi downstream record that Guinness granted to Michael Schnitzka and Bill Perdzock of Wisconsin, who beat the Kruger/Fons record by 29 minutes in 1989.

Verlen and Bob by the mold Verlen used to make their Mississippi Cruiser *(photo by Mark Przedwojewski)*

The Kruger team was more than willing to make the effort to take back the Mississippi downstream record. Verlen Kruger and Bob Bradford headed downstream to beat the record set by Verlen and Valerie in 1984, the Wisconsin Team's record, and anything else that stood in the way of a new World Record for the Mississippi. Verlen was 78 years old and Bob was 58. They left Lake Itasca the morning of May 5, 2001, with four other competing teams, all of whom were paddling kayaks. Some key competitors involved in the 2001 race, though they wanted to win, also wanted Verlen Kruger to regain his record!

Verlen's partner, Bob Bradford, said, "When Verlen invited me to partner with him for the 2001 race, I wasn't sure if I should. I knew of Verlen Kruger, but I also knew he had invited Steve Landick first. Steve couldn't go because he is a middle-school math teacher and could not take a month off during school. I had never paddled a Kruger Cruiser and it seemed to me to be a big boat. I went over to Verlen's and we launched in the snow from his river bank onto the Grand River for my first trial run in a Kruger Cruiser. Then I borrowed Verlen's old green Cruiser and my son and I paddled it about 300 miles up the Au Sable and down the Manistee Rivers here in Michigan. Then I paddled with Verlen twice more. He can stay right in time with you. I'm mostly a bow paddler and Verlen is real smooth. That's all it took to convince me. During the race, Verlen took the stern all the way to the Mile Zero marker with me in the bow. It was an adventure!"

Team Kruger and Double Helix above St. Louis *(photo by Stan Hanson)*

Though Steve Landick was unable to join Verlen as a paddling partner for this race, he showed up at Lake Itasca to be the official starter of the race. Since no one brought any black powder weapons, Steve inflated a paper bag and burst it with a dramatic loud pop for the official start. It worked. Stan Hanson said it was with a wishful expression on his face that Steve watched the competitors pass him and move on down the Mississippi.

(l to r) Stan Hanson, Mike Bradford, Bob Bradford, Janet Bradford (Dare Mighty Things T-Shirt), **Terry Norris, Nancy Norris, Jenny Kruger** *(photo by Verlen Kruger)*

Bob Bradford continues, "We left in May of 2001. That early in the year, on the big lakes you must cross in Minnesota, it is very cold, especially at night, and big winds can pick up from out of nowhere very quickly. The ice had just gone out, in some places it was still going, and you could not fall into that water without being a goner. Until you near Minneapolis, there are no lights to navigate by and it is difficult not to become lost. Without a map, compass and navigator, which Verlen was superb as, you simply wouldn't make it. Being lost at night is not life-threatening, but it is very frustrating because it slows you down in a race. I got lost on Rice Lake, in northern Minnesota, in the middle of the night while Verlen slept.

Team Kruger exiting Mississippi culvert shortly after start
(photo by Jon Young)

Team Double Helix at the headwaters of the Mississippi, awaiting launch
(photo by Lib Eid, courtesy of dreamkeeper.org)

He was a much better navigator than I and he always seemed to be able to feel where we were. I didn't want to wake him so I wasted over a half-hour paddling into dead end bays."

Bob continued, "As you progress down the Mississippi, the traffic increases dramatically. More barges and tugs, more recreational craft, more locks and dams, all combine to make your days more complicated. Being with Verlen, who had been through it all before, was a big plus. I learned a lot from Verlen. I had never canoed through a lock before, so Verlen made that easy. The water was so high that many of the locks were closed. There was enough water going over the spillways so many of them could be paddled right over. We'd usually talk to the lockmaster via radio and ask what kind of a drop we should expect in the river level as we passed over it. They would say things like, 'Oh, a foot or two,' and we were never sure what to expect. One night, while Verlen was asleep, I paddled over one that must have suddenly dropped about two feet. I couldn't believe how hard we hit. Verlen never woke up! Of course, we always had our spray-cover on at night to keep us dry and warm.

"Floating logs, trees, and debris were always a hazard. Sometimes they were so difficult to see at night that we would run right into them. Fortunately, they were traveling at the speed of the downstream current, which made it easier to extricate our canoe from those situations. We hit some nasty barge traffic, but we kept in touch with those barge captains via radio. They were very helpful to us, always describing how they would negotiate the next bend in the river, whether they would pass others to port or starboard, and they would even inform each other where Verlen and I were on the river. You never want to get on an outside bend of a big riverboat or barge. It will kick up a huge wave a few-hundred feet behind you that will tip you over when it reaches you," Bob went on. "We always tried to stay on the inside of barges on the river's bends.

"Verlen had Stan Hanson, our shore-crew captain, communicate with the locks and some of the tug-boats so they would always know where we were. Verlen, Clark Eid and Stan Hanson had done such a good job of alerting them along the downstream route that when we talked to them via radio they would respond, 'Yep, we knew you would be right along here somewhere. How are you doing?' Then you would hear one captain saying to another captain,

'Watch out for the canoe racing to the gulf!' and then they would give our approximate position. It was a great help and gave us confidence when negotiating the barge traffic. "

Bob smiled as he discussed Verlen. "He was so good natured that it made it easy to be with him. We never argued, just had fun. He was so upbeat, real positive and he just enjoyed being out on the river. I would watch him day after day, hoping that I would be of a similar nature and still paddling when I became 78. I'd ask him, 'What do you think of this situation Verlen?' He'd say, 'It doesn't get any better than this!' We had to have exchanged those exact words at least forty times during our time on the Mississippi.

Team Kruger enthusiasm shows up on the road team's wheels *(photo by Stan Hanson)*

"There were so many things that made Verlen a great partner. First, his experience on the Mississippi. He knew his way around. Then, his experience as a marathon paddler allowed Verlen to know how to pace. He always said, 'This isn't a race. It's survival!' We beat the old record by 39 hours in elapsed time, though we didn't win back the record because of the time the Coast Guard and Corps kept us ashore. That's no small accomplishment for a 78-year-old man! We were disappointed that the local authorities, Coast Guard, and Corps stopped us. They felt the high flood waters were too dangerous for us to be paddling in. Verlen and I felt unthreatened by them and wanted to maintain the substantial lead we had built up. We knew, however, that each of these government agencies had their own responsibilities to be enforced as they understood them. We acquiesced to their wishes, but didn't like it. Verlen simply understood the task and goal, and his use of the time and distance schedule enabled us to know exactly how we were doing all the way down. He also knew how to husband his energy. He called it, 'Getting the most from the least, the rule of maximum efficiency.' He would dole out his energy, never squander it in a short spurt, and he knew how to capitalize on psychological opportunities to influence the competition as well. I was amazed at how he kept up to our pace."

The portage below Blanchard Dam was very difficult *(photo by Stan Hanson)*

Bob added, "Verlen is famous for his nightmares. He is always dreaming about past encounters with bears and can get a little rambunctious when dreaming. Everyone who has ever slept with their tent near Verlen's can vouch for his dreaming in action. I can also vouch for the fact that he does exactly the same thing even when sleeping in the bottom of a canoe on the Mississippi."

"We had such an awesome road-crew! Stan Hanson, Jon Young, Mick Wood, Chuck Hasencamp, Dana Hanson and my son Mike and daughter Angie and my grandson, Michael, who passed away from ALD, was also out there with us then. We tried to make contact and stop with them between 30-mile and 60-mile intervals, more often 30. We usually saw them every 4 to 5 hours. Sometimes we would go ashore, but often would simply use the bathrooms, grab our food and hop back into the canoe, eating as we paddled. That was our call, Verlen and I. It depended on how we were feeling at the time. If the crew advised that a contact spot in the next fifty miles did not look possible due to flood conditions, we'd stop right away. That way we could replenish supplies, eat and take a break, and then get into a longer run. It was their advice on shore conditions that enabled us to keep pace with our time and distance schedule, which Verlen had laid out.

Rett supporters surprised racers repeatedly near New Orleans to cheer them on (photo by Clark Eid)

"The road-crew always adapted to our needs. No one can ever beat the standing records without a very good road-crew. Verlen and I are good paddlers and that's what we prefer to do. Stan Hanson, having been a career air traffic controller, knew how to make things happen. He could get locks to open, permission for portages, coordinate the press. Jon Young was right there too. While Verlen and I would eat ashore, Jon would empty the boat, clean it of candy and snack wrappers, dry it out and fill it up again ready to go. Verlen always encouraged a clean, dry canoe when he left shore. He felt it had to do with comfort, convenience, and your attitude while paddling. Jon made sure that happened throughout the trip. When we came ashore wet, we'd find our sleeping bags had been replaced with

Clark Eid sleeps beneath bubble as Kurt Zimmermann paddles his shift (photo by Johann Fembek, courtesy of dreamkeeper.org)

dry ones. Chuck, Mick, and Dana were the same way. Each had things to look after. As we'd paddle from shore back onto the river, everything had fresh batteries, had been fixed or replaced, and we were back in the condition we started the trip with at Lake Itasca. We used one headlight all of the time we paddled at night. When one went dim we'd switch to the other. Each time we were ashore the batteries had to be replaced."

Bob continued, "Food is very important on a marathon. I would average about 10,000 calories a day, and do that by eating every four hours, whether ashore or in the canoe. Verlen ate a little less because his metabolism is different than mine. In between those regular 4-hour meals, we would snack as the urge struck us. In the canoe, we always had water, juices, snacks of energy bars, candy, etc. Each time we made contact, the crew would hand us new snack bags for the bow and stern and retrieve our waste bags. Verlen has a unique pallet. I have never seen a man consume pancakes and macaroni and cheese as he does. His 'your stomach is a furnace' theory doesn't hold up in the court of nutrition, but it sure seems to work for him. Because of the amount we were both eating, bathroom stops and waste removal occurred regularly four times a day. That's mandatory when consuming close to 10,000 calories a day. Stan Hanson kept Verlen happy by cooking sausage or bacon and tall stacks of pancakes smothered in butter and syrup!"

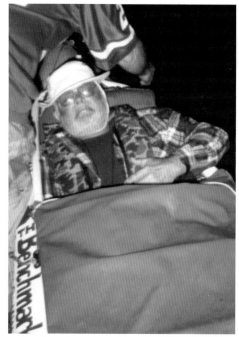

Mick tucks Verlen in for the rest of the night while Bob paddles on *(photo by Stan Hanson)*

Because of the extreme high water on the Mississippi during the race, the Corps of Engineers, which manages the dams, and the Coast Guard, which monitors safety practices on the River, caused some delay to all teams. Nearly all of the locks and dams to St. Louis were closed due to high water. The teams actually paddled over the tops of some of the dams at night. Then the safety officer, who had been recommended to race officials by the American Canoe Association to ensure it was a safe event, stopped the race for nearly two days. During that time, of all teams, only Double Helix was able to catch up with Team Kruger. The first delay was before the St. Anthony Falls Lock and Dam in Minneapolis where they were forced to overnight before the Coast Guard and the Corps gave the ok to continue. The second delay was at Dubuque, Iowa, where the Coast Guard had closed the river. They spent two nights on shore before they got the ok to continue, providing that Team Kruger and Double Helix (the only two teams that had made it that far south by then) agreed to paddle together until they reached St. Louis. Beyond that last dam they could race again and separate as the race dictated. If they would agree to that, they would allow them back onto the water. All agreed, and they started paddling again. The third delay came a little later when a local Sheriff forced the

Bob saying goodnight; Verlen paddles on during his shift *(photo by Stan Hanson)*

two teams off the river and made them overnight on shore before letting them go the next morning. The two teams paddled together to St. Louis, where the race began again.

Clark Eid said, "It was a lot of fun to paddle against Bob and Verlen. Much of the time was like playing 'cat and mouse,' always wondering where the other team was. The record flooding conditions of 2001 complicated the whole race, and we were forced to travel together from Minneapolis to St. Louis. However, this unity helped Verlen get through a rough section where his health slipped and he was going to quit. It was a race, sure, but more important was the fact that it was a charity event and we had become close friends." So friendly was this race after St. Louis between Double Helix and Team Kruger that, at one point, Clark and Kurt held back on their paddling for several hours at Nauvoo, Illinois, while Verlen recuperated from a stomach problem. When Verlen was feeling better, the race resumed.

Double Helix crosses wake of *Ambassador Norris* (photo by Johann Fembek, courtesy of dreamkeeper.org)

At the Mile Zero marker in the Gulf of Mexico, Verlen Kruger and Bob Bradford were plucked from the water at 10:51 pm on Tuesday, May 29, 2001, by the crew of the 55-foot fire boat, *Authority II*, and treated to a Cajun style champagne celebration. Ron St. Germain continued to write update articles for the Lansing State Journal. Stan Hanson, the team captain from O'Fallon, Illinois, was quoted by St. Germain, "This has been a once in a lifetime experience, but right now maybe we all just need some sleep." Their time for the 2,348 miles had been 24 days, 17 hours, and 51 minutes, which was 32 hours short of the Wisconsin Team's existing World Record. Verlen Kruger and Bob Bradford also broke the mark as the oldest tandem team to canoe the entire Mississippi River. Their combined ages totaled 136 years. At Nauvoo, Illinois, Verlen said that, for the first time, he might be willing to admit that he no longer belonged out there at his age, but he rebounded after dinner!

At the end of this race, almost immediately after the celebration, Verlen Kruger was hospitalized. He had been wrestling with prostate cancer for about eighteen years by then and the medicines he was taking caused him to retain water in his system toward the end of the race. He was hospitalized for about twenty-four hours and lost over thirty pounds of water.

Clark Eid commented, "I was very happy that Bob and Verlen finished. They and their support team were well organized all the way through." Stan Hanson of the Team Kruger road

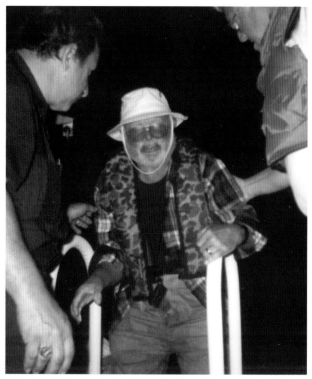

Verlen climbs from the Cruiser to the Mile Zero celebration boat about midnight *(photo by Jenny Kruger)*

Verlen and Bob posing with deckhands of the welcome boat, *Authority II* *(photo by Stan Hanson)*

crew said that there were occasions when they had invited the Double Helix paddlers into their trailer for shelter and rest, had fed them, and helped them to relaunch to chase Team Kruger. "Double Helix was the fastest boat out there, but also needed the most in terms of shore support—a bit of a double-edged sword there."

Clark continued, "What most impressed me about Verlen Kruger was that he helped my family by being part of both our 2001 and 2003 charity events. One of my favorite thoughts of Verlen would be that he lent me a helpful hand (and paddle) when others would have dismissed my ideas as being crazy and foolish."

Bob Bradford and Stan Hanson *(photo by Jenny Kruger)*

The Great Mississippi River Race for Rett Syndrome was summarized in a final press release in May of 2001: "Two Teams Survive World's Longest, Toughest Race. In true 'survivor' form, two teams of undaunted paddlers finished the longest non-stop canoe/kayak race in history when they arrived at where the Mississippi River enters the Gulf of Mexico, ending an epic journey of 2,348 miles that encountered everything from exhaustion to some of the worst flooding on record. Team Kruger, led by the renowned Verlen Kruger, placed first in their specialized canoe at 24-days, 17-hours, 51-minutes. Team Double Helix,

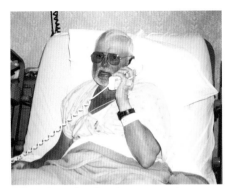

Verlen talks with well-wishers in New Orleans while hospitalized after finish *(photo by Jenny Kruger)*

The paddlers of Team Kruger back home *(photo by Janet Bradford)*

featuring the event's unique flagship kayak called the Double Helix, placed second at 26-days, 6-hours, 40-minutes. Team Alaska, who replaced a kayak lost in a rapids, remained on the river 707 miles short of the finish. Two other teams had withdrawn from the race after the first week. Special U.S. Coast Guard permission was granted to travel on otherwise 'closed' sections of the river. Unfortunately, negotiations for this cost the racers at least two days. The U.S. Corp of Engineers also permitted several locks and dams to be safely navigated by going over their spillways. Foul weather, combined with the unusually high flow rates, at times generated extraordinary paddling conditions. Although all paddlers experienced some physical trauma, only two required temporary hospitalization."

An article in the Delta-Waverly Community newspaper said, "Team Kruger's experience and familiarity with their equipment gave them an advantage." Verlen Kruger went on to say, "The average person doesn't know what makes the difference. Of course the other team was better, they were faster, stronger, a better team. But they didn't have the right boat." Kruger noted all of them prepared well for the event; short-distance racers would not have shown so well. "After 24 hours, it's a whole different ball game. You have to regroup your resources and try to find something that's in you. Sometimes it is, and sometimes it's not. There were times when I had to find something bigger than myself," he added. "There's no doubt in my mind at all that I wouldn't have done as well without prayer. I get a lot of spiritual help. Mankind is more than just a physical being—we also have a spiritual nature, and you can draw strength from that."

If the time they were forced off the water by the Corps of Engineers and the Coast Guard is deducted, Team Kruger beat the standing Wisconsin record by roughly thirty-nine hours. They didn't apply for the new World Record, though, because it would not be fair to do so since they were allowed to rest during the fifty hours they were held ashore by authorities. Instead, they began to plan a brand new effort to break the record. The new team intended to do it with a more dramatic margin and in a diligently recorded manner, which would be welcomed by Guinness.

Author's Note

The Double Helix, the flagship of the event, will be on permanent display at the Morial Convention Center in New Orleans starting in the summer of 2006.

About This Special Charity Event

The Great Mississippi River Race for Rett Syndrome, May 5–31, 2001, was an international charity event designed to raise awareness and research funds for Rett Syndrome. All proceeds generated in association with this event are directed toward the Rett Syndrome Research Foundation, whose website is www.dreamkeeper.org.

Rett Syndrome is a rare and devastating neurodevelopmental disorder affecting approximately one in 10,000—15,000 live female births. The majority of cases are caused by a spontaneous genetic mutation of the MECP2 gene, located on the distal arm of the X-chromosome, discovered in late 1999 by Huda Zoghbi and colleagues at Baylor College of Medicine in Houston. Girls with Rett Syndrome develop normally until they are between 6 and 18 months of age. They then stop learning new skills and enter a period of regression, losing speech and fine motor control. Most girls experience a cognitive decline and develop seizures, repetitive hand movements, irregular breathing, and severe motor apraxia. Severe scoliosis and muscle wasting often cause these girls to be confined to a wheelchair.

Pre-race celebration gathering. Amanda Eid sits on her mother's lap in the middle bottom of group. *(photo by Clark Eid)*

"About the great Mississippi River Race.
This isn't a race, it's survival."

VERLEN KRUGER

The Mississippi River Challenge for Rett Syndrome and Leukodystrophy, 2003

The Great Mississippi River Race of 2001 was such a success that founders Clark Eid and Mary Potter decided to get another one going. It would start in May of 2003. This time, it would be a dual charity event, with proceeds going to both Rett Syndrome and Leukodystrophy research.

Leukodystrophy is a group of demyelinating diseases, of which multiple sclerosis is probably best known. Verlen Kruger's partner for The Great River Race, Bob Bradford, had two grandsons diagnosed with Adrenoleukodystrophy (ALD). The oldest, Michael, who had been part of the shore crew for the 2001 race, passed away in 2002, less than a year before the 2003 challenge. Approximately one in 100,000 boys is affected by ALD.

This 2003 attempt to break the existing Mississippi River record would involve Verlen Kruger in a different manner. At age 81, Verlen would be Race Director and a member of Team Hope's shore team, which was again captained by Stan Hanson, veteran of the 2001 attempt. The paddling team would be probably the strongest to ever attempt it: Bob Bradford and Clark Eid. They had both paddled the Mississippi's full length in the 2001 event, Bob with Verlen in a Kruger Cruiser, and Clark with Kurt Zimmermann in the Double Helix racing kayak.

Backing them would be the most experienced shore team ever assembled for the Mississippi. That crew consisted of Stan Hanson, Dana Hanson, Jon Young, Janet Bradford, Denise Bradford and Mike Bradford. Dana Hanson acted as webmas-

Verlen with apprentice, Mark Przedwojewski, finishing Rett Cruiser (photo by Bob Bradford)

ter backup, when needed, and did much of the update writing for the website and sent news releases to Mary Potter, Clark Eid's wife and the webmaster for the event. Andrew Gribble also supported the team and had the primary task of documentation and GPS support for the website. Team Hope's shore-team members volunteered not only their time during the race, but the preparation time as well. The Hansons and Bradfords volunteered their personal vehicles for road crew use from the Canadian border to the Gulf. Additional support came from Kenton Spading, Clark's former college roommate, who was the official Army Corp of Engineers liaison for the race. Also helping the team were Bill Pullen, a retired police officer from St. Louis, Tony Swenson, a friend of Clark's from his hometown, and Angie Phelps, Bradford's daughter, her sons, David and Jacob, and her daughter, Jessie. At the beginning of the race, they also had some temporary help for a few days from Tammy and Bob Hanson and their daughter Rachel, who has Rett Syndrome. Tammy Hanson coordinated the Minnesota kick-off dinner in Bemidji, Minnesota and, Desiree Loeb-Guth, whose daughter, Lisette, has a form of ALD called Canavan Disease, coordinated the celebration dinner in New Orleans. Individuals too numerous to list here generously donated cash for gasoline for those vehicles. Bob and Clark assumed all costs and work not covered by sponsors to outfit the race boat and an identical backup Cruiser. Team Hope and sponsors also put out a special thanks to Verlen Kruger and Mark Przedwojewski, of Kruger Canoes, for building the two race canoes. This was a truly tough team of paddlers and support and they were all joined at the hip for this record attempt!

Bob Bradford takes delivery of Rett Cruisers for Mississippi *(photo by Mark Przedwojewski)*

Clark Eid and Bob Bradford on Mississippi below Itasca *(photo by Stan Hanson)*

Stan Hanson organized and scheduled the shore crew throughout the route and was always amazed at support of parents of children suffering from Rett Syndrome or Leukodystrophy. When they stopped on May 26 in Louisiana, about 30 parents and several children in wheelchairs showed up on the waterfront to cheer them on!

This was Team Hope. Their goal was to beat the previous Guinness World Records set in 1989 by Bill Perdzock and Mike Schnitzka, and the one set in 1984 by Verlen and Valerie Fons. This time they intended to take the record back, in a Kruger canoe, and do it with a substantial margin of time, documented beyond question.

Their hope was that the publicity generated by their efforts to regain the Mississippi Guinness title would also lend attention to the ALD cause, just as it had for Rett Syndrome in 2001. It did. In that race alone, over $35,000 dollars were raised for the ALD fund. All of the expenses of the race were donated by the participants, including the shore and support crews. Not one penny of ALD or Rett Syndrome donations was used for any of the Race costs.

With Verlen aiding them in the preparation of their planned time and distance schedule, Clark and Bob continued to train prior to the race. As they practiced, Stan Hanson and some of the shore team worked on logistics, planning, and sponsor acquisition. By launch day Stan had contracted with more than 22 sponsors.

Though Team Hope had seen it before, the Mississippi River is a fascinating route. Verlen, at 81, said, "It is my favorite river in America. I never tire of it. There is so much action!" The river's channel constantly changes from weather, flow, and volume of water. Even with today's technology, its length varies depending on who you listen to. According to The Mississippi River Challenge for Rett Syndrome website, the Itasca State Park at the Mississippi's source says the Mississippi is 2,552 miles long. I-Survey has published a number of 2,300 miles or 2,320 miles long, and the Mississippi National River and Recreation Authority says its length is 2,350 miles. As it leaves Lake Itasca, its width is only 20 to 30 feet with a depth of less than 3 feet. In New Orleans, its depth reaches 200 feet. At Lake Itasca, the average flow rate is 6 cubic feet per second; at New Orleans, it is 600,000 cubic feet per second. The river drops some 1,475 feet to sea level at the Mile Zero marker. The website also points out that the race route begins at Lake Itasca in northern Minnesota and ends ten states and 2,348 miles later in the Gulf of Mexico. This was Team Hope's route and challenge.

Team Hope's start was at 6:00 am on May 10, 2003, from Lake Itasca in the rain. Despite very low water conditions (about a fifth of the 2001 water flow through Minneapolis, according to the U.S.G.S.), they made good time throughout the day. Bob and Clark were a balanced team in Verlen's opinion. He said, "They were balanced in so many ways, physically, equally tough, equally experienced, and equally motivated by their causes, their children, as well as equally frustrated by their failure to break the Guinness record during the 2001 attempt. I had zero doubt that they would substantially beat the old record. This was a tough team, and they had the right boat. Comfort will make a huge difference to Clark in this attempt." Verlen did have his biases, but they were based on experience. Verlen also felt Clark would find using a bent-shaft

Bill Pullen, member of Team Hope, helps ready the canoe
(photo by Angie Phelps, courtesy of dreamkeeper.org)

Allowing them to launch without him was the hardest for Verlen
(photo by Angie Phelps, courtesy of dreamkeeper.org)

Oh, how he wanted to be in that canoe! *(photo by Janet Bradford)*

canoe paddle less stressful than when he paddled Double Helix in the 2001 event.

After that 6:00 am start on May 10, 2003, the paddlers and road team poured it on! The website updates and personal accounts for the next eighteen days looked like this:

May 10: Race start, 6 AM sharp, at the Headwaters of the Mississippi River, Itasca Lake Park, Minnesota, weather a little rainy, paddlers made good time through the initial sixty-five miles of swamps. It became cold and rainy in the evening. Covered one hundred miles in first twenty-four hours. Still intend to both stay awake until past Lake Winnipeg, then one paddler to take sleeping cycle while other paddled. The choice of who would do what would wait.

May 11: Rough overnight crossing of Lake Winni (the one on which Clark referred to wishing he had his kayak paddle). Paddlers are at least twenty miles ahead of 1984 record. While Verlen and Janet Bradford search Lake Winnibigoshish's black and windy surface for canoe lights around 2:00 am, Clark Eid watches bow paddler, Bob Bradford, go under water as they surf down the wave they are riding and plunge into the one ahead. Clark said Bob was totally underwater when the lights blew! Lake Winni is famous for its venturi winds that wreak havoc on much bigger boats than a Cruiser. As conditions worsened in the middle of the night, Verlen was very worried about them. Clark and Bob were not sure how far away they were from becoming a statistic.

By recording their daily GPS readings at scheduled daily times (GPS didn't exist during the 1984 record settings), and comparing them to the detailed records provided by Verlen and Valerie's record, they always knew where they stood with regard to breaking that record.

May 12: Bob takes the first sleeping break after leaving Lake Winni dam. After thirty-three hours of continuous and hard paddling, Clark begins to hallucinate, so he takes a nap for three hours while Bob paddles. Then, after another twenty hours of strenuous paddling, he said he really began to see some interesting things, like the faces of old men in the riverbank and Star Wars figures standing on the shore!

May 13: Dana says the paddlers are over a hundred miles ahead of the record by this evening. Verlen Kruger gives some great advice about getting over the Diversion Dams.

May 14: More paddlers join in and paddle with Team Hope to the Twin Cities, MN. Cold rain all day pushes Bob to hypothermic status. Had to fight high winds all day and Clark misses another sleep cycle. The whole team stops at Ken Ketter's Canoes for a short break. Paddlers nap on shore and then continue on to arrive at the first Lock and Dam at midnight.

May 15: The Lake Pepin daylight crossing is very smooth, but little or no current. Weather overall good. Verlen left at Sauk Rapids. Had to go home for medical attention and prostate treatments.

May 16: Through Lock and Dams 5, 6, 7, 8 and 9. Still well ahead of the 1984 record despite low water levels.

May 17: The paddlers record video and audio en route and average over one hundred miles per day through Lock and Dams #10, 11 and 12.

Team Hope's Bradford and Eid with Rett Angels in Bemidji, MN
(photo by Angie Phelps, courtesy of dreamkeeper.org)

May 18: Clark says they are now over 150 miles ahead of the 1984 record. The team gets more media coverage. Angie Phelps and gang are leaving the road crew but will be back for the end. Don Bradford, Bob's brother, shows up for moral support. Portaged Lock and Dam #16 in Muscatine, Iowa, by dragging canoe a couple hundred yards.

May 19: Team Hope is at least through Lock and Dam #20, maybe 21, by the end of this day. Paddlers are requesting ice, it's getting hot. Clark is taking sneaky pictures of Bob for the website 'later.' The crew pulls together with the help of tug boat captains and the Lock and Dam #20 master and let the paddlers go ahead of a couple of tugs with their barges. Bob clips a buoy as Clark sleeps.

May 20: 190 miles ahead of the 1984 record in the morning. Very windy conditions. Rudder cable snapped at night, during a storm, and while we were trying to outmaneuver a barge and tow! Paddled over the top of Dam #25 in afternoon.

Bob Bradford paddled bow the entire race
(photo by Angie Phelps, courtesy of dreamkeeper.org)

May 21: While paddling in for a pit stop, a two-foot fish jumps into Clark's lap in the canoe! Dana Hanson and Jon Young join the road crew. Over 200 miles ahead of the 1984 record.

May 22: 409 miles ahead of the 1984 record. The Coast Guard is calling and wants updates as the paddlers go through New Orleans. Arrived at Tiptonville, Baton Rouge, found ferry landing very flooded. Mike and Denise arrive. Lots of flooding going on, so it's hard to meet the paddlers. Janet's van punctured a gas line on a remote road. Paddlers arrive in Memphis, Tennessee, at 3:00 pm.

May 24: Bob is clocked paddling 10 mph solo! Bob and Clark are 556 miles ahead of the 1984 record. Clark avoids a tug and barge traveling upstream over flooded land!

Clark paddled stern *(photo by Angie Phelps, courtesy of dreamkeeper.org)*

May 25: Lots of floating debris during night.

May 26: 600 miles ahead of the 1984 record. Baton Rouge or bust. Bets are being taken for final time estimates. The paddlers are too fast to catch. Clark and Bob averaged 160 miles a day for several days in a row! Coast Guard Cutter escorts canoe through Baton Rouge.

May 27: Desiree has joined the road crew. Paddlers are facing heavy fog this morning. In section between Baton Rouge and New Orleans, heavy barge traffic encountered. Clark hates this section and thinks that no small craft should ever be permitted there. The barges are getting nasty, winds are high, waves are rough.

May 28: Arrived at Mile Zero Bay after an intense night. Sprinted last ten miles. 2003 record set at 18 days, 4 hours, 51 minutes!

The new World Record had been established by Bob Bradford and Clark Eid. Team Hope had beaten the record by 5 days, 5 hours and 29 minutes. It meant a great deal to all of Team Hope's members that Verlen Kruger was their inspiration, advisor, and enthusiastic supporter of their cause of Rett Syndrome and Leukodystrophy. All this had been accomplished during May of 2003, the worst recorded month of May on record for tornadoes, and record low-water levels on the upper Mississippi. The paddlers had nothing but praise for their shore team.

Team Hope during shore lunch
(photo by Angie Phelps, courtesy of dreamkeeper.org)

Stan Hanson, captain of the shore team, said, "Verlen Kruger always expected his records to be beaten and was always willing to try to take them back. That's what canoe racing is about. Beaten fairly, within the framework of the rules and documentation, Verlen Kruger would always have been the first to applaud anyone who beat him."

On September 1, 2005, according to the Guinness website, Clark Eid and Bob Bradford were informed by Guinness that they had indeed been issued a new Guinness World Record for the Mississippi River. That record stands at 18 days, 4 hours, 51 minutes. It was accomplished in the identical canoe hull with which Verlen Kruger and Valerie Fons set their record in 1984.

Bob Bradford writing in his journal before paddling on into the night (photo by Stan Hanson)

Verlen Kruger was pleased to see the new record.

"That's what records are all about," said Verlen. "Now let someone else work on beating this 2003 record, playing by the same rules with which it was set. I will be the first to congratulate them if they win using them." Verlen always expected records to be beaten. He knew if challengers adhered to the same parameters of performance that he had when he set them, many of those records would stand for some time because he knew what it had taken to establish them. He knew that even his 100,000-mile mark would eventually be taken by someone. (He even thought some of them were predictable. Steve Landick, Verlen's UCC partner, has accrued more than 70,000 miles and is still a young man by Verlen's standards.) "But," he said, "it may be a while before someone takes up the Grand Canyon from Steve and me, or up the Mississippi." Those who knew Verlen well were never surprised at the help and information he would freely give to anyone he considered a valid challenger, even those who might take his records from him. He loved competition and respected the results it produced.

Clark established another record with this event. I believe he is the only man who has paddled the entire Mississippi top to bottom, in both a kayak and a canoe, with both a double kayak paddle and a single canoe paddle. With that experience, he makes some interesting comments.

May 13, Little Falls Dam. Donita Baker brought pizza and pop. Her twin daughters have Rett Syndrome. *(photo by Angie Phelps, courtesy of dreamkeeper.org)*

Clark said, "For me, the biggest difference between using a kayak paddle versus a canoe paddle dealt with nerve compression in my hands. (I also feather my kayak paddle, but have never had a problem with my wrists or shoulders.) You don't change your grip holding a kayak paddle and after 500 (continuous) miles your hands become off-and-on numb. At the end of the 2001 race, my hands were always numb, and it took 2 months for the feeling to come back. No numbness developed using a single-blade paddle in 2003. I also prefer a single blade for the ability to change grips on a long run, but I'd switch back in a heartbeat to a double blade in rough water. In 2003, Bob and I had to deal with massive waves on Lake Winni, using single blade paddles. I recall twice that I had to throw my torso into a towering, rear-quartering wave as a crude high brace because my paddle was on the wrong side at the time."

Verlen never argued about a double kayak paddle being better in rough conditions; in fact, he praised Steve Landick's superior abilities with one on many occasions during the UCC. He did in fact try kayak paddles on numerous occasions, but found he preferred a canoe paddle. His bias was, over long-distance, a kayak paddle was physically more stressful, especially on a newer paddler, than a single canoe paddle. Verlen said, "Over a long haul, a kayak paddle can really tear you up." Verlen felt that many choose a kayak over a canoe because it is cool, rather than beneficial to a marathon paddler. Even he felt that a kayak going by with synchronized kayak paddle strokes looked cooler than a canoe.

Finish line at Mile Marker Zero! *(photo by Bill Pullen, courtesy of dreamkeeper.org)*

Clark was experienced, highly trained, and physically adapted to the kayak stroke, which, at the time, he preferred over a canoe paddle. He also felt at the time, the kayak stroke would prevail over the canoe. He still feels that was a possibility without other conflicting idiosyncrasies of the 2001 trip. Clark also bears out Verlen's long held theory of comfort being one of the mainstays of successful marathon racing. He readily admitted to more comfort in the Cruiser than in Double Helix.

"In regard to contrasting my two runs, it isn't fair to draw too many hard and fast conclusions. The race itself is extremely complicated on many fronts. Different partners with different skills, different boats, different paddles, different road teams, different weather. For instance, there's a good chance we could have beat Bob and Verlen in 2001 if our road crew had just kept together on the lower Mississippi." Clark went on, "Kurt and I also took more time out from the race to meet with families en route, at one point traveling twenty miles farther than Bob and Verlen to do so, because we were more tied into the charity aspect of the event (naturally). Also, Kurt and I elected to keep back and keep together with Team Kruger when Verlen's health failed at Nauvoo, Illinois. What would have been the result if we had said goodbye to them at that point? So many things to consider. Verlen's canoe was much easier to sit and sleep in than my kayak was, but mine was far faster, but that depended on who was paddling and at what time"

Success! A new World Record for Team Hope. *(photo by Bill Pullen, courtesy of dreamkeeper.org)*

Bob, Stan and Clark at post-race celebration in New Orleans
(photo by Janet Bradford)

Clark ended with, "So again, it is hard to do a direct head to head comparison between the Kruger Cruiser with canoe paddles, and the Double Helix with kayak paddles."

The ongoing discussions about kayak versus canoe and kayak paddle versus canoe paddle will likely go on for some time.

Bob Bradford's second grandson, Justin, sitting in grandpa's bow seat *(photo by Angie Phelps, courtesy of dreamkeeper.org)*

Michael G. Bradford
December 21, 1987
August 30, 2002

God's Garden

God looked around His garden,

and He found an empty place.

He then looked down upon this earth

and saw your tired face.

He put His arms around you,

and lifted you to rest.

God's garden must be beautiful,

05.28.2003

Bob stayed motivated with encouragement of grandson's photo on bow deck. (Note shadow of Bob's head and cap.) *(photo by Andrew M. Gribble)*

"The secret is circulation. Get your body moving and you will feel lots better. Tiredness is a residue in the muscle system. Increasing the pumping action of the heart rejuvenates the body."

VERLEN KRUGER

Yukon Odyssey

Back together, Verlen and Jenny's relationship thrived. Verlen's apprentice, Mark Przedwojewski, said Verlen always talked about another paddling adventure. He wanted to do a big one with Jenny. He began to talk about the Yukon again and finally decided, with Jenny's enthusiastic approval, to invite all the people for whom he had built canoes to join him for the Yukon Odyssey in 2002. This canoe trip would transit the Yukon River from its source in Carcross in the Yukon Territory to the Bering Sea. It would be a 2,080-mile, 84-day canoe trip, a flotilla of Kruger canoes, with an eightieth birthday celebration for Verlen Kruger in Dawson City on the Yukon. While he and Jenny had done a good deal of paddling together, Jenny had never done a trip of this length. Verlen wanted her beside him on the entire journey. He decided they would each paddle a Sea Wind, catamaraned together, for comfort and convenience. Jenny was seventy-five at the time. About twenty-five people committed and ultimately nineteen showed up in Whitehorse for the group meeting in the Robert Service Campground before the trip. There were seventeen Sea Winds, one Dream Catcher, and one Kruger Cruiser, as well as two Chesapeake Light craft kayaks and their occupants at the meeting. Eight of the group, due to lack of time, would end

Dan Smith leading "North to Alaska!" *(photo by Ron Bolt)*

Signpost village, Yukon Territory *(photo by Stan Hanson)*

Loaded in Whitehorse for shuttle to Carcross, the Yukon River source
(photo Jenny Kruger)

Yukon Odyssey (l to r) Nick Newhouse, Dan Smith, Ron Bolt, Chris Adolph, Steve Newhouse, John Young, Brandon Nelson, Jim Witinski, Mel Herrera, Verlen Kruger, Dan Pahman, Mark Przedwojewski (above), Jenny Kruger, Stan Hanson, Emily Drouin, Andy Witinski, Joanne Peterson, Phil Peterson, Bernie Bast *(photo by Phil Peterson)*

The Yukon Odyssey team takes a break in Liard Hot Springs for an IQ test (l to r) Jon (hear no evil) Young, Dan (see no evil) Smith, Ron (speak no evil) Bolt *(photo from Kruger Archives)*

Brandon and Heather Nelson married after the Odyssey. He raced this kayak in the Yukon Quest a few days after this picture. The following year they circumnavigated Lake Baikal in Russia. *(photo by Verlen Kruger)*

their participation in Dawson, roughly 550 miles into the trip. The others would go on with Verlen and Jenny to the Bering Sea. My wife and I joined them for as far as Dawson. We, too, couldn't steal enough free time for the whole trip.

One of the neat things about tripping with Verlen was the type of people that were attracted to the trips. Verlen's rule was that everyone was independent, that is, responsible for themselves. This meant that each member was fully equipped to separate from the group for a day or two at a time if they chose, or were forced to do so by weather or storm. Each had their own gear, water source, food, first aid, maps, compass, GPS, and whatever else they would have brought had they started the trip alone. By establishing that degree of independence, no one was responsible for anyone else. Even though most of the time the group was together, or within several hours of each other, they were on their own. The other rule was that if you did plan on separating, you told others in the group so no one would worry about what happened to you.

That's how it worked. And we did have people forced to separate from the rest of us by high winds on Windy Arm above White Horse on the Yukon. It took them a day to catch up after winds forced them ashore on an island and remained too strong to launch again until the next day. During the evening mealtime, you would see seventeen different people cooking their own meals. Sometimes those meals would be shared as in a smorgasbord, but each took care of them. Knowing that each was capable of self-care and of sustaining themselves for the entire trip created a freedom for everyone. No one was burdened with the needs of another, yet would leap to help any at any time with whatever they were doing. At lunch stops, most were quick to share coffee, a snack, or a taste of their latest creations, but if the need for space from the group arose you might not see them for a day or two. If an illness or an emergency requiring more than first aid occurred, people would rally as needed. It was as though these rules had been set up by a master of the rivers. They worked.

In some towns, the local press would pop up in the camps to interview Verlen. Many had seen him on his earlier trips on the Yukon, so it was almost like a reunion. Local radios did interviews and newspapers wrote stories. Verlen treated Jenny like royalty, as he had since they remarried. Each night the group would muster to help erect the palace, which housed Verlen and Jenny. It was the largest tent on the Yukon Odyssey and one that everyone on the trip learned how to pitch before reaching the Bering Sea. After the tent was up, Verlen would go off in the underbrush with what looked like a camouflaged turkey stand. It turned out to be the ladies' room.

"German" Chris Breier in his inflatable stealth-boat paddled partway to the Bering Sea with Verlen and Jenny and the Odyssey crew *(photo by Stan Hanson)*

(When nature called, the men of the Odyssey would quietly and casually drift off into the brush on what everyone referred to as a "morel hunt." During the 2,080-mile event, no one ever returned with any mushrooms.)

Author's wife Joanne, a.k.a. "Wildflower of the North," taking a rare nap *(photo by Dan Pahman)*

"Wildflower," Jenny, Verlen and Phil say goodbye in Dawson
(photo by Jim Witinski)

Yukon scenery, Verlen and Jenny under sail *(photo by Dan Pahman)*

Passing by the unique variety of Yukon scenery *(photo by Stan Hanson)*

Nick Newhouse takes a break *(photo by Dan Pahman)*

Verlen never unhooked the two Sea Winds from catamaran configuration because, he said, "I wanted Jenny beside me from start to finish." Consequently, he paddled harder than any other paddler on the Odyssey. During some of the first days, Jenny would sometimes rest, but Verlen always paddled. Jenny, however, got tougher every day. Before the Yukon Odyssey group reached Dawson twenty days later, most had acquired photos of Jenny paddling while Verlen napped! One day, we stopped at a riverside tourist resort. Verlen and Jenny were bringing up the rear and, as they reached our location, the current tried to sweep them on downstream. There was a tiny island about fifty feet off shore. Verlen quickly turned the catamaran in beneath the end of the island, aimed upstream and allowed one hull to be on each side of the slipstream of current leaving the bottom end of the island. Then he casually paddled upstream to the end of the island, made a 90-degree turn toward us, shot across the downstream current, and landed right beside our boats on the shore. We had all expected him to be swept a couple of hundred feet down below us. No one could read the river better than Verlen and he always knew what to do with it.

Each time we camped, or passed a historic spot, cameras came out and paddlers would try to casually have their photos taken with Verlen and Jenny. There was a lot of hero worship, disguised by all of us present as, "Oh, I don't know why I came. I just thought it would be fun, I guess." The truth was each of us owned Kruger canoes. We had bought them because they were designed and built by *the* Verlen Kruger, and we were each now paddling the Yukon River with that Verlen Kruger. We were all where we had wished we could be as we read about his life and adventures over the years. Jenny even wrote a letter to each of us that signed on for the Odyssey and in it said, "He's always been my hero, too!"

Each day, some would spend time paddling with Verlen and Jenny, asking questions they always wanted to ask. When the answers would come from Verlen, everyone leaned in close to hear. Verlen didn't talk a lot, but when he did, everyone listened.

When on the Yukon, or elsewhere in Alaska or Canada, he often dreamed of bears. One day, over lunch on the shore, Jenny told us, "Don't be alarmed when you hear Verlen at night. He'll be dreaming of bears." One night, my wife and I had pitched our tent near Verlen and Jenny's. In the middle of the night we awoke, sitting up with a start, to hear Verlen bellowing, "G'wan, get out of here!" Then, "Get! Get outta here!" even louder. Then, a calm voice said, "Verlen, Verlen, you're dreaming again." Then it was quiet. Having read of, and heard Verlen's bear stories, his nightmare wasn't a big surprise. Some of those who paddled the Mississippi with him and the support team talked of Verlen's dreams as well. Both Bob Bradford, Verlen's paddling partner, and Stan Hanson, of the support team, have told me stories of Verlen becoming active during a dream and actually taking a swing at the sleeping body next to him. Nearly everyone on the Yukon Odyssey heard Verlen hollering at bears at sometime during the trip, and usually in the middle of the night.

Verlen didn't get his feet wet on the whole trip! (photo by Dan Pahman)

Verlen spent an enormous amount of time paddling alone throughout his life. Yet, he enjoyed company. It is my judgment that he preferred good company when available, but never let the lack of it stop him from going. Being alone didn't upset him. When paddling alone he would manage to find others to talk to along his path. Usually, people along the rivers had already heard that he, or he and

Bernie Bast and Dan Pahman wondering where the mosquitoes went (photo by Jenny Kruger)

Dan Smith chasing frogs (photo by Jon Young)

a partner were coming. There was always someone ready with a question and Verlen was always ready with an answer. He was a good listener, too, and gave his full attention. He listened more than he spoke. It was the lifetime learner in him. He knew everyone had a story; by listening to them, he was learning. He was never bored—ever—and had little patience with those who were. "How can you be bored," Verlen would say, "when you are surrounded by life? If you look, you see, if you listen, you hear, and you are surrounded by

Jon Young filtering the daily water *(photo by Stan Hanson)*

Jim and Andy Witinski breaking camp *(photo by Jenny Kruger)*

Lunch by a native fish wheel; (l to r): Jon Young, Dan Smith, Dan Pahman, Nick Newhouse, Mel Herrera, Jenny Kruger, Verlen Kruger, Chris Adolph, Steve Newhouse *(photo by Stan Hanson)*

The "Ladies Room" being set up by Mel Herrera, Dan Smith and Verlen *(photo by Jenny Kruger)*

things to see and hear." He used to say his thousands of paddling miles gave him opportunity to think more often and deeper on any subject, and he would often rethink the same things through again and again. He felt most people on the treadmill of society didn't have much time to just think. They were moving too fast and didn't have the free time a long-distance paddler did to ponder. 100,000 miles of paddling, portaging, and camping-time, at an average of three miles per hour, equals at least thirty-three-thousand hours of thinking time.

The young and restless, even some of the old and restless of the Odyssey usually wanted to go faster, or farther, than Verlen seemed to want to go. Some, who had barely squeezed enough time from the demands of their other lives, were concerned they wouldn't reach Dawson in time to catch their scheduled transportation home. When they would express their concern to Verlen he would simply respond, "We'll make it as scheduled." We were dealing with a master of time and distance schedules. In addition, Verlen knew that as soon as we reached the end of Lake Laberge, the river current, in what the old river boat captains called the thirty-mile, would grab us and increase our average speed by some four miles per hour. We reached Dawson with time to spare.

Verlen and Jenny paddling hard, still headed north (photo by Jon Young)

Bob Vincent and Bob Bradford won the 2002 Yukon Quest in an 18-foot Jensen canoe (photo by Jenny Kruger)

The mayor of Dawson gave Verlen and Jenny the Key to the City and held a party for his 80th birthday (photo by Stan Hanson)

In Dawson, the mayor gave the Key to the City to Verlen and Jenny, and threw a birthday party with cake and goodies for the general public by the waterfront. While we were in Dawson, Verlen's former Mississippi partner, Bob Bradford, and his fellow paddler, Bob Vincent, paddling a Jensen 18 tandem canoe, placed first in the Quest race from Whitehorse to Dawson.

Verlen and Jenny checking in at Dawson's historical house of ill repute *(photo by Stan Hanson)*

The mayor of Dawson put Verlen and Jenny into the rumble seat of the same type of car used for their first blind date *(photo by Stan Hanson)*

Brandon Nelson and John Weed placed second, but first in the kayak class. The Odyssey group was there to cheer them all in. Then we all took up a collection and rented Verlen and Jenny a room in a former historic Dawson Brothel for the night. The next day, Verlen and Jenny were guests of honor in the rumble seat of an old Ford coupe in the annual Dawson parade.

The Yukon Odyssey continued from Dawson. Over the next sixty days, they encountered everything the Yukon offers. Hot, cold, wet, dry, bugs, wind, sandstorms, mud, bears, combined with one of the most beautiful rivers on earth. Verlen broke a tooth, requiring a two-day visit to the nearest dentist. He and Jenny also were able to visit their youngest daughter, Sarah Sparkes, with her husband and children, who had moved to Fairbanks, Alaska. This dental trip and visit occurred while the rest of the Odyssey party camped where the Prudhoe pipeline crosses the Yukon. They found it to be a big mess, so while

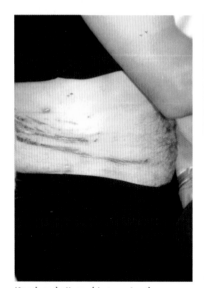

Kayak cockpit-combing was tough on the hide for bow paddler John Weed
(photo by Jenny Kruger)

Brandon Nelson and John Weed reach the finish line of the 2002 Yukon Quest in second place *(photo by Jenny Kruger)*

They made it! *(photo by Verlen Kruger)*

Chris Adolph and Nick Newhouse towing Verlen and Jenny into headwinds. They thought they might miss their plane at Bering Sea. Verlen said he could never figure out why they were in a hurry. *(photo by Verlen Kruger)*

waiting for Verlen's return, staged a two-day clean up and celebrated with one of the largest bonfires ever held at that location! Some of the Yukon crew described a dust storm, which incapacitated most of their tent zippers and infiltrated all of their gear—both inside and outside the tent. Progress slowed to a snail's pace as they neared the Bering Sea due to headwinds. Soon some of the paddlers again began to worry about reaching their destination in time to catch the chartered flight that was to return them to Whitehorse. At one point, there were two Sea Winds towing Verlen and Jenny's catamaran, which by then had been nicknamed the Love Barge. Verlen continued to advise they would be on time, but tolerated being towed for half a day. They were on time. Getting all those Kruger boats into the aircraft proved a task, but all were deposited in Whitehorse at the exact time planned. That trip will forever be one of the highlights of the lives of those who attended Verlen's Yukon birthday party.

Quiet Water Symposium Verlen Kruger Award at Michigan State University, in March of 2003 to Yukon Odyssey group (some missing). This award is now an annual event.
(photo by Terry Norris, courtesy of Kruger Archives)

*"Tough, fast, capacity, diverse,
seaworthy, comfortable."*

VERLEN KRUGER

Verlen Kruger and His Canoes

Verlen continued to build and sell Kruger canoes in Michigan. He never really wanted to be a canoe designer and builder. He had drifted into the field when he and his canoe racing partners could not find the canoes they wanted commercially available. As his exploits and reputation grew, however, more and more people began to ask him to build them a custom canoe. He became known among his following of trippers and wannabe-trippers as the builder of the toughest canoes made. That reputation is intact today. At first, each was a custom model with new ideas Verlen periodically added. As the demand grew, Verlen recognized the need to standardize the line of canoes he would offer and to establish pricing at which he could afford to sell them. His standard line became the solo canoes called Sea Wind and Dream Catcher, and the tandem canoe called the Kruger Cruiser.

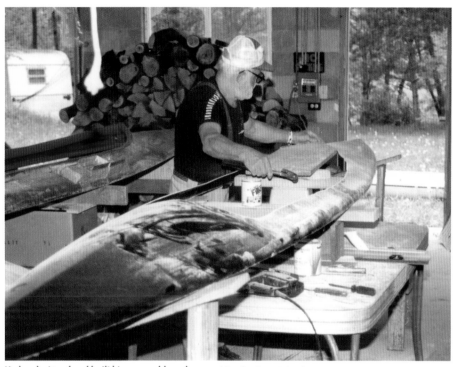

Verlen designed and built his own molds and canoes (photo from Kruger Archives)

The reason Verlen designed his canoes into their existing configuration was because he had paddled and tested them himself for thousands and thousands of miles. He tested his canoes more thoroughly, and for greater distance, than most canoes are ever paddled. Much of Verlen's design talent came from the combination of studying nautical design and his flight training, which taught him about friction, flow and drag. Then, the thousands of hours of paddling in all conditions gave him the intense hands-on focus that made his canoes so practical. Verlen said, "First they must be fast. Second they must be tough. Third they must be seaworthy and capable of handling the roughest of waters. Then, too, they must be efficient, thus the incorporation of rudders. It is crucial that they have adequate capacity to easily store and locate, as needed, their 300 pounds of gear." Eventually, he moved comfort way up on his list of canoe attributes needed for a good tripping canoe. Weight, contrary to designs of canoes commercially available, was not as high on Verlen's

KRUGER CRAFTED

The Kruger Crafted logo with a Monarch butterfly
(photo from Kruger Archives)

Early Sea Winds were built in a variety of colors *(photo from Kruger Archives)*

list. He knew that to provide speed, toughness, seaworthiness, efficiency, capacity and comfort, his canoes would have to be a little heavier.

Initially, he built with fiberglass, but as soon as Kevlar became commercially available he began to use it almost exclusively. He used a lot more Kevlar than most manufacturers. Usually, it is formed on each side of a foam core—composite sandwich fashion—made famous by the Gougeons of Michigan who pioneered so many of the glassing techniques of the boating world. Verlen, however, did not want a foam core in his boats because of his demand for toughness. His boats were all hand-laid of Kevlar and used up to twelve layers. He wanted canoes that could be dribbled on the rocks by the waves. "You never know when weather and sea conditions will try to snatch your canoe from you as you make landfall or launch." Verlen said. "Bringing in a 300-pound canoe onto surfing rocks is no easy task. Tripping is not casual paddling and you must be able to deal with whatever demands the environment makes upon you and your canoe. You are always into new surroundings where you don't know the safest routes to take. It is easy to get into more trouble, when trouble is what is already forcing you ashore. When you are blown off the water, and must make landfall to survive, you don't get to pick the soft, sandy little spot you would normally seek to beach your canoe. You make do with what you find and your boat must survive whatever that is."

Verlen was planning his Paddle-to-the-Sea Venture when he added words to the bottom of his Sea Wind: "Please put me back in the water." *(photo from Kruger Archives)*

Verlen and his partners had abused his boats in the worst of ways. His canoes had been buried for the winter atop the Chilkoot Pass of Alaska and pitch poled end-to-end down surfing beaches, even while catamaraned. They had been slid and dragged over rocks down mountain passes, often while fully loaded with gear. His canoes, containing not only the paddler but another 300 pounds of gear, were dragged ashore, sometimes on sand, sometimes mud and grass, but often sharp and jagged rocks. Verlen had seen his canoes, even when loaded, blowing about on the shores of a Chilean lake like a kite and then landing again on rocks. All of these happenings dictated the design and construction of Verlen's canoes, which are built for tripping. Thus, the toughness of Kruger canoes.

Finally, he wanted his canoe to be quick and easy to load and unload and to carry on the portages he was so famous for. (Verlen Kruger has portaged farther than most will ever paddle.) The November/December 2005 issue of Paddler Magazine said it best when they compared four of today's best decked touring tripping canoes. They said that Verlen's Sea Wind, which is still sold today as it was designed in the early eighties, was "the most fully outfitted boat on the market." They continued on to say "the seating comfort was superb," and that it had "cavernous storage," "bombproof construction," and more. They described it as "the only portage-friendly boat." Not a bad evaluation of a twenty-five-year-old design. They finished with, "He (Verlen) called it the ultimate tripping canoe. He was right."

Verlen felt his original Loon lacked adequate buoyancy aft, so over the years, added volume and buoyancy to his new designs. The Sea Wind, which had the same hull water-line as the Monarch, but more internal space beneath the decks fore and aft, had more buoyancy than either the Loon or the Monarch. The Sea Wind provided more internal storage and what he considered ideal buoyancy. Eventually, he made Sea Winds available in either shallow or deep versions, preferring the deep hull himself when tripping. He felt the hulls to be equal in speed, but was willing to sacrifice the slight additional windage the deep hull had for the additional space it provided inside. Mark Przedwojewski says the shallow versus deep Sea Winds now sell about 50/50.

Early designs used a single cross arm to catamaran. All now use two.
(photo from Kruger Archives)

While Verlen built some great racing canoes, they weren't for tripping. He wanted as much of the speed of his racers designed into his trippers as possible. Verlen and partners established eleven Guinness World Records in Kruger canoes that he designed.

Seaworthiness of his designs also came from practical experience. During those thousands of miles of hands-on paddling, Verlen's mind was honed to produce some of the most seaworthy and practical canoes afloat. The bow, cockpit, and stern decking arrangement, with the spray- and wave-deflecting cockpit combing, made for a dry boat. The ability to cover the elongated comfort cockpit with both soft and hard coverings (hard for open sea) made them even more weather resistant. Keeping water out of the boat at sea was always a priority. Seaworthiness also demands a low center of gravity, which in all Kruger canoes is provided by the height-adjustable, tractor-style seats. Three optional seat heights can be chosen, based on the water conditions. That low center of gravity minimizes the likelihood of capsizing. Verlen also designed his boats to be slippery. Paddling troughs, with the waves abeam, is a pleasure in a Kruger boat. As the approaching wave lifts your canoe, the boat just slides sideways, down the sloping, fronts of the waves. Verlen designed his canoes to have everything rounded, no sharp edges or angled chines for waves to grab. It is also said by those who paddle Verlen's designs that the more weight put into the craft, the better they handle. Adding foot-pedal rudders to aid crossing currents of wind and water also ensures that each of the thousands of paddle stroke efforts goes exclusively to propulsion and not to steering, which adds efficiency to seaworthiness.

The top Sea Wind is the deep hull, higher capacity version Verlen began making in 1997 *(photo from Kruger Archives)*

Another seaworthiness addition was the ability to join Sea Winds into a catamaran on demand. When the weather becomes threatening for single Sea Winds, they can join with the connecting sleeves of each boat, converting them into a single catamaran. The Kruger design enables hooking up Sea Winds without corrupting the water-shedding spray covers on each boat. This catamaran capability has saved Verlen and partners from threatening weather on many occasions. It also provides the opportunity for one partner to sleep while the other paddles, and to cook and prepare meals on the water.

Then there was the comfort issue. Verlen Kruger was recognized as one of the best marathon canoeists in the country long before he began to build canoes. As canoe racers and associations began to zero in on what made canoes go fast, they seemed willing to sacrifice anything they could to make the canoe go faster. Canoe racers are a tough breed of folk. Comfort, on a canoe race, is one of the last things they expect to run across! As new designs evolved, they became more like spears than boats. Their narrow beams left inadequate space for the paddlers to sit upon and were only precariously balanced upright when underway with paddles stroking. New rules evolved to try to bring standardization into racing designs, just as they did in sailboat racing. As new rules surfaced, racing canoes were warped and tortured into some pretty strange configurations, which all bowed first to the need for speed, seldom to comfort.

Verlen did his time in the racing circuits and built racing canoes while there. As his dreams began to grow, his practical mind was seeing different needs for tripping than for racing. His marathon experiences while racing in Canada showed him that comfort during a long-distance canoe trip was extremely important to the paddlers; the longer the trip, the more important comfort became.

Bob Bradford and his daughter and son-in-law admire the tandem Cruiser he raced on the Mississippi
(photo by Janet Bradford)

Verlen always said that the most important thing he learned in his military flying experiences was "The rule of maximum efficiency. The ability to get the most from the least. There is so much wisdom in that rule and it can be applied to any physical effort, mental too. It's simple: the more comfortable you are, the less energy you expend fighting discomfort and, therefore, the more energy you have to paddle, which is why you are there in the first place." Verlen used the term comfort in canoeing to cover physical comfort, as well as convenience to the paddler. For instance, the tractor seat makes your butt comfy. One can paddle with their butt in an uncomfortable position for only so long before they begin to expend energy, wiggling around a variety of muscles, trying to ease the discomfort. By adding an adjustable tractor-style seat for comfort, he eliminated the discomfort (even though it meant a little more weight to the canoe). By having an elongated cockpit, the paddler can easily change his position, stretch his legs, lie down, or anything else in that less-restricted amount of space. Verlen also designed and built rain roofs and Velcro netting tents, which kept the occupants dry and critters and bugs outside their boats while in the second continent.

Another comfort to a paddler on a long-distance venture is convenience. A long-distance race must be paddled according to a time and distance schedule. That means you cannot stop and beach every time you need to find something in your canoe. The cockpits of

Kruger canoes and their removable spray covers enable a paddler to ransack nearly the entire boat from the paddler's seat when necessary. While the decking of his canoes is in some ways similar to kayak designs, a Kruger canoe suffers none of the loading and unloading restrictions of kayaks. There are no separate watertight compartments requiring separate entry or access lids. Those conveniences are important in a marathon event, where even a small inconvenience can mushroom into a major irritation over time and distance. When that happens Verlen says, "You begin to waste energy being irritated, instead of using that same energy toward positive propulsion. I learned in combat flying if you act with maximum efficiency, the results will always improve. Most people never discover, or fail to recognize, the many ways they waste energy on whatever it is they are doing."

Verlen could go on for hours about the design technology of his craft. There were very specific reasons for every facet and feature of his boats. His designs initiated while he was paddling and were then honed into his vision of perfection in his shop. Everything about the boats was there for a reason. Nothing was done because it was traditional, nothing was built to look like something that proceeded it and everything was done to capitalize on the rule of maximum efficiency and comfort. Verlen described his designs: "The Sea Wind design and concept is a break with tradition and form. It is an innovative, functional departure from conventional ideas of what a canoe should look like and how it should be handled. In January, 1975, I designed and built the Loon. A lot of water has passed under the hull since then. No canoe was ever built with more love and personal feelings and such intense commitment to function. Function can be beautiful. Every line, every curve, every square inch from stem to stern was thoroughly analyzed, evaluated, re-evaluated and agonized over. I wanted the Ultimate Solo Canoe. I had big dreams! Above all, the boat had to be comfortable to maximize my enjoyment.

"The Sea Wind was conceived with the sound of the ocean in my ears and the feel of the

Mark Przedwojewski finishing a Sea Wind in his new shop in Irons, Michigan
(photo from Kruger Archives)

Early undecked version of Cruiser. Expedition model is decked fore and aft. (photo from Kruger Archives)

sea breeze in my face, in anticipation that this was the canoe in which I would soon be crossing the Caribbean and rounding Cape Horn. The Sea Wind is a decked canoe; consequently, it is not affected as much by the wind. The Sea Wind is more efficient and drier than an open canoe. The Sea Wind makes an excellent sea kayak. My 'canoes' have traveled thousands of miles as 'kayaks' while using a double blade. My canoes even roll quite well if the paddler encloses the cockpit down to kayak size or uses a seat belt. The Sea Wind form has no straight lines or flat spots anywhere. The Sea Wind is all curves. Curves are stronger and smoother in function. The total design is very forgiving, very stable and self-righting because of its continuous flare all the way up to the gunwale line. The rounded hull responds easily to being yanked or pried sideways to avoid an obstacle. There is sufficient curve and rake in the bow to make it self cleaning. Combined with paddle power, the Sea Wind can jump over obstructions and climb up on a beach."

Verlen never claimed to have superior designs, nor did he really care much how people felt about his boats. He always felt that kayaks would win sprints and shorter distance races. They were more streamlined, narrower of beam, and could absolutely be paddled faster for short distances than canoes.

In races like the Mississippi's 2,000 miles, he felt that most times a canoe paddle stroke would win. Verlen knew that there were kayak paddlers who were so determined to defeat his claimed canoe advantage that one day some kayaker would win long-distance races against canoes. "But," he added, "I'll bet that when that happens they will still have used more energy to do so than the single-bladed craft. At some point, they may design a kayak whose hull is so efficient in the water that the canoe stroke advantages are neutralized. Then it will be a different ballgame."

He said his later designs became almost more kayak than canoe, but he did feel the bottom portion of the hulls of all his boats started out as canoes. After all those mold changes, the bottom half of all Kruger canoes are still almost identical to the original canoes. When he would talk to kayakers, he would frequently find strongly biased arguments in favor of the kayak versus the canoe.

His argument was never canoes against kayaks. His argument was always, "Which one best accommodates the rule of maximum efficiency?" Then he would go out and paddle a few thousand miles to prove his point. Verlen applied that rule to most things he did, because it saved him time, money, effort, and energy, and nearly always produced better results.

Verlen was not a sophisticated, play-in-the-waves paddler. To whatever degree possible, he would avoid the waves. He did not have an adopted brace stroke and he didn't know how to roll—both considered nowadays to be essential to achieve the status of a kayaker. His approach was more of a blue collar than white collar style of paddling. His paddling was unendingly basic and practical. His canoes never contained a fitted cockpit area, with knee

Sea Wind #44 many years and many miles old
(photo from Kruger Archives)

and hip pads, which secure today's kayak paddlers as they "wear" their boats. It was his ultra-practical approach that sometimes frustrated Steve Landick, because Steve trained and practiced paddling sophistication, which he believes could have been easily added to Verlen's arsenal if Verlen had been less stubborn about it. In contrast, however, in terms of marathon distance paddling, Verlen was sophisticated beyond most of today's kayakers. He couldn't swim and he didn't like to get wet; he felt rolling to be impractical and unnecessary, and would seek a kelp bed to rest in rather than wrestle with waves. Yet, when necessary, he aptly wet launched or came ashore in surf in heavily loaded canoes hundreds of times. Verlen's sophistication in paddling tied to his rules of efficiency. In his thousands of paddling miles, he discovered, tested and practiced the minute, almost invisible, secret differences between the strokes using less energy per mile than the competition he left behind.

Verlen's last canoe shop. *(photo from Kruger Archives)*

He said, "Let's just talk of paddling. Generally, a double-bladed kayak paddle weighs more than a single-blade canoe paddle. If that is true, during a single day of paddling, the user lifts that extra weight on every stroke of the paddle. Sixty strokes per minute equals 3,600 strokes per hour. In an eight-hour day that equals 28,800 strokes. Just for example's sake, let's say the difference in the weight of a double kayak paddle and a canoe paddle is one ounce. During that eight-hour paddling day, the kayaker has lifted 28,800 extra ounces, which equals 170 extra pounds of weight. That may not seem like much, but it is more complicated than that. When stroking with a double kayak paddle you generally lift both arms higher than you do with a single canoe paddle and the arc of the stroke, I believe, requires more energy than the stroke of a single blade. Since each of your arms probably weighs more than your paddle and you use both of them more in a kayak stroke, what extra weight does that represent when converted to pounds through the same arithmetic and how many pounds does that equal? Add that to the extra weight of the paddle.

Verlen demonstrated one of his and Bob's Mississippi tandem Cruisers for a gentleman from Bozeman, Montana, in September of 2001
(photo from Kruger Archives)

"Through this process you can rough out the approximate number of extra pounds lifted per eight-hour day, which now is probably approaching several hundred. There are other factors too, like the number of muscles used to do a kayak-stroke versus a canoe-stroke, but it takes some study. The point I am making is that, between the kayak and the canoe paddles, one person is lifting several hundred pounds more per eight-hour day. That requires more energy. Some strong arguments can be made in favor of single bent-shaft canoe paddles in a power racing stroke versus a kayak stroke. I believe, assuming the blade surface area that contacts the water is equal in size and shape, the single-blade canoe power stroke provides more propulsion than the kayak paddle. This is another argument that will likely go on for several years. I have drawn my conclusion from the races I have been in, and won, paddling my way versus race-designed kayaks using kayak strokes, and with younger and stronger crews in them. People will have to draw their own conclusions."

Author's Note

As I wrote this chapter, Steve Landick, Verlen's former UCC partner, was again racing the Quest Race in Alaska, from Whitehorse to Dawson. He had won it more than once, paddling a Jensen 18 tandem canoe, and he intended to do it again with his paddling partner from the Texas Water Safari group. This year, however, he and his partner came in third, twenty minutes behind two racing kayaks! I anticipate there will soon be a substantial battle to make the Quest rules fairer to both kayaks and canoes regarding their water lines. It would be most interesting to see identical tandem kayaks, paddled by seasoned race teams, one with double kayak paddles and the other with single canoe paddles. Maybe some day.

"People will have to draw their own conclusions."

"It seems like the most natural thing to do. The contentment I feel while paddling tells me I am where I want to be. I'm following a dream."

VERLEN KRUGER

Friends of Verlen Kruger

During the last months I was working on this book I began to receive touching comments from people about their feelings for Verlen. I've included some here.

"Verlen had that quiet, careful attitude that encourages 'survival' when the chips are down. I wonder if people realize how significant it was that he and Clint Waddell crossed some of the most complex stretches of the Boundary Waters Canoe Area at night, with a small scale map and a tiny Silva Huntsman compass. That Verlen was a fighter pilot instructor in the days before GPS etc. prepared him well for wilderness travel."

CLIFF JACOBSON: RENOWNED AUTHOR OF MANY OUTDOORS BOOKS, RECIPIENT OF THE ACA LEGENDS OF PADDLING AWARD, GUIDE OF ELABORATE AND FAR OUT CUSTOM CANOE EXPEDITIONS, A CONSTANT SPEAKER AT PADDLING EVENTS, AND ESPECIALLY, A FRIEND OF VERLEN.

Cliff Jacobson

"When I asked Verlen what his favorite place to paddle was, he said, 'The Grand River in front of my house.' The greatest of long distance paddlers loved his home the best."

BRAND FRENTZ: CO-AUTHOR OF *THE ULTIMATE CANOE CHALLENGE* BY VERLEN AND BRAND FRENTZ.

"Verlen was always the kindest man I have ever met. He never said anything behind anyone's back or talked down about anyone. He was so supportive of anyone who showed interest in the sport of paddling. I think he often lived through those who would go off to find peace and solitude a wilderness river offers."

NORM MILLER: NORM MILLER WAS A FRIEND OF VERLEN'S FOR SOME YEARS. DURING THE LEWIS AND CLARK CELEBRATION IN 2004, HE PADDLED A KRUGER SEA WIND FROM ST. LOUIS, UP THE MISSOURI RIVER AND THE YELLOWSTONE, WHICH IS JUST ONE OF MANY TRIPS HE HAS MADE IN VERLEN'S CANOES

Brand Frentz

"During the 1993 Finlandia Clean Water Challenge, the 800-mile race from Chicago to NY, I was camped next to Verlen's tent. Early in the morning, I heard him mumbling in his sleep. I sat up to listen and heard him say, clear as day, 'I fear the seals.' He was dreaming, but it somehow humanized him even more and made his stunning journeys all the more amazing since he was, on one level, confronting the fears that limit us all. Only he didn't let it get in the way. He was and continues to be an inspiration to lots of us paddlers."

JOE GLICKMAN: JOE, WHO IS FROM BROOKLYN, NY, PADDLED FOR 800 MILES IN THAT RACE WITH VERLEN, HAS ALSO PADDLED FROM MONTANA TO CHICAGO, AND IS AN AVID PADDLER TODAY.

Norm Miller

Joseph Harwood

"Verlen was a friend of my father, and an inspiration to me. As I spent countless hours working on his portrait, I was driven to finish, knowing Verlen would never quit."

JOSEPH D. HARWOOD: JOSEPH IS THE ARTIST THAT HAS PAINTED A BEAUTIFUL REMEMBRANCE PORTRAIT OF VERLEN AND HAS CREATED THE MODELS FOR THE VERLEN KRUGER BRONZE MEMORIAL TO BE ERECTED ON THE GRAND RIVER OF MICHIGAN.

"Verlen was just plain happiest when he was traveling by canoe. Just to be moving, to see what was around the next bend, that's what he wanted to be doing. He didn't care where, or even if, he camped. He didn't seem to plan that. He just ended up, for that day, wherever, and then was perfectly happy with it. When we paddled the Yukon, he was a different man than the one I worked with in the canoe shop every day. I can't put it into words. He was just happy in a way I can't describe.

"Verlen's favorite Bible verse has impacted my life. Verlen often used his favorite quote, 'All Things are Possible with God,' to explain how and why he did what he did. Especially in times of great challenge, God was the force and energy that made it possible for Verlen to accomplish any and all of what he chose. He always gave full credit where it was due, to God. He taught me to travel as he did, and to build his canoes as he did, to high standards. All of the work I now do in life was started by Verlen. I will always be grateful for his input into my life. I will forever miss him."

Mark Przedwojewski

MARK PRZEDWOJEWSKI: MARK APPRENTICED UNDER VERLEN AND TOOK OVER THE BUILDING OF KRUGER CANOES WHEN VERLEN RETIRED. HE ALSO PADDLED THE YUKON AND SEVERAL OTHER RIVERS WITH HIM. HE IS THE OWNER/OPERATOR OF KRUGER CANOES TODAY, IN IRONS, MICHIGAN.

"From Verlen I learned that the greatest obstacle to success is the limitations that we accept, be they age, fear, or paddling up the unpaddleable river. That with preparation, perseverance and faith anything can be achieved, because something always works out."

DAN PAHMAN: DAN PADDLED A SEA WIND WHILE CIRCUMNAVIGATING LAKE SUPERIOR, THEN DID THE YUKON RIVER TO THE BERING SEA WITH VERLEN AND JENNY.

Dan Pahman

"Verlen would always go the extra mile for anyone. Even when he was in his seventies and eighties he always would try to do more than others. If we all had to pile into the back of a pickup to get to our canoes, Verlen would be one of the first to jump into the back of the truck instead of the front seat. If we had to carry, he'd pick one of the heaviest loads, even when he was older and his knees were bad. If there was a dirty job to do in camp, Verlen would be the first to have at it! He didn't want credit or recognition for it. He was always just quietly teaching others how to make things work with group dynamics. Working on the chemistry, he would call it."

"Verlen loved the long haul. Being on the water ten to twelve hours or more is what he lived for. He taught me I could do the same. A mentor in canoeing and all walks of life, Verlen was always there to help me or anyone he could. He will forever be missed. A best friend."

Dan Smith

DAN SMITH: DAN SMITH, OF PORTLAND, MICHIGAN, HAS PADDLED WITH VERLEN FOR YEARS, PROBA-BLY MORE THAN ANYONE OTHER THAN VERLEN'S PARTNERS ON THE MARATHONS. HE PADDLED SEVERAL CANADIAN RIVERS, AS WELL AS THE YUKON AND THE BUFFALO WITH VERLEN.

"Verlen has been so special in my life! As a tribute to him and my father's memory, in September of 2005, my sixteen-year-old son, Jacob, and I accompanied Larry Rice, Dan and Scot Smith, and Mark Przedwojewski on a canoe trip back to the White River where my father was lost all those years ago. My first trip there was with Verlen twenty-three years after my father's loss. This time we prayed for them both, by the same cross Verlen Kruger helped me erect in 1998. Verlen has been so special in our lives."

TODD CESAR TODD IS THE SON OF JERRY CESAR, WHOSE STORY IS IN CHAPTER SIX.

"Learning of Verlen's untiring perseverance with the paddle has motivated me to approach life's challenges with greater determination. His example helps me to focus upon goals instead of doubts and turn challenges into commitments.

Todd Cesar

BERNARD BAST: BERNIE PADDLED THE FIRST LEG OF THE YUKON ODYSSEY WITH VERLEN AND JENNY AND FRIENDS AND HAS BEEN SHOOTING RAPIDS OF CANADIAN RIVERS IN A SEA WIND FOR YEARS.

"Verlen and I were kindred spirits from different worlds. We shared a common passion and a common dream. He shaped my life in many ways... none more profoundly than by having a daughter who became my wife."

STEVE LANDICK: STEVE PADDLED THE ENTIRE ULTIMATE CANOE CHALLENGE, BOTH WITH AND WITHOUT VERLEN. THEY WERE BEST FRIENDS AND ONE OF THE STRONGEST CANOEING TEAMS IN HISTORY.

"My English writing is very very bad! Verlen did show me that All Things Are Possible, if you really want it. I was thinking to quit traveling because I thought I was getting too old, but Verlen taught me that age is not the limiting factor, it's your will. If you think you can do it, so it is."

Bernard Bast

CHRIS BREIER ALIAS GERMAN CHRIS: CHRIS HAS COME FROM GERMANY TO PADDLE THE YUKON SEV-ERAL TIMES. THAT'S WHERE HE MET VERLEN ON HIS 80TH BIRTHDAY YUKON ODYSSEY.

"Loving husband and father, obsessed and driven to explore, adventurer, writer, canoeist, visionary, designer, and photographer and lecturer. He was a wise man who was forgiving and forgiven, tough yet kind, who found and brought out the best in everyone, tolerant, a humble role model, unpretentious, thoughtful, never complained, loved and was loved, fulfilled and fulfilling,

a hero to many, patriotic, and loved God. He was my mentor and mentor to many without trying to be. He loved life to the fullest. He is missed!"

> STAN HANSON: STAN HANSON WAS THE SHORE CREW CAPTAIN, WHO SPENT MONTHS OF ACTIVITY IN SUPPORT OF VERLEN'S AND BOB BRADFORD'S 2001 GREAT MISSISSIPPI RIVER RACE. STAN WAS ALSO THE SHORE CREW CAPTAIN DURING THE MISSISSIPPI RIVER CHALLENGE FOR RETT SYNDROME AND LEUKODYSTROPHY IN 2003 (WITH CLARK EID AND BOB BRADFORD SETTING THE NEW GUINNESS WORLD RECORD) FOR WHICH VERLEN WAS THE ADVISOR. HE ALSO PADDLED THE YUKON AND BUFFALO RIVERS WITH VERLEN AND JENNY.

Joannie McGuffin

"*We camped near the Beaufort Sea with Verlen in 1986. Together we marveled at the Mackenzie River's ice breakup. Then big goodbye hugs. Verlen was heading for South America and ourselves for the Atlantic.*"

> JOANNIE AND GARY MCGUFFINS: AUTHORS OF INSPIRING BOOKS FOR THE PADDLER'S WORLD WHO HAVE MANAGED TO FILL SOME VERLEN'S BIG FOOTPRINTS WITH THEIR OWN FAMILY'S ADVENTURES!

"*I first met Verlen on the Mississippi River, with the St. Louis Arch as the backdrop, while I was poring over his river maps in 2001. It took only a few minutes of conversing with him to understand why he had such an incredible influence on people! (For those who knew him, do you hear the humble 'hnnnnnn' in the background?!)*"

> DANA HANSON: DANA WILLINGLY LENT HER HUSBAND STAN TO VERLEN TO MAKE SEVERAL LENGTHY RIVER TRIPS. SHE PROVIDED LAND AND MAP ASSISTANCE FROM ST. LOUIS TO MILE ZERO FOR THE GREAT MISSISSIPPI RIVER RACE IN 2001; SHE SAID SHE WILL FOREVER CHERISH THE PADDLE HE GAVE HER AS THANKS. DANA WAS ALSO PART OF THE SHORE TEAM FOR THE 2003 MISSISSIPPI RIVER RACE.

Gary McGuffin

"*I will miss sitting around the campfire with Verlen. He didn't talk much, but when he did, people listened. Verlen taught mostly by example. All you had to do was watch and learn.*"

> JON YOUNG: JON WAS PART OF THE SHORE CREW ON TWO OF VERLEN'S MISSISSIPPI VENTURES AND ALSO CANOED THE YUKON AND BUFFALO RIVERS WITH VERLEN AND JENNY.

"*Verlen Kruger knew how to deal with adversity, keep his spirits high, and remain composed. Making friends was his second nature. It is no wonder he is so admired.*"

> CHRIS ADOLF: CHRIS WAS A MEMBER OF THE YUKON ODYSSEY

"*Verlen's enthusiasm for adventure and passion for paddling the 'Water Highways' of the world inspired me to pursue a lifelong goal of paddling the largest lakes on the planet. That dream has now taken me around the world, paddling a number of these remarkable freshwater resources, as well as inspiring me to work with others in creating the Great Lakes Aquarium in Duluth, Minnesota. I deeply miss being able to call him and share our mutual excitement for paddling*

Jon Young

in freshwater, but often feel his presence as I gaze out across lake Superior or watch a sparkling river disappear into a distant landscape."

John Anderson

JOHN H. ANDERSON: JOHN WAS THE KEY ORGANIZER AND CO-LEADER OF THE SUPERIOR-BAIKAL CONNECT, A SEA KAYAKING EXPEDITION ACROSS THE WORLD'S TWO LARGEST FRESHWATER LAKES, LAKE BAIKAL IN SIBERIA, AND LAKE SUPERIOR IN NORTH AMERICA, AND A FRIEND OF VERLEN. HE PADDLED BAIKAL AND HAS ESTABLISHED AN IMPRESSIVE LIST OF OTHER WORLD-STATURE PADDLES, WITH THE INSPIRATION AND SUPPORT OF VERLEN AND JENNY.

"Verlen and I were both 1922-born World War II Veterans living on the Grand River, but while he paddled upstream and down in all kinds of weather, I mostly waved from the bank. The last mile Verlen ever paddled took him by my house."

JAMES WOODRUFF: JAMES WAS A TEN-YEAR FRIEND OF VERLEN'S WHO LIVED JUST UPSTREAM OF VERLEN AND JENNY'S GRAND RIVER HOME.

"Verlen was definitely the 20th Century's top Wilderness Adventurer and Canoeist. I am proud to have had the world's greatest paddler as my friend and advisor. His belief that 'God is Good' is so true. Verlen and I were indeed 'Kindred Spirits.'"

Clayton Klein

CLAYTON KLEIN: CO-AUTHOR OF *ONE INCREDIBLE JOURNEY*, THE STORY OF VERLEN AND CLINT'S EPIC SIX-MONTH RECORD FROM MONTREAL TO THE BERING SEA, AND *COLD SUMMER WIND*, BOOKS THAT MAKE YOU WISH TO PADDLE.

"Whenever a story came in about Verlen, we knew it was going to be good, something that would make us yearn to get away from our editing tasks and get outside into the wild. We'd go to him when we needed quotes about other expeditions, comments on designs, or simply to chat about the state of the sport. In January, 2000, Paddler listed him as one of 100 Paddlers of the Century, and he still belongs near the top of that list."

EUGENE BUCHANAN: PUBLISHER/EDITOR-IN-CHIEF, *PADDLER/KAYAK* MAGAZINES

"Verlen took me in the Great Mississippi River Race in 2001. With the knowledge I received from him, it inspired me to race the Yukon Quest in 2002, and to race the Mississippi in 2003 for a World Record with Clark Eid."

Eugene Buchanan

BOB BRADFORD: BOB BRADFORD WAS THE BOW-HALF OF TEAM KRUGER IN THE 2001 GREAT MISSISSIPPI RIVER RACE WITH VERLEN. HE AND CLARK EID CURRENTLY HOLD THE NEW GUINNESS WORLD RECORD FOR THE MISSISSIPPI FROM LAKE ITASCA TO MILE MARKER ONE.

"'I always laughed when those writers would call me the King of Pain,' Verlen said as I sat on the ground next to his chair, on the bank of the upper Yukon River. Jenny walked over and handed him a bowl of steaming hot macaroni and cheese. He smiled at her as if they'd just met, then

Brandon Nelson

Heather Nelson

Clark Eid

looked out over the slow moving river. 'It is not about enduring pain,' he went on. 'It is about being in total comfort.'"

BRANDON NELSON

"While Brandon sat on the ground near Verlen's feet, looking up at his hero, relishing every word, I dreamed that Brandon and I might still be out enjoying the wilds like this when we were 70 or 80-something. A King and Queen of Comfort."

HEATHER NELSON

BRANDON AND HEATHER CANOED THE FIRST LEG OF THE YUKON ODYSSEY. BRANDON AND TEAMMATE, JOHN WEED, WON THE KAYAK RACE FOR THE YUKON RIVER QUEST THE SAME YEAR. BRANDON AND HEATHER ARE ACCOMPLISHED TRIPPERS, HAVING MOST RECENTLY CIRCUMNAVIGATED LAKE BAIKAL IN RUSSIA IN 2003. VERLEN HAS LONG BEEN THEIR INSPIRATION.

"What most impressed me about Verlen was that when I called him for advice on running the Mississippi River as a charity event, he said that he wanted to be there doing it, too! His kindness helped my family and many others struggling with Rett Syndrome and Leukodystrophy. He went the extra mile."

CLARK EID: PADDLER OF THE DOUBLE HELIX RACING KAYAK IN THE 2001 GREAT MISSISSIPPI RIVER RACE, AND CURRENT CO-HOLDER OF THE NEW GUINNESS WORLD RECORD FOR THE MISSISSIPPI FROM THE 2003 EVENT.

"Verlen Kruger welcomed me to the Grand River and encouraged me as a new paddler. This began many wonderful memories. He was truly an inspiration, and I feel blessed to have called Verlen my friend."

NANCY HAMLIN ANDERSON: NANCY IS A FRIEND AND IS ON THE VERLEN KRUGER MEMORIAL FOUNDATION COMMITTEE.

"When I stand by the Erie Canal, Mississippi River, Oregon Coast, or the Phantom Ranch along the Colorado River, I see Verlen paddling by! He loved to see new places and enjoyed the serenity water imparts to a traveler. Watching Verlen paddle up the Grand River was a lesson in timing and grace. I take his zest for life on any journey I make!"

JIM WITINSKI: JIM PADDLED A KRUGER CANOE FOR YEARS AND ACCOMPANIED VERLEN AND JENNY ON THE FIRST LEG OF THE YUKON ODYSSEY.

"Verlen was just the guy Donna and I were looking for. Like ourselves, he used his wilderness tripping background as a spring board into racing. Then it was back to tripping at an elevated level."

JOHN AND DONNA BUCKLEY: JOHN AND DONNA RACED WITH VERLEN FOR MANY YEARS.

"I went from vicariously living Verlen's travels to actually experiencing them on the 2002 Yukon trip, all because he asked me to 'Come along and make the dream come true.' My hero, my inspiration, my friend... Verlen Kruger."

STEVE NEWHOUSE: STEVE, SENIOR ENVIRONMENTAL MANAGER, INDIANA DEPARTMENT OF ENVIRONMENTAL MANAGEMENT, AND NICK, HIS 25-YEAR-OLD SON, WHO SPENT THE FOLLOWING YEAR IN MILITARY DUTY IN IRAQ, PARTICIPATED IN THE YUKON ODYSSEY ALL THE WAY TO THE BERING SEA WITH VERLEN AND JENNY.

Nancy Hamlin Anderson

"I remember 'kick back, end-of-the-day campfires' when this soft-spoken man became the storyteller. Verlen passed on his own, and accrued, philosophy, mixing it in like salt and pepper with a bear encounter or two. This River Guardian will be missed."

JOANNE PETERSON: JOANNE, WIFE OF THE AUTHOR, PADDLED WITH PHIL AND THE KRUGER ODYSSEY GROUP ON THE YUKON AND BUFFALO RIVERS.

During some presentations I have made on Verlen Kruger while working on the book, I have frequently been asked, "How did Verlen's family feel about him after all that happened between he and Jenny while they were younger?" Here are some responses from the Kruger family:

"Verlen was always willing to help others in so many ways. He was a leader, and encouraged others to always do their best. He was a loving husband and father. Above all, he loved the Lord Jesus Christ."

JENNY KRUGER, WIFE OF VERLEN

Jim Witinski

"Thanks Dad, for being my father, my hero, my mentor, my spiritual guide, my brother in Christ, and my friend. I will miss you badly, until the day we meet again. Love, your son, Phil."

PHILIP KRUGER, SON OF VERLEN AND JENNY

"As a daughter, the greatest impressions my dad stamped on my life were unconditional love for family and a deep faith in God. These characteristics were exhibited through tough choices, proud accomplishments and everyday living."

CHRISTINE PROUT, DAUGHTER OF VERLEN AND JENNY

Donna and John Buckley

"Verlen was an awesome man. He has done so much in his lifetime. If you knew Verlen, you knew he loved the Lord. The love of his life was Jenny and he loved her as no other could. Their love was so strong for each other that you could see it in their eyes. He loved his family so much and he made sure his children were raised as Christians."

CONNIE KRUGER, DAUGHTER-IN-LAW OF VERLEN AND JENNY

Steve Newhouse

Joanne Peterson

Jenny Kruger

"On Sundays, Dad woke us kids by yelling up the stairs in a great booming voice, 'Everybody up, time to get up, IT'S A BEAUTIFUL MORNING!' I loved that. I still hear his voice every morning when I wake my own children. I cherish it. The older I got, the more I enjoyed being with him and the older he got, the more I was sorry I couldn't be with him more. I miss our talks, walks and teasing, but the memories I'll have forever. When canoe racing, we kids were all a part of it, cheering him from the banks! He was so involved, yet through it all I always knew he loved us."

SARAH SPARKES, YOUNGEST DAUGHTER OF VERLEN AND JENNY

"Dad, Thank you for being an example of love, kindness, patience, wisdom and stubbornness! Thank you for taking the whole family to church to hear about God and His love. Thank you for teaching us, by your example, how to give of ourselves, how to love our spouses and how to paddle a canoe! I know we will see you again in Heaven, with a paddle in your hands! Thank you, Dad, for being you. I love you. Your first-born.

NANCY NORRIS, VERLEN AND JENNY'S OLDEST DAUGHTER

Author's Note

We did not have room for all respondents, so inserted them chronologically, by date received. Sorry if you were not included.

It is difficult to find anyone who has heard Verlen Kruger complain, or be angry with someone. He knew anger was one of the least productive methods of teaching. Verlen had tremendous patience. He could watch someone new to canoeing make an error, in how they loaded, launched, paddled, or portaged. Then without saying anything, he would quietly demonstrate with his own canoe how it might be easier, more stable, faster, or safer. Where words might create resistance in the student, Verlen taught by example. Many have heard Verlen say, "The most important thing is to make the chemistry between the partners of the trip work." He taught everyone, by walking his talk.

Verlen lived beyond the norm and touched a lot of lives, some profoundly, some casually, most good, some bad, sort of like the rest of us, but far more dramatically. Even a brief and casual communication with Verlen became a moment to remember for most. People wanted to hear from him. While working on this book we would sit at his kitchen table in Lansing, listening to his response to questions. His phone would ring, he'd answer, and then you would hear, "Well, in later years I switched almost exclusively to the black graphite paddles. The Black Bart is great, and every year improvements come out. Be sure to use the bent-shaft style for ergonomics, they are more efficient and that's important." Then he'd ask, "Where are you going?" After listening to the speaker's answer, he would say, "Well I wish you the best of journeys and let me know how you come out." Then he would hang up. Jenny would ask, "Who was that?" He would say, "I don't know." Verlen always had time to answer questions he'd heard a thousand times. And, when he did, you would swear you were the first to ever ask him that question. When Verlen responded, you always received his undivided attention. Those blue eyes would be looking directly into yours and he would give you the best advice he could.

Christine Prout

Sarah Sparkes

Nancy Norris

"There's always another portage."

VERLEN KRUGER

Verlen Kruger and Animals

Early in life, while still working the farms in Indiana, Verlen Kruger fell in love with the Monarch Butterfly. He would see them occasionally come through his region on their annual migration. The Monarch migrates from Mexico to North America and beyond, while actually chasing milkweed plants, which they thrive on as food and lay their eggs on to create the next generation. That milkweed tends to be more prolific in the north, so each year, after hibernating in Mexico for the winter, millions and millions of Monarchs fly from their wintering grounds in Mexico way up into the States and the southern edges of Canada. After arriving in the north, they lay their eggs only on milkweed plants, then pass on to wherever Monarchs go when they die. New, hungry caterpillars hatch on those milkweed plants, and they start to eat. Then, they morph into Monarch butterflies, one of the most beautiful butterflies on earth, for the return trip home during August, September and October, all the way back to Mexico. An insect, weighing less than a single gram, makes up to a 5,000- or 6,000-mile migration across North America to Mexico and returns the following spring to give birth to the next generation. This is an amazing accomplishment. Verlen Kruger thought so too. He told me once, "I think I may have some Monarch blood in my veins." He loved Monarchs. So much so, that the logo for his canoes was a Monarch silhouette with the words

Verlen Kruger loved the accomplished Monarch butterfly *(photo from Kruger Archives)*

Kruger Crafted beneath the image. He placed that logo on both sides of the stern of every canoe they made over the years. He always had time to have a discussion about Monarchs and he readily used their photos in many of his presentations.

Verlen had a healthy respect for all animals and would go out of his way to avoid conflict with them. He had an above average insight into animal behavior because of his years working with animals on the farm. He was usually alert to their presence—especially bears. He didn't like what he called camp bears: the bears that had discovered food where people camped. In Alaska and the territories, there are signs that say "A fed bear is a dead bear." Once a bear finds food in a camp full of people, they will continue to seek food in the same places. Verlen felt camp bears became more aggressive after successfully attaining food in camps, more stubborn and harder to intimidate, just as farm animals can if you become the obstacle between them and the food they want. He was always on the lookout for such critters and would often avoid camping in a place if he thought a camp bear might be in the vicinity. That's one reason he had so few encounters in the large amount of time he spent in their neighborhoods. He did have some close calls though.

He loved to photograph wildlife (photo from Kruger Archives)

Verlen once paddled solo from Fairbanks to visit his daughter Sarah's homestead, 150 miles west of there, on a branch of the Tanana River. At his last campsite before Fairbanks, he camped close to the junction of the Tanana and Kantishna Rivers, on a flat spot, five or six feet above water level. He thought it just right for a small campsite and he could pull his loaded canoe right up near the tent on the grass. He tethered his canoe to the bushes with the hull about halfway out of the water, unloaded and set up camp. After a good dinner of the old favorite macaroni and cheese, he retired.

Early the next morning, something woke him. He sat up, wondering what had alerted him. He looked out through his mosquito netting door, which was facing away from the river, through an eye-level hole in the rain fly. He was face to face with a young grizzly, definitely larger than an adult black bear. The bear had his nose pushed through the opening in the rain fly and right up against the mosquito-netting. He wanted to know what Verlen was doing in there and what he might have to share in that tent. The first thing Verlen did was say, "Don't panic, Verlen!" Beside him was his bear gun. He always carried a 12-gauge with slugs, and his flare gun as well. All of a sudden, the bear looking in was pushed aside by a bigger bear, which seemed to tower above the door to his tent. Behind that one, which he thought was the mother, was another younger bear. This was turning into the story of the three bears!

Verlen never wanted to have to shoot a bear. He yelled at the bears, "G'wan! Get out of here!" but they ignored him, seeming unafraid. The two young bears were pushing each other aside to get the first look into the tent. He pointed his flare gun at the second bear, whose nose was now against the netting, but was reluctant to shoot because he did not want to injure the animal. He decided he must do something to scare them away before they got braver. He aimed a little high at the bear's forehead and pulled the trigger. The discharged flare went through the netting, glanced off the bear's forehead, and left a hole in his tent's mosquito netting! The bear didn't panic, just backed off a few feet. The larger mother looked back behind her to see that the other two were ok, but remained near the front of his tent. Verlen then lowered his voice and began to

There were frequently swans swimming in his "million dollar view" *(photo from Kruger Archives)*

just talk to the bears. He had been told once that animals did not like the sound of human voices. His constant talking seemed to back them down more than his shouting had. He had a canister of bear spray in his hand, but didn't want to use it while in the tent. The mother began to slowly back away. Verlen suspected it may have been from the flare gun's smoke, but that was only a guess.

Verlen watched as the bears seemed to circle around the campsite, then went out of sight. He immediately zipped down the tent's back door and threw everything he could into the canoe: his bear bag, the mace and the shotgun, sleeping bag mattress and the collapsed tent without rolling any of it. He wanted out of there! Then the bears reappeared on the other side of the tent's ground tarp. He left his chair and tarp at the campsite, leaped into his canoe and pushed off into the river. The tent and tarp are still there. He admits to being semi-terrified for a few minutes. After that event, he always repeated, during his slide show presentations, that people in that region should be on the lookout for a bear with a lawn chair with the name Kruger on it. Nearly everyone who has ever paddled with Verlen has heard him dreaming at night, saying, "G'wan! Get outta here!" This is the bear story that routinely inspires that same dream. His granddaughter, Jessie Sparkes, said it best with her Three Bears drawing.

Another time, Verlen was with Clint Waddell on the Grand Portage trail above Lake Superior when a black bear decided he wanted the oatmeal and raisins Verlen was about to eat on the last portage of their eighty-hour trip from International Falls. They had taken no tents, sleeping bags, or excess baggage; just the canoe, their clothing, and enough food to sustain them to Grand Portage. At the head of the Grand Portage, they built a quick fire to boil oatmeal and raisins. They had just swallowed the first spoons full when a black bear appeared and circled them, sniffing the air. He smelled raisins! The bear appeared brazen, behaving as a camp bear. This bear, however, had never run into the likes of Verlen Kruger and Clint Waddell!

Verlen and Clint found these pups during the CCCS *(photo by Verlen Kruger)*

When the bear got within two canoe lengths of them, Verlen stood up, intending to reverse the intimidation, but the bear slowly continued his approach. When Verlen did not back down, the bear stood up. They were eyeball to eyeball, about twenty feet apart, and Verlen was not going to give up his breakfast. Clint, whom the bear hadn't seen yet, made a move that attracted the bear's attention. As the bear realized there were two humans to deal with, he stopped his approach. Verlen threw a sizable branch at him, which spooked the bear into a short run, but he continued to circle their location, growling and grumbling all the while they finished eating. Finally, when Verlen and Clint resumed their portage, the bear disappeared into the woods.

Verlen has always kept his food away from bears, instead of keeping bears away from his food. Contrary to most modern bear advice, he did so by keeping much of his food either in his tent, or in his boat. He and Clint almost regularly ate their evening meals within the tent to get away from mosquitoes, but never had bear problems during the Canoe Safari. He felt his presence in the tent most times kept them away, and that he could scare more aggressive bears away from his tent if necessary. He has had occasional "whops" to the side of the tent, sniffing around the edges, and bear

Yukon black bear *(photo from Kruger Archives)*

tracks around his tent in the morning, but no bear has ever aggressively entered his tent. He felt hanging food in packsacks in trees simply advertised its presence, as the aromas wafted on the wind from the treetops to attract more bears. Even "bear-proof" containers don't always keep bears out. It was his opinion that people were the biggest deterrent to bears. When considering the incredible number of miles and days Verlen paddled and camped, it becomes difficult to say he was absolutely wrong in his rationale.

He felt that in bear confrontations, there is fear on both sides. He learned early on the farm that there were benefits in being perceived as the alpha male and dominant participant in animal/human confrontations. He demonstrated his dominance by reacting with the confidence of being unafraid and in charge, which in the military is sometimes called command presence. Verlen always kept this reserve arsenal of shotgun, flare gun, and bear spray in what he called his bear bag (on the Yukon he carried two bear bags) for that extreme emergency in which command presence might fail him. He never had to fire a shot other than that single flare, but came close a couple of times. He felt there was usually some form of bluff charge by bears, sort of a trial approach to measure effect, to see if you will resist. Then he said, most times the would-be attacker backs away from the perceived alpha dominance. (It is important to note that this was how Verlen felt about him handling a bear confrontation. He did not suggest that others do it. And he never criticized modern day bear advice.)

Right or wrong by today's standards, Verlen's critter rationale enabled him to do his incredible miles and years without more encounters and more serious outcomes. He never made claims that his approach was better and should be used by others. He simply did what he thought was best for him and his paddling partners. Verlen took risks, but he always thought they were risks he understood

This swan attacked Verlen all summer long until the county removed it from the Grand River (photo from Kruger Archives)

Early morning moose on the run (photo from Kruger Archives)

"Man has a spiritual side.
Much strength can be gained from prayer when needed."

VERLEN KRUGER

The Last Portage

Matthew 19:26, Mark 10:27 and Luke 1:37 refer to Verlen Kruger's favorite Biblical quotation, "All Things Are Possible with God." In the middle age of his life, he frequently displayed his faith in this scripture by displaying "All Things Are Possible" on his tripping canoes. He frequently used this quotation when he autographed posters, books, and other items. He believed so strongly in this quote, he seemed to demonstrate proof by things he accomplished. He seemed to believe in it even more strongly toward the end of his life.

Whenever he spoke or received an award or honor, he would quickly pass on the credit to his higher being. His World Records, his Guinness, his accomplishments, his reuniting with Jenny, his reconnection with the family, and his continued adventures late into life with Jenny, were his proof in his belief.

Not all of his partners shared his deep faith. Verlen knew this, but was also aware each of his partners was a Christian before they tripped. With Clint or Steve, he generally prayed alone, only praying aloud at meals, which all partners accepted. Each of his partners gave him all of the space he needed, and respected his faith. Verlen returned that space and respect in mutual fashion. He understood that religion is a very private thing with some.

As a child, Verlen's parents were not Born-Again Christians. His dad was neutral, not a practicing Christian. Verlen did have some experience with praying, though. His mom would encourage it at bedtime with, "Ok kids, say your prayers." Bedtime prayers were something he and Jenny continued daily while raising their own family.

Bow of one of Verlen's early canoes *(photo from Kruger Archives)*

While in the military, Verlen was not a practicing Christian, but his mother's encouragement to pray stuck with him. When he was in his older teens he would occasionally pray for and about things. "He didn't know his Lord then as he does now, but he did get baptized while a teen," said Jenny. From that time on, he prayed when he felt he needed to, even though he really didn't know how. He said he taught himself to pray, as he taught himself most things, and also discovered his feelings of response to prayer. He continued on with what he was doing with greater faith after praying. If he felt he did not receive a response, he still felt he had been heard.

While in the service, he began to read the Bible on his own. He shared a room in the military with another serviceman whose father was a minister. That roommate, though the son of a minister, was not a practicing Christian. Verlen wound up motivating him to pray and to become a Christian. Verlen read the Bible and other literature on world religions while in the military. When he returned to the states and married Jenny, he tried to encourage Jenny to pray with him in their home. She really wasn't yet into it to the degree he was. She had never been encouraged by her parents to be a practicing Christian, but she had been "saved" as a teen at an evangelical service, but then kind of let it go. She was a bit more cautious than Verlen's normal 120% approach.

While attending a local Lansing Church, they eventually became Born-Again Christians, a common occurrence in the Baptist church of those times. Jenny said, "The year after Verlen got out of the military (1948), Verlen and I attended the Walker Bible Church. It was there that Verlen was saved, or born again, and I rededicated my life to the Lord. About two months later, and on the same day, Verlen and I were both baptized again!" From then on, their lives changed dramatically. They could pray together, and as they raised their nine children, prayer at meals and bedtime was a constant in their family life.

Dreamcatcher hangs in front of "million dollar view"
(photo by Phil Peterson)

Mark Przedwojewski, who apprenticed with Verlen first, then later purchased and managed his canoe business, said, "Verlen always told me, especially in times of great challenge, that God was the force and energy source of his strength that made it possible to accomplish what he did. He said, 'It makes a difference who is important in your life. I have always been drawn to Jesus, out of respect and admiration, not just doctrine. If your heroes are the right people, you behave better. But, as hard as I have tried to practice accordingly, I have still made some grand mistakes!'"

When Verlen prayed and asked for guidance, he felt he always received it. Prayer gave him confidence and made him trust his own judgment more. After praying, he believed the Lord would not let him take the wrong steps, though he admitted some of his personal choices went far astray. Just the act of praying, and the time it took, focused more time and attention onto whatever he was thinking about. Whatever feedback Verlen received through prayer was adequate to cause him to pray with regularity and intent throughout his life, and to pass that practice on to his children and friends. When he raced the Mississippi at age 78 and needed more energy midway through the challenge to continue, he prayed, and received it. He said, "Without that help, I would not have finished that trip."

Verlen prayed quietly, humbly, and unobtrusively in restaurants, bars, roadside inns. I watched him quiet a roadside pub in Alaska, while many were drinking beer and talking. Verlen prayed, the bar quieted, until he finished saying grace over the meal before us all, then resumed their normal behavior. No one was offended, many bowed their heads in participation, those who you might guess likely never prayed, were quiet until he finished. He didn't wear his religion on his sleeve, just calmly witnessed in his own way. It was often refreshing to see his faith in operation in public.

Verlen was willing to accept the risk, and pay the price it would cost, to reach the goals he dreamed of. "Show me a man who has made no errors and I'll show you a man who is doing nothing." He and his canoeing partners took risks, but they were calculated risks. Verlen was not a gambler.

What Verlen called his "million dollar view" from his office at Kruger Base on the Grand River
(photo by Phil Peterson)

He felt everyone needed a supreme being. He never wanted to go with a partner who did not have a supreme entity, a higher authority, to fall back on when needed. Collectively aiming at a higher cause leaves less room for immediate and local concerns. He never faulted other religions or flaunted his over others. Verlen's relationship with God seemed to transcend any single denominational approach. He, in fact, had been at considerable odds with his own church over their feelings about the Ultimate Canoe Challenge when they wanted him to cancel the trip. He felt it was God who was encouraging him to go, as his church stripped him of his deacon's status for not staying home. Verlen never changed his mind about that situation, even after it separated him from Jenny for twelve years; when they remarried, it was in a different church.

One thing Verlen never did was blame anything that happened to him on God or anyone else. He owned his own mistakes, all of them. Sometimes you hear "God caused all of that to happen and I've always wondered why," but not from Verlen. Verlen wanted no part of an easy escape from personal responsibility. He believed God offers choices to all, but he also felt those choices are made by us. In his UCC book, he spoke of his involvement with Valerie Fons, which ultimately separated him and Jenny: "I have to say that, in my obsession with continuing the trip, I did not see the personal ramifications of taking on Valerie, who had been unacceptable to my partner Steve from the first time they met. Personally, I say, this was the worst decision of my life. The whole thing was wrong. I knew better. But the trip was warping my judgment. And that was the biggest mistake I ever made."

What a disappointment it would have been had Verlen blamed God for those errors. Verlen may have seemed borderline-hypocritical with the conflict that developed between his professed Christian beliefs and his own broken commitments during what he called his "crazy years." It was a many-year paradox during which he could not see the trail of debris behind his route. And he did not see it until the same thing happened to him. But he blamed only his own obsessions, no one else.

The sign that still hangs above Verlen's home-base deck on the **Grand River** *(photo from Kruger Archives)*

Verlen knew he was dying of cancer for years. He just never knew how fast it might come. He actually fought it for nearly eighteen years. During the last three or four years, his visits to the doctor increased, as did his medicines, headaches and pain. He hid it well from most. But his faith never questioned his status. One day, we were working at his kitchen table when I said, "Verlen, how are you feeling?" He said, "It's difficult to know how I'm doing right now. All these doctor visits and medicines, but I never come away from the doctor knowing any more than when I went in!" He sensed my concern about how long we had to finish our work and wanted to give me an encouraging answer. He said, "I'll fight this thing as long as I'm able, but if God wants me now, I'm ready."

With everything he was going through, his faith was never shaken. He absolutely believed. He was Verlen Kruger.

I asked, "How would you like to be remembered?" He gave me that blue-eyed look, then said, "I haven't done any great things for mankind. No one owes me anything. I do hope I'm remembered for trying to get people to appreciate the rivers of earth, to care for them, to not pollute them. My canoeing accomplishments, while unique, are no great gift to anyone, but should prove insightful for some. I don't think I can explain it to people any better than those who climb Mt. Everest can, but those people can probably understand why I did 100,000 miles of paddling."

Kruger Base in high flood on Grand River *(photo from Kruger Archives)*

Verlen always felt he was destined to accomplish something more. Many were fascinated by his amazing confidence and philosophy because they knew some of what he had already accomplished. They wanted to know how he did it. They wanted to be around him, to learn from him, and to perhaps attempt similar things themselves. They believed he was capable of more than most. They expected more from him, and more from themselves when they were with him.

He believed in lifelong learning. In an interview with *Heron* magazine, he said, "The concept of lifelong learning is more than a concept. It should be what everyone experiences. By learning, you continue to live. It's like life itself. It seems to be one of the principles of life. If you don't use it you lose it. You either grow or you dissipate, largely by choice, rather than just that some people do and some people don't." Verlen tried to teach that a full life comes from making a decision to have it. He observed that many do not make a choice about life, but rather simply accept it as it comes. The older he got, the more he appreciated his favorite teacher and that message she drummed into him: "You can!" Verlen felt people should recognize the opportunities that surround them. Those opportunities should not be avoided because they are hard or difficult; the difficulty is their price. But if people pay it, they get to have the results of those opportunities.

He would laugh when he spoke of the number of times he had been told, "You can't do that. It's not possible!" He said, "It happened to Clint and me, it happened to Steve and me, it happened to Valerie and me, it happened to Jenny and me, and then we would just do it!" He felt much well-meant advice, so freely given by others, was frequently ignorant. Verlen said, "Most of the rapids that local people told us we could not possibly paddle through, we could paddle. Most

Derelict racing canoes, designed, built and raced by Verlen, still rest at Kruger Base. *(photo by Phil Peterson)*

of the portages they said we couldn't possibly do, we did. Most of the distances they said couldn't be done, we exceeded. They had never attempted it, and had heard for years it couldn't be done, so they believed it. Sometimes they were so convinced they were right, they resented us even trying it against their advice."

Basically, he felt there was only a small percentage of people who question, or challenge, their own thought processes. "Our minds will deceive us, and sometimes the erroneous advice of others helps it do so," he added. That's why Verlen felt lifelong learning so important. "There is no logical reason why we should ever stop, no matter our age," he said. He felt one could always use the philosophy he and Steve used going up the Grand Canyon. "Look at each past accomplishment in your life as an added boxcar to your train, and use that lifelong strength and condensed inertia to keep moving forward, always learning something new as you go." To Verlen that was living life.

When asked about the hardships he had endured while tripping he would usually respond, "It depends on how you look at hardship." In Rod MacIver's article in the *Heron*, Verlen said, "It toughens some and weakens others. The same experience that will make one person stronger and positive, will almost destroy someone else. I find that extreme effort seems to make me grow. Toughen up. But it seems to wear some people out." He saw his adventures as opportunities for growth. Verlen's attitude was that his cup was always half

Most of the distances they said couldn't be done, we exceeded.

full. He knew he was tough, but also knew that after finishing the next challenge he would be tougher.

Verlen felt many undertake marathon canoe trips for the wrong reasons. Some go to prove how tough they are, to show their macho side, and to be able to display their hardships and accomplishment to others later. It is the aftermath they seek, rather than the act itself. Verlen went in near opposite fashion. He wanted to enjoy it: every paddle-stroke, every portage, in good or bad weather. He never wasted energy regretting where he was, or wishing he was elsewhere. He felt that wherever he was and no matter the circumstances, he was exactly where he belonged.

Verlen and Jenny in 2003 (photo by Phil Peterson)

When asked how he could afford to do the things he did, Verlen usually responded, "Money was never very important to me. I usually just wanted enough. I wanted enough to raise my family and to cover our needs, but I never had a desire to have more." He put his view of money into perspective in his interview with *Heron* magazine: "There have been things I could have done over the years to generate income, but I didn't do them. When I left home on the Ultimate Canoe Challenge, I had signed contracts for over a million dollars. I dropped them and left. It was time to go! That was the peak of my business career. If I had stayed home, I would be comfortable now financially. As it is, I am zero financially, but comfortable otherwise. I made the right decision."

He never regretted not having more money for himself, and only occasionally for others—especially for Jenny as they grew older—but they seemed to manage to do what they wanted. He did sometimes worry about the cost of his cancer treatments. He was quoted in the *Heron* as saying, "I can remember back when I was a kid on the farm, one day we killed the last chicken in order to have something to eat. I can remember when I didn't have a pair of shoes. But we never felt poor. We always had a happy family. Nine of us kids and I never felt deprived. While I have little money now, I don't regret the way I have lived my life. I am wealthy in experiences and have lived a very full life. Much of it I lived as I was called upon to do, on the farm, in the military, and much of it as I chose to do. While I made some mistakes along the way, who has not? But mine were big."

I don't believe Verlen ever really forgave himself for what he had done to Jenny and his family prior to their 12 years of separation. One day, about six months before he died, he and Jenny and I were sitting around his kitchen table having lunch. I looked at both of them, who seemed so happy together, and said, "It is so great that the two of you got back together!" Verlen responded, "Yeah, and now she gets to be my caretaker!" Jenny had just laid out the pills he was to take with his lunch. From the time they got back together again, Verlen put Jenny back onto the pedestal she had occupied for so long, but it seemed he felt he could never do enough to make up for their years apart. He certainly didn't want her to have to care for him. He wanted to take her on the rivers of the country he had so far missed and to share more life with his Jenny. That evening, as we sat in his office he said, "I don't want to leave Jenny, but if the Lord wants me, I'm ready."

He had been treating for prostate cancer for over eighteen years, taking more medicine when his PSA numbers went up, less when they went down, and later forms of oral chemo. For more than five years, he suffered from excruciating headaches and intense pain, but only a few could tell when he was suffering. It was with his cancer, and the pain and headaches that he continued building canoes, training apprentices, and paddling. He canoed the Yukon with Jenny and friends for his 80th birthday, the Buffalo River at 81, again with Jenny and friends. They spent time on the Mississippi and paddled under the Mackinac Bridge beneath the Governor's March on Labor Days. As word spread of his cancer's impact, old friends began to call and show up at his home. No one wanted the world to be without Verlen.

Verlen paddled nearly every day on the Grand River by his home. He told me, "No matter how bad I feel from either my cancer or the medicine I continually take, I always feel better if I paddle." Just a month before he died, there had been a lot of rain and the Grand was in near flood stage. He went out paddling with John Slawinski, a good friend and frequent fellow paddler, while Jenny went grocery shopping. She knew he was going paddling, and that he usually paddled upstream and then drifted and paddled back down to their home. Verlen and John had done that again this day, and while paddling upstream, John got ahead around a bend. Separating was not unusual when paddling with Verlen—that was part of the freedom of paddling solo canoes he enjoyed. They would catch up farther along. While trying to go through a group of small trees that had been flooded, a branch knocked Verlen's paddle from his grasp. When he grabbed for it, the current turned his canoe sideways in the trees and in typical fashion swept his canoe out from under him, just as it had done to Jerry Cesar so many years before. Verlen found himself neck-deep and swimming beside his Sea Wind, to which he was tethered. He wasn't concerned; he had been there before.

Steve and Verlen share a melon in 2004; lots of history and smiles still there (photo by John Slawinski)

Being not too far above his home, he decided to just drift-swim downstream beside his boat, which contained flotation to keep it on the surface, until he reached the shallow water by the island in front of his home. There, he would right the canoe, drain it, climb back in and paddle to his dock just 100 feet away. The flood waters had brought some large trees downstream and they rafted into a tangled mess near the upstream point of the small island across from his dock. As he and his boat drifted up to them, the current grabbed his boat and began to pull it beneath the trees into the tangle of logs. He tried to hold it back, but the current was too strong. It was the tug on his life jacket that reminded him that he was still tied to his canoe. He tried to disconnect the tether from his life jacket, but the pull was so intense that he couldn't loosen it. The pull only tightened the knot! He decided to cut it, but then found he didn't have a knife in his pocket. This was getting serious. He was hoping John would return to discover his plight, but didn't know how far ahead he had gone. Several minutes went by as he continually braced and re-braced against the boat's pull. At this point, there was little else he could do but hope John or someone else would see his plight. It took all his concentration and strength to keep the canoe from pulling him into the logs and underwater beneath them.

The first canoes showed up at the church *(photo by Phil Peterson)*

Verlen knew an eighty-two-year-old man in the last throes of cancer was soon going to run out of strength. Jenny had not yet returned home, so was unaware of Verlen's predicament. Verlen tried to get out of the life jacket, but because of the boat's pull, couldn't make it happen. He said, "I was beginning to think that this might be a lousy way to end things," when all of a sudden the county rescue boat came into sight. A homeowner along the Grand had seen Verlen drifting down beside his boat in the water, and called 911 to report it. "By the time they got there, I was about finished," he said. "Then, before I realized it, they had cut loose my boat and dragged me into theirs. I hurt a rib or two something fierce in the process, but I'm here!" By the time John had paddled back down to Verlen's dock, Verlen had been ambulanced to the hospital. He saw Verlen's canoe lying on shore beside the trees, where the rescue squad had left it. John had no idea what had happened.

Three weeks later, at the age of 82, on August 2, 2004, Verlen Kruger died of cancer in his hospital room, where the day before, his children and grandchildren had sung hymns around his bed to help ease his pain.

His funeral was held at the same DeWitt church he had helped to start fifty years before, the same one for which he split his weekly earnings with the minister, Orval Heinebaugh. His funeral drew the largest crowd the church had ever seen. Car after car arrived, nearly 200, and more than forty of them with one or more Kruger Canoes on top. Word had gone out to carry your canoe in tribute to Verlen. The ceremony was conducted by Pastor Shawn Smith of Heritage Baptist Church, formerly East DeWitt Bible Church. Pastor Bob Prang of Grove Bible Church spoke about Verlen, and Pastor Ted Jameson of Calvary Baptist Church gave prayers.

As part of the eulogy a very good friend, Pastor Bob Prang, said, "Verlen and Jenny both loved kids and proved it beyond all doubt. One, two, three, four, five, six, seven, eight and nine! The kids have many memories. They remember Dad playing bear with them. He would turn out all the lights and growl and hunt for them in the dark. Then there was the time when Mom had the house all cleaned up and Dad came home and played bear. The bear tore things up. Pillows were everywhere, the cushions were pulled off the couch and out of the chairs. Mom was working in the kitchen, but when she saw the living room all tore up she was exasperated and chased the 'bear' with a wet washcloth until she could slush him in the face. The kids were delighted and cheered for both of them.

"Birthdays were special. Dad chased the birthday person with the broom. If the boys went up a tree or climbed up the beams in the barn he went after them. The girls might have had it a little easier. They didn't have a TV, but they knew how to have fun. Every Easter everyone got measured as to how tall they were and their name and age was written beside the mark on the wall. On Sunday morning the kids woke up to hear shoes that came flying up the stairs to hit the metal clothes hamper and then to hear Dad holler, 'Up and at 'em, rise and shine. It's a beautiful day.' After breakfast, it was mass production. The boys were in one line and the girls in the other. Dad did the boys and Mom did the girls. Sometimes Dad did both lines, scrub neck, ears, face, hands and arms. Big families are often late for church. There was

More and more Kruger canoes kept showing up (photo by Phil Peterson)

And more! (photo by Phil Peterson)

And yet more! (photo by Phil Peterson)

Verlen Kruger was brought to his last portage with military honors
(photo by Dan Pahman)

Graveside paddle salute for the last portage *(photo by Dan Pahman)*

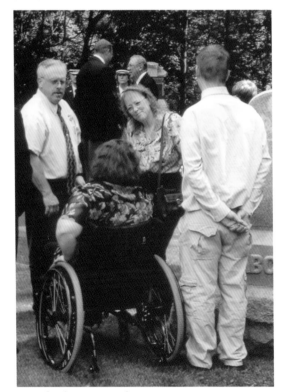
Kruger family congregates for ceremony *(photo by Dan Pahman)*

real time and Kruger time. Sometimes they would forget one or more children at church and someone else would bring them home. On one of the camping trips they forgot Debby at the Grand Canyon. On the same trip they left Jon another place and Dan another place. They never lost any. One Sunday morning the car wouldn't start, so Verlen got all of the family into the cab of the '62 Ford pickup (between 9 and 11 people) and made it to church."

Verlen and Jenny's son, Philip, spoke at his father's funeral. "I wanted to tell you of a few memories of my dad's past. My dad was raised in a large family of nine children on a farm in Indiana. Dad says it was a great experience growing up there. He liked it so much he decided to duplicate this by raising a large family of his own nine children in De Witt, Michigan. All of us kids had different experiences with my dad as we grew up, but these stuck in my memory.

"I found it to be fun growing up as a plumber's kid. We would always play hide and go seek in the barn that had all the plumbing supplies in it. While in the house, at night, after we did our nightly devotions, we could talk Dad into playing hide and seek in our house. Dad would pretend he was a growling bear that was going to eat you up. I was very young, but I loved it! When I got older, my dad built this homemade camper. It seemed huge. I was able to help him in some areas of the construction. Shortly after that, our family started to take a few vacations. Mom and Dad would take us all over the country and it seemed like it lasted all summer. All of us kids learned so much about North America. I remember our family's first big canoe trip. We went across a few lakes in the back woods of Canada. We spent a week or two camping out in tents with the black flies. We all enjoyed ourselves, biting flies, and roughing it. On the return trip, my dad wanted to get home quickly to tend to his plumbing business. He lashed our two aluminum canoes together and made a sail out of a large poncho and two long tree branches. Wow! We really sailed across those lakes coming home! Us kids had to hold up these long poles for so long against the wind. I thought my arms were going to fall off.

"After that trip, my dad got bit by the canoeing bug. He started hanging around those canoe racing guys. He learned all he could and even got into his first race shortly after that.

He then decided to build his first canoe. He had these things called formers and he built his first cedar strip canoe. He said it looks great, but it weighs like a tank. He improved on his canoe building skills every time he built a new one after that. He always wanted lighter, faster, and improved functions with high quality.

Military flag honors (photo by Dan Pahman)

"Around this time, Dad started racing canoes professionally and we traveled in many areas of Canada and the lower 48 states in our camper to many races each year. Bank running is a term only used by canoe racers and their support team. Our family did a lot of bank running. Dad raced canoes from the time he was about 42 until about 80 years old. He began taking big trips when he was 48. Dad read a lot of books and talked to a lot of people and he got very interested in our environment and water quality around our state and local waterways. He tested the water and sent samples to laboratories helping with studies nationwide.

"Dad's last 40 years encompassed his life with canoeing, designing and building canoes, studying the watershed from his canoe, or just for fun, putting his canoe in the water and crossing paddles with friends. Dad loved to teach others about the joy of canoeing. There was something about that self powered boat that really made him happy. My Mom always was supportive of my dad, even if she was home alone with all of us kids frequently.

"Overall, my dad has certainly done a lot of interesting

The folding (photo by Dan Pahman)

things in his life. He makes me proud of him for being a member of 'The Greatest Generation.' This generation built our country into a great nation. My Father served his country proudly in the Army Air Forces during WWII. He was a pilot and a fine officer. He flew P51 Mustang Fighter planes. He named his fighter plane after his best friend and sweetheart, his Sweet Genevieve, my mom. He became an instructor and taught other pilots how to fly in combat.

"Dad was human, and he made mistakes during his life. We all do. When he discovered his mistake, he would ask for forgiveness and would make every attempt to make things right. Dad was a very giving man. He helped all of us kids, most of his brothers and sisters, and his Mom and Dad during hard times. From my point of view, one of the most important things Dad and Mom accomplished was raising all of us 9 children in a Christian home, instilling in us values, morals, and strong Christian principals. Above all things, Dad loved our heavenly Father and I look forward to the day that I will again be able to give him a big hug and see his smile.

"Dad, you will be missed by all who knew you here on earth. But, I know there is huge rejoicing in heaven, welcoming you home to the streets of gold. If there are rivers in heaven, I am sure we will find you on them, crossing paddles with other Christians that you have shared God's Word with.

"Dad says: 'Happy are they who dream dreams and have the courage to make them come true!' He also said, 'All things are possible with God.'"

After the ceremony, the funeral procession drove twelve miles to the cemetery, only three blocks from Verlen and Jenny's home on the Grand River. The procession filled the cemetery and both sides of the adjacent road in front of it as they parked. Near the grave site, a number of Verlen's friends had set up a display of the actual canoes Verlen paddled on the UCC and the TCCE. Because of his military background, part of the graveside ceremony included uniformed officers of the U.S. Air Force performing a flag-folding and presentation to Jenny Kruger. During the ceremony, those who had brought along their canoes shared their paddles with any in the crowd who wished to participate in the

Presentation of flag to Jenny Kruger *(photos by Dan Pahman)*

paddle salute offered for Verlen at the grave site. Jenny, with their nine children and thirty-four grandchildren, accepted the U.S. flag in Verlen's honor, surrounded by a paddle salute as much in her honor as his. Here and there in the crowd was someone in a suit and tie wearing a Tilley hat. It is difficult to find photos of Verlen without his Tilley hat.

After the graveside ceremony, all returned to the church for a gathering, food and beverage, and conversation that went on for hours with many who had not seen each other in years. It was Verlen's goodbye.

Once in a while a man comes along who is loved for what he did, forgiven for what he didn't, admired for his magnitude of life, and held in reverence by those he touched. Such a man is Verlen Kruger. He was an icon to the paddling world: bigger than life as icons must be, but an inspiration to the common man. He felt he was simply an ordinary man who had been given an opportunity to be living proof that ordinary people can do extraordinary things, if they will just believe it is possible and agree to pay the price.

"Verlen was like an adopted father to me." Dan Smith
(photo by Phil Peterson)

We must all paddle on without him now, but he won't be far away. As you paddle, watch the water drip from the blade of your paddle. You will see a hint of the intense blue of Verlen's eyes and favorite flower, feel a smile you miss, and softly hear "you can do that—you should," and then, as the drops hit the water's surface, perhaps see a reflected Monarch, and again hear, "avoid my mistakes, but fulfill your dreams."

"All things are possible with God."

Verlen loved blue morning glories
(photos by Mary Kruger, courtesy of Kruger Archives)

Epilogue: A true story

My wife, Joanne, and I were driving across the top of Lake Michigan on September 7, 2005, to Lansing to work one last time with Jenny Kruger before I finished this book. About ten miles west of the Mackinac Bridge on Highway 2, as we were driving along the beautiful sand beaches we have loved for years, a Monarch Butterfly landed on my driver-side windshield wiper. I was moving about 55 miles per hour, but that Monarch hung onto the top of the wiper arm for probably three miles. In my entire life, a Monarch has never landed on my windshield. I said, "Look, Joanne, a Monarch! Look at how it's hanging on to the wiper arm at this speed!"

Two days later, I was sitting at Jenny Kruger's kitchen table where I had worked so many times with Verlen. She was telling me about the Verlen Kruger memorial paddle. Jenny didn't paddle, but had brought a Kruger Cruiser on top of her van for her sons, Jon and Daniel, to paddle. Each Labor Day weekend, a number of Kruger canoes gather beneath the Mackinac Bridge and, while the Michigan Governor and a crowd of people walk across the bridge, the paddlers paddle across the Straits of Mackinac beneath it. It's a fun event and quite an honor for Verlen's memory. Jenny, at age 78, had driven her camper with a Kruger Cruiser atop to the event by herself. Coming home from the bridge, her son Jon rode home with her. She said, "Phil, I have to tell you what happened. As Jon and I headed south on I-75, just as we were approaching St. Johns, a Monarch Butterfly landed on my windshield wiper. I couldn't believe it! And it stayed there so long as I drove down the freeway. That has never happened to me before. Jon and I watched that butterfly and we laughed and laughed."

I said, "Jenny, let me tell you what happened to Joanne and me as we drove over here to see you...."

Phil and Joanne Peterson, lonesome friends of Verlen Kruger.

Author's Note

The title of this book, *All Things are Possible*, is from Verlen's favorite biblical quote. It is expressed in the chapters of Matthew 19:26, Luke 1:37, Mark 10:17-31. The statement made by Jesus was in response to the question by the disciples about who can be saved. He responded that it was easier for a camel to go through the eye of a needle than for a rich man to enter the kingdom of God, prompting the disciples to ask again who could be saved. Jesus looked at them and said, "With man this is impossible, but with God all things are possible."

OPPOSITE: "Until we meet again." *(photo by Jenny Kruger)*

Some Awards and Records of Verlen Kruger

1969

Verlen and Clint Waddell hold the Boundary Waters Canoe Area of Minnesota (BWCA) record for paddling its full length from International Falls on Rainy Lake to Lake Superior, a distance of 262 miles. They paddled it in 80 hours and 40 minutes. Record stands. Never applied for Guinness.

October 10, 1971

Verlen and Clint Waddell are the only two people in history to paddle the full fur trade route by manpower alone in less than six months. Record stands. Never applied for Guinness.

October 10, 1971

Verlen and Clint Waddell also hold the record for the most miles ever traveled in a tandem canoe in less than six months. Record stands. Never applied for Guinness.

1981

Verlen and Steve Landick hold the speed record down the Missouri River, from Red Rock, Montana, to St. Louis, Missouri, a distance of 2,575 miles. They paddled it in 37 days. Record stands. Never applied for Guinness.

May 11, 1981

Verlen and Steve Landick hold the record for paddling upstream on the Mississippi from the Gulf of Mexico to Lake Itasca, Minnesota, a distance of 2,350 miles. They paddled it in 83 days. Record stands. Never applied for Guinness.

1981

Verlen and Steve Landick hold the record for the longest continuous canoe journey. They paddled 17,260 miles from Red Rock, Montana, to Skagway, Alaska, without a layover.

1983

Verlen holds the record for the most miles one canoe has ever made. He paddled his Loon for the entire 28,043 miles of the Ultimate Canoe Challenge.

1983

Verlen and Steve Landick hold the record for paddling the entire West Coast (Pacific Ocean), a distance of 4,275 miles from Skagway, Alaska, to Cabo San Lucas, Baja California, Mexico.

April 27, 1983

Verlen and Steve Landick hold the world record for the only recorded upstream passage of the Colorado River in the Grand Canyon. They paddled 237 miles upstream (1,900 vertical feet) in 21 days.

1983 Guinness World Record

On the Ultimate Canoe Challenge, Verlen and Steve Landick paddled canoes from Red Rock, Montana, to Lansing, Michigan, a World Record distance of 28,043 miles between April 29, 1980 and December 15, 1983. This is the longest canoe journey ever.

1984 Guinness World Record
Verlen and Valerie Fons paddled from Lake Itasca, Minnesota, to the Gulf of Mexico, between April 27 to May 20, 1984. They set the record at 23 days, 10 hours, 20 minutes.

March 1, 1989
Verlen and Valerie Fons hold the record for the second-longest canoe trip in history. They paddled 21,246 miles, from Arctic to Antarctic, Bering Sea to Cape Horn, in just over three years. Record stands. Never applied for Guinness.

September 1997
Verlen receives the American Canoe Association Hall of Fame Award. He is inducted into the Paddlesport Hall of Fame "In Recognition of His Legendary Contributions To Paddlesports."

2001
Verlen is the only person known to have raced the full length of the Mississippi River three times.

2001
Verlen and Bob Bradford hold the record for the oldest combined-age team to race the full length of the Mississippi River in a tandem canoe. Their combined age was 136 years!

2001
Verlen is the oldest person to race the entire Mississippi River at age 78.

2005
Verlen's name is added to the bronze plaque of the Au Sable Canoe Monument.

Many additional awards were given to Verlen for his canoeing accomplishments. He was a member of the world-renowned Explorer's Club, listed in Who's Who in the State of Michigan and appointed as a Citizen Ambassador for the State of Michigan. His travels have been written into the Congressional Record. He has been made an honorary member of Partners of America, People to People, life member of numerous canoe clubs and honored with countless awards, plaques and keys to cities on both the North and South American continents.

Verlen Kruger was best known for the Cross Continent Canoe Safari with Clint Waddell in 1971, the Ultimate Canoe Challenge with Steve Landick in 1983, and the Two Continent Canoe Expedition with Valerie Fons in 1989. He is also remembered for his Mississippi Challenges with various partners, and the additional thousands of miles of races, training and canoe trips accrued during his lifetime.

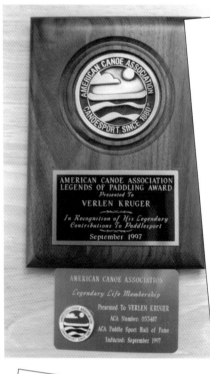

AMERICAN CANOE ASSOCIATION
LEGENDS OF PADDLING AWARD
Presented To
VERLEN KRUGER
In Recognition of His Legendary
Contributions To Paddlesport
September 1997

AMERICAN CANOE ASSOCIATION
Legendary Life Membership
Presented To VERLEN KRUGER
ACA Number: 033487
ACA Paddle Sport Hall of Fame
Inducted: September 1997

City of LANSING
LANSING, MICHIGAN

TERRY J. MC KANE, MAYOR

Proclamation

WHEREAS: Verlen Kruger and Steven Landick of Lansing, Michigan shared a great dream of adventure, endurance and physical accomplishment; and

WHEREAS: Verlen and Steve undertook the challenge of canoeing some three times further than any man before, a distance greater than that around the earth, requiring three and one-half years to complete; and

WHEREAS: This adventure/journey included being the first men to canoe the length of the Mississippi upstream, to canoe the Colorado through the Grand Canyon, and to canoe the Pacific coast line from Alaska to Mexico; and

WHEREAS: The canoes had to be portaged over 600 times, with a total distance to be traveled of over 500 land miles, including terrain as rugged as across ice sheets near the Arctic Circle, and over the continental divide in Wyoming; and

WHEREAS: The trip took Verlen and Steve into 44 states and 8 Canadian provinces; three of the world's four oceans and all five Great Lakes; and through every type of climate, hardship, and test of human spirit and endurance; and

WHEREAS: The "Ultimate Canoe Challenge" has received national attention, creating for Steve and Verlen an identity as modern day explorers and pioneers; and

WHEREAS: On this date these two men have completed a challenge so dramatic, that most Americans, accustomed to today's life of conveniences, could not adequately visualize; and

WHEREAS: Lansing, Michigan is proud to have these two honored sons home again, after canoeing over 28,000 miles.

NOW, THEREFORE, I, TERRY J. MC KANE, MAYOR OF THE CITY OF LANSING, by the power vested in me, do hereby proclaim Thursday, December 15, 1983, as:

"VERLEN KRUGER AND STEVEN LANDICK, ULTIMATE CANOE CHALLENGE DAY"

in Lansing, and urge all citizens of this community to join with me in applauding the outstanding accomplishment of these courageous and adventurous men.

Given under my hand and the Seal of the City of Lansing this fourteenth day of December in the year of Our Lord one thousand nine hundred and eighty-three.

Terry J. McKane
MAYOR

RALPH W. CREGO PARK
KRUGER'S LANDING
CITY OF LANSING

STATE OF MICHIGAN

State Board of Education

This
Certificate of Appreciation
is awarded to
Verlen Kruger
For Outstanding Service to Education
and in Recognition of Significant Personal Efforts to Increase The Educational
Opportunities for the Youth and Adults of The State of Michigan

Donald L. Bemis
Superintendent of Public Instruction

GUINNESS SUPERLATIVES LIMITED

RECORD CERTIFICATE

This is to certify that VALERIE FONS and VERLEN
of
The Eddie Bauer Mississippi River Challenge

Downstream River - Mississippi

20th day of May

Canoeing the full length
Lake Itasca, Minn., to
Mexico, in 23 days 10 hrs

Norris McWhirter

THIS CERTIFICATE DOES NOT NECESSARILY DENOTE AN ENTRY

COMMEMORATING
A 28,000 MILE CONTINENT CIRCLING CANOE VOYAGE
BY TWO LANSING ADVENTURERS, VERLEN KRUGER
AND STEVE LANDICK. THEY COMPLETED THEIR
WORLD RECORD ODYSSEY IN THREE AND ONE-HALF
YEARS LANDING AT THIS SITE ON THE GRAND RIVER
DECEMBER 15, 1983.
A MICHIGAN HERITAGE MEMORIAL
BY THE
MICHIGAN OUTDOOR WRITERS ASS'N

CARL LEVIN
MICHIGAN

United States Senate
WASHINGTON, D.C. 20510

Feb. 8, 1984

Mr. Verlen Kruger
2906 Meister Lane
Lansing, Mich. 48906

Dear Mr. Kruger:

I thought you might like to see the attached tribute to you which I recently put into the Congressional Record.

Again, my congratulations.

Sincerely,
Carl Levin
Carl Levin

Quiet Water Symposium

In Memory of Verlen Kruger, River Guardian
1922 – 2004

"Happy are those that dream dreams,
and have the courage to make them come true."

KRUGER
CANOES

AuSable
River Center
NEMCSA RSVP

VERLEN KRUGER EXHIBIT
FRI - SAT
12:00 - 4:00 PM

In memory of those who paddled and finished the

- FRANK "BUD" ELSIGNEYER
- DONALD J. FELDHAUS
- ROBERT J. FULLERTON
- VERLEN E. KRUGER
- EUGENE JENSEN
- IRVIN "BUS" PETERSON
- WILLIAM J. STAPLES
- HUGO F. WOJAHN

Donated by: Oscoda-AuSable

GUINNESS WORLD RECORDS

CERTIFICATE

VERLEN KRUGER AND STEVEN LANDICK
PADDLED CANOES FROM
RED ROCK, MONTANA TO
LANSING MICHIGAN, USA
A WORLD RECORD DISTANCE OF
28,043 MILES BETWEEN
29 APRIL 1980 AND 15 DECEMBER 1983

Keeper of the Records
GUINNESS WORLD RECORDS

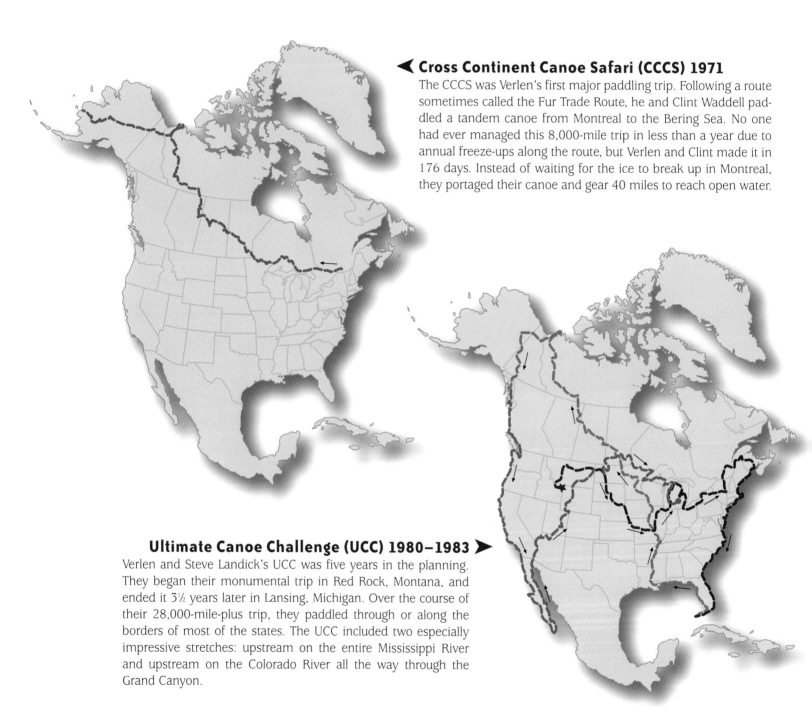

◄ Cross Continent Canoe Safari (CCCS) 1971

The CCCS was Verlen's first major paddling trip. Following a route sometimes called the Fur Trade Route, he and Clint Waddell paddled a tandem canoe from Montreal to the Bering Sea. No one had ever managed this 8,000-mile trip in less than a year due to annual freeze-ups along the route, but Verlen and Clint made it in 176 days. Instead of waiting for the ice to break up in Montreal, they portaged their canoe and gear 40 miles to reach open water.

Ultimate Canoe Challenge (UCC) 1980–1983 ►

Verlen and Steve Landick's UCC was five years in the planning. They began their monumental trip in Red Rock, Montana, and ended it 3½ years later in Lansing, Michigan. Over the course of their 28,000-mile-plus trip, they paddled through or along the borders of most of the states. The UCC included two especially impressive stretches: upstream on the entire Mississippi River and upstream on the Colorado River all the way through the Grand Canyon.

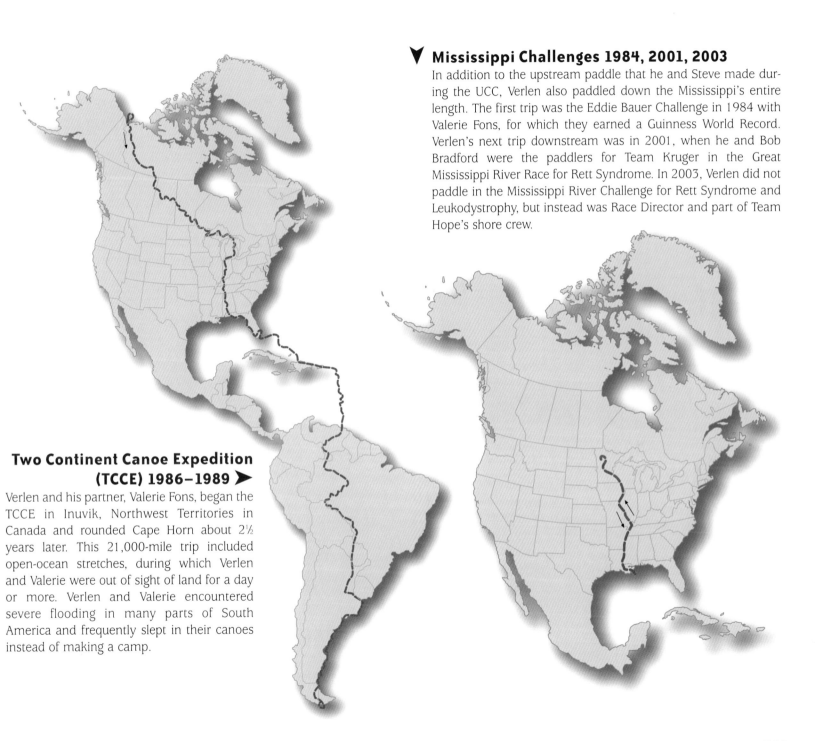

Mississippi Challenges 1984, 2001, 2003

In addition to the upstream paddle that he and Steve made during the UCC, Verlen also paddled down the Mississippi's entire length. The first trip was the Eddie Bauer Challenge in 1984 with Valerie Fons, for which they earned a Guinness World Record. Verlen's next trip downstream was in 2001, when he and Bob Bradford were the paddlers for Team Kruger in the Great Mississippi River Race for Rett Syndrome. In 2003, Verlen did not paddle in the Mississippi River Challenge for Rett Syndrome and Leukodystrophy, but instead was Race Director and part of Team Hope's shore crew.

Two Continent Canoe Expedition (TCCE) 1986–1989 ➤

Verlen and his partner, Valerie Fons, began the TCCE in Inuvik, Northwest Territories in Canada and rounded Cape Horn about 2½ years later. This 21,000-mile trip included open-ocean stretches, during which Verlen and Valerie were out of sight of land for a day or more. Verlen and Valerie encountered severe flooding in many parts of South America and frequently slept in their canoes instead of making a camp.

Suggested Reading and Viewing on Verlen Kruger

Fons, Valerie. *Keep It Moving*. Washington: The Mountaineers, 1986.

Frentz, LeRoy Brand and Verlen Kruger. *The Ultimate Canoe Challenge*. iUniverse of Nebraska, 2005.

Klein, Clayton and Verlen Kruger. *One Incredible Journey*. Wilderness Adventure Books, (3rd printing), 1990.

Kruger, Verlen (producer). *Never Before, Never Again*. 1990.
A 90-minute DVD of Verlen Kruger and Clint Waddell on their 1971 canoe trip from Montreal to the Bering Sea.

Verlen Kruger Memorial

Artist's rendition of the statue.

As a memorial to Verlen and his remarkable accomplishments, a life-size bronze statue will be situated on the banks of the Grand River in Portland, Michigan. Derek Rainey, of Portland, Michigan, is the sculptor. You can support the Verlen Kruger Memorial by purchasing a brick. These bricks will be used as part of the landscaping around the statue. For a brochure about the memorial, or to purchase a brick, contact:

Verlen Kruger Memorial
P.O. Box 533
Portland, MI 48875-0533
(517)647-5788
krugermemorial@yahoo.com
www.verlenkrugermemorial.org

Support Rett Syndrome and Leukodystrophy

Verlen participated in two Mississippi River Challenges to support Rett Syndrome and Leukodystrophy research (see pages 220–243). To support these causes as he did, contact:

Rett Syndrome Research Foundation (RSRF)
www.rsrf.org; (513)874-3020

United Leukodystrophy Foundation (ULF)
www.ulf.org; 800-728-5483

Author's Note

The first time I heard of Verlen Kruger was in an article about paddling Lake Superior. We lived in Grand Marais in the 1970s, and I heard of him and Clint passing Grand Marais on the Cross Continent Canoe Safari. When Verlen and Steve passed through Seattle, I was working for a company based in Seattle, so I heard of him again. I read Clayton Klein's book, *One Incredible Journey*, and continued to read of Verlen in the paddling magazines over the years. I finally contacted him in 1997, asking him to build me a custom expedition Cruiser. I picked it up from his home in 1999, and finally met the man I'd read so much about.

We spent the better part of an afternoon talking as though we'd been close friends for years. It was a treat to share, with *the* Verlen Kruger, stories of my own canoe trips. Knowing the BWCA and Quetico turf made it easy for us to communicate.

In 2001, Verlen invited us, along with other Kruger canoe owners, to celebrate his 80th birthday as part of the Yukon Odyssey, a canoe trip from the Yukon's source to its end. My wife and I spent the first 21 days with them and the rest went on 2,080 miles to the Bering Sea. The following year we paddled again with Verlen, Jenny and friends on the Buffalo River in Arkansas. The better I came to know Verlen, the more I felt his inspiring story had to be told.

After the Buffalo River trip, Verlen called one day and said, "Why don't you come over for a day or two to talk about this book." I did, and you are reading the results of that trip and the dozen more that followed during the next two years.